CLOBBER!

CLOBBER!

Bridging the Gap Between Casuals and their Clobber

Roo Oxley

Copyright © Roo Oxley 2023

The moral rights of the author have been asserted.

All rights reserved. No part of this publication may be reproduced, stored in or introduced into a retrieval system or transmitted in any form or by any means, electronic, mechanical, photocopying, recording or otherwise without prior written permission from the publisher.

Published by Vulpine Press in the United Kingdom in 2023

ISBN: 978-1-83919-539-6

www.vulpine-press.com

This book is dedicated to my children, Luka and Mia. Let's hope it's a best seller because this is your inheritance 😊 And well deserved after all the peace and quiet you gave me whilst writing this haha. I love you both. It's all for you.

For Nana, Pa, Grandma and Auntie Jill.

Stoke RIP:

Matthew Shaw
Chris Steele
Carl Smith
Danny McCoy
Matt Giannitto
Dean Wood
Craig Bowman
Stacey Rhodes
Mark Morris
Eliot Howell
Jay Lovatt
James Morgan
Chris Kelly
Martin Wilson
Ant Jones

Contents

Foreword	i
What Does She Know About Terrace Culture?!	1
Introduction	4
Part 1: The Past; Nostalgia and the Golden Age of Terrace Culture.	11
1| What Is a Subculture: Here Comes the (social) Science Bit…	13
2| Just In Case You Didn't Know; Terrace Culture and the Birth of the Casuals	15
3| The New Football Hooligans; the Lads	18
4| Stoke City's Terrace Culture; Be Loyal, Be Proud, Be Stoke	21
5| Don't Believe the Hype	26
6| Back in the Day, Before the Cliche	32
7| The (Brand) Consumption Back Then	34
8| Paninaro, Oh, Oh, Oh	37
9| From Bowie to Boss, Laaa	40
10| Music is the Answer (To Your Problems)	45
11| Northern Monkeys V Southern Fairies; The Influences in the Geographical Divide	47
12| Hackett Off	50
13| When Two Tribes Go to War	54
14| Smooth Operators	58
15| End of the (Nova Checked) Line	60

16| Clone Island	64
17| Symbolic Consumption	66
18| Consumption Communities	68
Part 2: The Present: The 808 State of Terrace Culture Today	71
19| 'Death' of Terrace Culture	73
20| Credit Card Casuals	76
21| Post Subcultural Turn	78
22| Where Have all the Subcultures Gone?	81
23| Post Fandom: Did Subcultures Die Years Ago Anyway?	86
24| Authenticity: Against Modern Football Part 1	88
25| Brand Identity; Clobber for the Jilted Generation	91
26| Terrace Culture and the Dawn of the Digital Age	95
27| #JointheCult	101
28| Nouveaux Casuals	104
29| Brand Loyalty in Millennials; Consumer Behaviour Now	107
30| 80s Casual (Classics)	111
31| Doing it for the Gram	115
32| If Everybody Looked the Same; the Dilution of the Brands	118
33| I've Got 99 Problems but A Coat Ain't One	124
34| Wake Me Up Before You Go Go; Smart Marketing for the Woke Generation	130
35| Vive La (Consumer) Resistance	135
36| The Vintage Connection	139
37| 'Daduals' and Mini Mes	145
38| Brand Longevity; Where Has all the Faconnable Gone?!	150
39| Silk Slut; Social Media & the Evolution of Marketing	157

40| Luxe Brands; Living the Dream or Social Media 'Mare 163
41| Fast Fashion; Check out my Discount Code Boohoo.Com/Rooey25 166
42| Stop, Collaborate and Listen 172
43| An Oud; RIP Casual Culture (for good this time) 181
44| #Getthebadgein 184
45| #Takethebadgeoff? 187
46| Covid-19 Sucks 191
47| Apocalypse (N)ow! 193
48| How Brands Survived Covid; Survival of the Slickest 198
49| Get the (Post) Covid Look; Hooligan Rennaissance Classics 201
50| Stop Press; the Media's Role in Vilifying the Casuals. 206
51| Ultras; the International Scene & Football Fandom 211
52| Against Modern Football Part 2; All Cops Are Bastards (Acab!) 215
53| Casual Ultras 221
54| Auld Enemies; By Order of the Peaky Fucking Blinders 231
55| "SCRUFFY FUCKS" 237
56| A Whole New World 243
57| Admit Nothing 247
58| Gold Rush 250
59| Just Say No; Clobber Addicts & Fanatics 256
60| "Fashion Fades, Only Style Remains the Same." 262
61| Modern Day Dressers; How to Spot an Original Casual Today 266
62| Get the S(m)ock In 269
Part 3: The Future Terrace Renaissance? The fate of Casual Culture 273
63| The Spezial One 275

64	Darwen's Theory of Evolution	280
65	Mama Miglia: Going Back to My Roots	283
66	Casual-Lites; the Age of Jacomo & the New Alternatives	286
67	Made In Italy; The Italian Job	290
68	Ol' Money, Mo Problems	297
69	Casual Core	299
70	Independent Day	302
71	This Thing of Ours	306
Reclaim the Game	314
Bibliography	318
Acknowledgments	331

Foreword

This book adds significantly to our understanding of the rise and ongoing appeal of the casual subculture. Its unique perspective from one of the few female participants adds a distinct and personal dimension to our understanding of how casuals have subverted ideas of class and masculinities through their bricolage approach to dress.

– Andrew Groves, Professor of Fashion Design, University of Westminster

What Does She Know About Terrace Culture?!

Supporting Stoke City is shit. Proper wank. A thankless task that us chosen ones were unfortunately born into. A lifetime of cold, wet misery; flashes of wins here and there, a trip to the Premier League if we are lucky, but predominantly following mediocre Championship football in the coldest, windiest ground in the Midlands. Neat.

My family has always had a deep connection to Stoke City Football Club. They established Hanley Glass & China in the Potteries, which was a successful business distributing our wares to the region and beyond, with all of us having a stint selling the seconds at Stockport market every Saturday. Hanley Glass & China sponsored the Victoria Ground (Stoke's first ground and spiritual home), with my nana, pa and uncle all attending every game in suites at the ground. I used to often go with them, Pa letting me have a bet first and generally being spoiled rotten. The seeds of this lifelong love affair were being planted. Add this initial interest in football and the local club to teenage passion and a perfect storm of club/football/lads/clobber began to develop.

My enduring love-in with the nineties terrace label stalwarts Stone Island and CP Company started early doors, and soon, trips to Life in Manchester and Tessuti in Chester would become the hunting ground for new pieces. Henri-Lloyd was a big staple in my early Casual wardrobe too, along with Napapijri, Thomas Burberry, Paul & Shark and

Aquascutum, which luckily local shops (Infinites, Terraces, Review and even Gemini) could provide. The big hitters, these Casual brands were, in my opinion, at the top of their game during these years, epitomising the Casual scene of the late nineties. An era where we earned our stripes, saving up to buy a big thick knit green label Stoney, the same as I would save up to buy albums from Portishead, The Verve and Oasis from Mike Lloyd Music. These carefree days would soon be ending, and along with the vibrant club scene such as Golden in Stoke, I just about managed cling onto and experience the last of the decent subcultures. These days, seeing the snides, the pretenders, the wannabees wearing my regalia, with no thought to its heritage makes my toes curl. It's not living in the past, it's a lifestyle, a way of life. You've either got it or you don't. You can either wear the labels or let the labels wear you. And if you're not game as fuck, then don't even bother.

Can she do it on a cold Monday night up the Britannia Stadium? Course she can! It's where it all started. Against the mighty Chesterfield. Walking up the concrete steps with my brother who took me, I inhaled the atmosphere; not crackling due to any tension or fighting, but an air of anticipation. This is where I would sit and watch, fixated by the waves of Burberry and Aquascutum caps, the lads, the coats, the camaraderie, the clobber.

Notts County away would be the next game, aged approximately 15. This is where I saw some of the lads flexing. Loved it. I had by now started to go out in town (Newcastle-under-Lyme), so I was starting to mix with people (boys) other than the ones at my school. I was in the mix, starting to know and be known. Notts County was a step up and most definitely in the right direction.

Late nineties, Stoke lads were already infamous from the earlier Naughty Forty firm, but even the younger lot that I knew and was knocking round with were making a name for themselves. How I wished I was a boy whilst watching the skirmishes, the bravado, the rows. I would have been game as fuck, no mither, getting rate stuck in. As a girl on the side-lines, I could only watch with a kind of primal desire and energy and keep an eye out for any rogue Old Bill or cranks from other firms.

Female Casuals are a rarity and are not always welcomed, particularly on away days when the lads would have to babysit or keep an extra eye out or get stuck in if any other lads started being a bit fiendish towards us. Let's just say West Ham fans had a delightful chant they sang at me when Stoke played them at the Olympic Stadium.

I drag my arse up to most home games, but definitely prefer the away days, with more recent fixtures even enticing some of the older lot to come out of retirement. I want to be where the action is. Cap on, head down, come on Stoke let's have it. Casual.

Clobber!

Introduction

Blah, blah, blah. Heard it all before, have we? Football Casuals and their memoirs have fast become way too prevalent and almost bloated caricatures of themselves. Going from a rose-tinted, nostalgic view of the Paninaro-inspired Casuals, every watered down hoolie was spilling his guts through the medium of a memoir, which then became a pissing contest, a dick-off, to decide who was the biggest and hardest.

The phenomenon of football hooligan memoirs has, however, brought the lifestyle into the popular culture. This ironically begs the question of when does a subculture stop being a subculture when it has been so deliciously lapped up and integrated by the mainstream?

Traditional football hooligan memoirs have been drawn from a more 'hit and tell' perspective, perceived as a right from the horse's mouth recollection, or an oral description susceptible to the defaults of a failing memory and/or ego boosted tale telling. My book, on the other hand, is a collection of not just football hooligan memoirs, but also a curation of the state of play today, of terrace culture as a subculture. More precisely, we know this subculture officially died many years ago, but the unofficial affiliations with Casuals and football hooligans is very apparent. I will be researching how this 'subculture' is still consuming 'their' brand and why.

The 'golden age' of terrace culture has long since gone, which we will cover in depth, but has Covid and its aftermath partially brought it back? And if it is back, does it still consist of iconic dressers?

I originally investigated this research for a master's degree dissertation more than a decade ago. I was intrigued to revisit and see what and how much has changed.

It is rare for terrace culture research to be undertaken from a female perspective, particularly one who is extremely au fait with this lifestyle and heavily connected to key players, Casuals, football hooligans, brand owners, and a mixture of all.

In this testosterone-heavy, male peacock prancing world, I am more than comfortable, enabling me to get right into the mix, to get information many others would not be allowed access to or be privy to. I have been forging and strengthening my links these past ten years; not just with the Stoke City football scene but other cities and firms also.

This perspective and attitude follow in the footsteps of journalist Caroline Gall who believed, as did Steve Redhead, that by being easy going and on the 'periphery' of some of the 'lads' she knew, it would make it easier for some of the interviewees to tell their story.

And now, post pandemic, are there any parts of this subculture – or any subculture – that still exists and have not been fragmented by, as some people see it, brutal and restricting lockdowns? How can they survive? Online communities surely must have had an extremely important and significant role in nurturing brand identities and relationships?

Also, we need to investigate the alleged rise of far-right nationalism in eastern Europe and its potential correlation with the increase of their more hard-line hooligans, or 'Ultras', who can arguably be blamed for the dilution and regression of labels that English fans have long since dispensed with. It is also fascinating to research the role of these Ultras in the Russian invasion of Ukraine – two countries where the die-hard Casual approach was adopted and later utilized for actual combat in battles. After an interview with CP Company President

Lorenzo Osti, I learned that one of their biggest markets was Korea, and some of their biggest and most loyal online fans were from Indonesia, so these territories and fanhoods must also be researched further.

There is undoubtedly a resurgence of football culture – at least in the media's eyes, heightened by the delayed Euros 2020. This book will aim to pick up where my last research left off in 2011. Buying habits and consumerism have changed beyond recognition this past decade, along with the world itself. So how does this subculture consume their brands? Does it vary regionally, nationally and internationally?

In today's frenetic, fast-paced, Covid-drained, postmodern world, the way in which consumers around the globe buy products, or in fact the reasons behind the act of consumption itself, is becoming increasingly difficult to predict or understand for marketeers, retailers and researchers alike. The decision-making process behind consumer behaviour, in particular of football Casuals, has always been of a personal interest to me. My master's degree dissertation explored this, as well as the concept of consumer collectives and symbolic consumption; why people of similar race, gender, class or background choose to buy similar products as an expression of identity.

Terrace culture is a subculture that was born on the terraces of post-Second World War, pre-corporate football stadiums; yet it is not just the act of football which is significant, more the whole culture and way of life which arguably encompasses those who experience it at football matches.

Growing up surrounded by the football hooligan eruption in the early nineties, I have often wondered about the traditions, rituals, clothes and behaviours of these football hooligans, and whether these were the predominant characteristics of terrace culture.

But how does anyone consume brands in the era of online living and digital-only experiences, replacing real life shopping habits and physical quests for one-off items? Back in 2011 and researching my dissertation, e-commerce was most certainly in its infancy, online communities a concept only hesitantly being discussed, brand identity and consumption a topic only getting bigger. So much has changed since then in terms of technology, innovation, human relationships and societal evolutions, but I will look into how exactly these seismic global events have impacted on the Casual scene. Nowadays, it appears brands are vying for customers in such a saturated market space but with ironically fewer independent shops, faceless high streets and soulless retail parks. These mainstream-dulled brands and ever slick marketing campaigns are desperate – their holy grail is cutting through the marketing noise of every brand on the planet, so how do the old faithful 'Casual' brands keep their longevity within the hearts of this culture; do they engage with this (once looked down on) sector of society? And how does brand consumption vary geographically, not just within regions and cities of the UK, but also does it change from country to country? And are these up and coming 'hoolie' territories abroad now responsible for a Casual brand's success/failure?

With a notoriously territorial approach to whom appropriated whom, geographical styles most definitely change throughout regions, but who owns the brand? Who wore it first? The brand itself? The loyal Casuals? Ironically, Casuals themselves appropriated the style by copying old money/high class luxury European sports brands and adapted it for themselves, but is this authentic rather than reinterpreted?

With so many questions I decided to ask them all myself by researching to seek patterns in observations and to collect data relevant to the topic. This subject area is not a topic that can be understood through a scientific approach as it involves not just in-depth academic reading and literature reviews, but also asking people themselves for their own personal accounts, stories and beliefs. Human beings are not flawless; in order to gain access to people and crucially their trust, it is necessary to expect any interviews or accounts to be open to interpretation and exaggeration. Despite this, I still believe that people's accounts are extremely important, particularly when trying to understand the psyche of a youth subculture; the hooligans' accounts may be self-important in the hoolie-lit and the interviews, yet they were witnesses to the culture, at the epicentre of the Casual movement. Thus, first person accounts are crucial as they tend to contain a wealth of central and fundamental material not available elsewhere. This is a research topic where the main goal is to gain a greater understanding of the subject of brands and clobber. Put simply, which kind of people bought them, why and how do they consume them now? I also acknowledge my presence as a researcher and writer is arguably just as important as the research itself, and that it is impossible to remain totally impartial due to my knowledge of, and position within this community. The new punk on the writing scene, *l'enfant terrible* (ish), my writing is intentionally irrelevant and intended to be self-deprecating for me and the whole of Stoke; I'm City 'Till I Die! Obvs!

By asking previous Casuals, modern-day Casuals, brand owners, authors, experts and by reading a huge amount of academic research, I hope to present some valid points and a shared vision of Casual brands in the future. But this will all be tied up in a controversial bow of it coming from MY perspective with tongue firmly in cheek and a healthy dollop of impartiality. Snowflakes! If you don't agree with anything in this book that's cool, everyone's entitled to their opinion. I have collated enough broad and wide-ranging data from first source narratives to unchallenged scholarly articles, that I hope the book presents a balanced view on Casuals and their clobber today. I ask these key individuals themselves whether terrace culture even exists anymore, whether it is just another stylistic youth subculture which was retired long ago, or whether post-Covid, there is now about to be a resurgence, a kick start, a breath of fresh air to this tired subculture due to fresh blood, a new vigour after being like caged tigers during a global lockdown. How they show this (collective) identity in terms of brands, either through traditionally Casual brands or new ones, underpins this work and is one of the main motivations behind the research process.

I am obviously not a football hooligan, but I have a great deal of knowledge, experience, 'beguiling' female charms, on the 'periphery' but much more than an outsider looking in. This insider, this keen aficionado is looking outward to the bigger world outside this once so favoured subculture and presenting a collation of key players who can aid this 'oral history of an oral history', as Redhead, the aforementioned and celebrated academic, once described it.

*

The world is undoubtedly saturated enough with football hoolie-lit, but *Clobber!* is so much more than that. It combines scholarly articles and facts, first-hand accounts from football Casuals, interviews with brand owners, and my own (female/Casual) take on the world of Casual clobber today. These are not myths, but recollections from those that were there, my job being to decipher what has cultural value or not regarding this book, whose stories to tell.

Here's a brief recap to help better understand our study of Casuals and their clobber, through the lens of yesterday, today and tomorrow. With this recap, we will be able to put forward a theory of terrace culture brand consumption in the 2020s and map out any trends for the future.

Part 1:

The Past; Nostalgia and the Golden Age of Terrace Culture

1|

What Is a Subculture: Here Comes the (social) Science Bit...

It can be hard to define concisely the actual meaning of *subculture*; Hebdige believed that the meaning will always be up for discussion. Yet he also had the opinion that the explosion of youth culture after the Second World War polarized this new, wealthier generation, which led to significant youth styles in fashion and music. Indeed, subcultures appear to go hand in hand with style, as a means for 'the young, the black, the working class to make something of what is made of them – to embellish, decorate, parody.' There is a long history of post-war youths having a succession of distinct groups, all with their unique subcultural styles, from the early teddy boys, mods, punks and skins; all these styles were adopted by the working class, but then often became too popular and mainstream, which Willis believed meant that a new symbolic, creative stylistic output had to be achieved for the look to be different once more. The working class have always used fashion as a means of expression; a one-upmanship game with them, the subordinate class, against the bosses or exploiters, evident even from the Victorian times when the young workers copied their masters, and also the Teddy Boys emulating their Edwardian forbearers, with stylish, eloquent suits and coiffed hair as described in Thornton's 2003 book, *Casuals*. Certainly, King also agreed that the working class have often used style as a type of resistance; and this feeling of resentment against authority, whether it be parents, employers or political parties, was heightened in the post-Second World War years, along with a strong desire by working-class youths to reaffirm their identity. Willis' iconic work researched into this link between social class, identity and consumption, an area of research that is crucial as it supports any further in-depth analysis on consumer behaviour, in particular its depiction of how certain groups will band together in a subculture such as the Punks, Mods, and later the Casuals. For example, post-modern communities that developed after the breakdown of traditional social hierarchies, such as the church, the government, and importantly, the nuclear family; their distinct style a method of differentiation and a way of 'winning cultural space for young people,' as described by Willis.

2|

Just In Case You Didn't Know; Terrace Culture and the Birth of the Casuals

Each subculture has their own distinguishing styles, clothes, rituals and behaviours; Muniz and O'Guinn write that in modern society some subcultures can be linked by their consumption of products and labels. With terrace culture, it was this typical love for certain fashions and brands that made this particular subculture stand out as arguably more brand conscious than the previous male-dominated subcultures. Terrace culture is the umbrella name for a whole way of life: working-class men going to support their local football team, which spawned the Casual youth culture movement in the late seventies. The Casual movement took over where another infamous subculture had led, the Skinheads. The Skinheads were first seen in London in the late sixties and would be seen by most to be the epitome of football hooliganism. However, with their uniform of denim jeans, braces, checked Ben Sherman shirts, and their love and instigation of football violence, this look, and indeed this trend, would soon become copied up and down the country in response to the perceived disruption of immigration and the redevelopment of local communities and housing, as documented by Hall and Jefferson. They found a connection in watching their local football team, and those strong loyalties that come with the relationship is one of the foundations of terrace culture. A working-class game, for working-class people in a working-class neighbourhood, the violence, passion, and endurance of a football match were reflective of the qualities of a working-class lifestyle itself.

Now, here is where the territorial pissing comes into play; before all the Casuals get their knickers in a twist, this is speculative, with many sides to the narrative. There is much lively debate over which particular city the first Casual style originated from, with the majority of academics and hooligans insisting Liverpool was the rightful birthplace, agreed on by both Thornton and Redhead, with inevitably some (mostly the home-grown hooligans) insisting it was either London or Manchester. Arguably, the trend spread after football fans went to away game matches and saw and were impressed by what the opposing fans were wearing. Merseyside football fans were renowned, however, for looking particularly sharp, as they brought back home luxury European sportswear labels from their trips abroad for away games in Europe. The names for this new, stylish football fan ranged from the Scally, the Perry, then mainly the Casual; the latter name withstanding time and is the name most commonly used to describe lads, or more precisely, hooligans, at the football match. There became many regional differences between how Casual firms dressed, which then became a game of one-upmanship at the football games; to have the best, most distinctive and elusive clothes or labels. To win this 'game' could be said to be a sign of victory or strength against the rival fans; Mclaughlin and Redhead pre-empting as early as 1985 that football's style wars were about to begin. The type of clothes these new Casuals favoured at the start of this terrace subculture in the late seventies, early eighties, were so far removed from the stereotypical image of a football hooligan – the boorish, uneducated skinhead. Instead, the new style began as 'post-mod'. This clean cut smartly dressed image confused the authorities; it was now harder to pinpoint a troublemaker or football hooligan as the traditional style of the Skinhead football hooligan was evolving into a well-groomed, sharp, slick lad who on first glance, their style would have more in common with a young Tory than a football hooligan, according to Redhead. Yet violence and hooliganism are ingrained in terrace culture; the growth of football hooliganism would rise simultaneously with the spread of the Casual clothes; a new tribe was emerging, one that would be dressed impeccably, but with the main aim to engage with violence before, during or after the football match.

3|
The New Football Hooligans; the Lads

Looking back at the origins of any youth subculture, there will always be dispute or confusion about the reasons for certain looks or trends. There is the belief that the new bourgeois style was adopted by this particular scion of football fans to lessen or avoid any police attention when on the prowl at the football match, or when trying to enter the opposing set of fans' end of the stadium to cause trouble. Others recall that at the time, there was no defined name for this Casual youth culture; that it was a style started on the streets, with the working-class boys working on their style through trial and error; yet once again, it is the violent, organized and disruptive aspects of these new Casuals, as well as their unique style, that will make them more feared than the previous generation of football hooligans. There has been a long history of football hooligans; known even to have been present at some of the earliest football games in the late 1800s, as researched by Dunning. For many cities, where there exists a strong magnetic pull to the local football teams, football hooliganism was simply a part of many men's lives and indeed remains a constant element of modern-day football. Hobbs and Robins believed the 'tribalistic customs' of more recent football hooligans were just the latest generation of working-class males who enjoy fighting at football matches, and the type of fashion and violence was just a way of creating their own elite group. Whether or not this is still the case, and if so, what brands/clothes they consume and how in order to portray this higher, elevated, gentrified version of themselves, is the crux of this book.

The massive changes to British football post-Hillsborough meant there were seismic repercussions for football hooligans. Gone were the terraces, which were a gathering place for the 'lads'. Instead, the authorities introduced all-seater, clinical stadiums in order to avoid the tragic disasters of Hillsborough and Heysel in which many fans were crushed. There was also a conscious effort to raise the image of football, thus families were encouraged to attend, prices rose to attract the middle classes and there was intense police presence. These new outlines threatened the very being of the football hooligan; by pricing them out of a game which they effectively saw as their own, not only were they being denied the actual football itself, but the arena and atmosphere in which their endearing, and enduring, relationships were forged. Furthermore, as King also wrote, this entirely new way of consuming football, in general, threatened the lads' act of fandom itself.

Paradoxically, Dunning discusses how this 'bourgeoisification' and 'internationalization' of the game as a commodity started to alienate the working-class fans, and actually resulted in more acts of football hooliganism as it pushed together a group who felt isolated and frustrated with what was happening to their game. The Casual subculture, with its distinctive clothes, codes of practice and loyalty, grew within the lads; the creation of the corporate and later the marketing of the football clubs with all the team colours, strips, merchandising and new (that is, inauthentic) fans, created increasing simmering resentment within the lads. Terrace culture became even more important for these football hooligans as a way to have a territory, a style and a movement they could call their own and not have anyone take it away from them. The self-conscious styles of dressing became a subconscious desire to distinguish themselves from the new army of fans invading their terrain.

4|

Stoke City's Terrace Culture; Be Loyal, Be Proud, Be Stoke

Obviously being a born and bred Stokie, the first Casuals I got to know, and later researched, were those affiliated with Stoke City Football Club. As a notorious firm with a predilection for violence and penchant for smart attire, I investigated the reasons why they have/had allegedly such a reputation for violence, and to see how strong their terrace and Casual culture is. There is not so much academic research on Stoke-on-Trent's hooligans; the following literature is from published factual books, memoirs and newspaper articles. The lack of scholarly articles is another reason why I am looking into this; there are many regional differences among football hooligans. There is, I believe, more to each football firm's style than is universally described. The first-hand narratives collated from a number of Stoke City Casuals has helped contribute to this section, but bias alert (!), Stoke City FC always gets overlooked as a key football team in England. We are one of the oldest! We helped form the Football League! Yet hardly any in-depth research has been written about the Potteries team as clocked by Martyn Dean Cooke and Gary James in their own findings. We also never get any credit in terms of footballing's early existence, or our position in the Casual culture hierarchy. Even on BBC1's *Match of the Day*, Stoke are predominantly shown last whichever league we are playing in. Even in the 'heady' Premier League/Tony Pulis days, the producers would always put our game last. For example, if we won (a mythical) 10 nil, only begrudgingly would the Stoke victory be shown first. So even with first-hand accounts, we have minimal academic research, aside from my own, to reinforce the factual and historical background for the formation of Stoke's terrace culture scene. But we go again.

Police intelligence once claimed that Stoke-on-Trent's football firm, named the Naughty Forty, was one of the most violent and organised firms in the early nineties, validated by the research of Lowles and Nicholls. Later, BBC News wrote in 2010 that even with the development of a new generation of football hooligans, Stoke City had been highlighted (along with several other West Midlands Premier league clubs) as one to keep an eye on, particularly as the region was well known for its hooligan element. Mark Chester – also known as 'Jasper' – was one of the original members of the Naughty Forty, and as he describes, not only in his semi-autobiography *Naughty* but in other publications also, that Stoke-on-Trent's male population are predominantly working-class, have a strong identity, renowned humour, like fighting, and are proud that they come from such a dilapidated city. Go 'on Stoke!! 😊 Jasper whilst advising me behind the scenes never fails to sign off messages with 'We're Stoke!' and 'Casual!' because that's who we fucking are!

In the nineteenth century, it really was a hard knock life for the Staffordshire city and encompassing six towns – the birthplace of the Pottery industry, a smoggy kiln underpinning the industrial revolution. There are references to football activities being undertaken in the region, prior to the creation of the early football association. Interestingly, these football games and matches are only mentioned whilst linked with any kind of accidental, or more frequently criminal, incidents. A pre-cursor to the Stoke Casual scene, perhaps? Maybe it's something in the water?! And apparently, we have always given it the big 'un and exaggerated loveable folk tales; 'local and oral histories resulted in multiple exaggerated and, often false, narratives emerging, particularly surrounding the origins of the region's two prominent professional football clubs,' discover Cooke and James. Hmmm. Always thought SCFC was established in 1863 but even this proud Stoke self-declared fact is 'sketchy' apparently.

Despite the 'moody' early connotations of Stoke City Football Club, it cannot be denied that Stoke and football and football and Stoke are intrinsically linked and have been from the very beginning.

One of the original Naughty Forty (Stoke City's notorious firm), Paul Walters remembers how addictive SCFC was in terms of pulling him and others into this way of life.

Paul explains:

'My Grandad took me when from age of five years old. We used to go to the Boothen End at the end of the match and loved it. From the age of 15 that was it. Lived it, breathed it, football violence. From then on it was Stoke City. All we ever talked about.'

The new way of life had started for many of Stoke's firm in the eighties, all banding together, not arsed, often outnumbered, never giving a fuck. Stoke City's Naughty Firm were living up to their name and had an infamous reputation. Why? Because they were fucking naughty.

Paul adds:

'I was a great hooligan, fearless and ran coaches to away games.'

Stoke and other firms' awaydays started to become legendary, iconic times caught up in the heady zeitgeist of fashion, music, politics and culture. Many lads began documenting clobber they wore on certain occasions/rows/matches/all the above in photographs, diaries or scrapbooks.

Me:

'What is one of your favourite pieces or items of clothing and why? Do you have a photograph with you in it?'

Paul:

'A Manchester City FC lad who was getting into mither and I saved him from a beating, he gave me a Lacoste T-shirt. Had it before anyone else.'

The decision to visually record key items of clothing from Casuals' wardrobes is to prompt them to regale any memorable or unique story they have about where or when they wore that particular item, again giving me knowledge and access into their lives. Additionally further insight was offered to me; one of the football hooligans gave me a scrapbook filled with newspaper articles charting the trouble of Stoke City football fans off and on the pitch, along with photographs and police orders which bars the respondent from cities in England because of their hooligan activities. Apparently, and as Hobbs and Robbins discovered, this desire to keep and record all football related troubles and details is quite common in football hooligans, despite these semi-autobiographies often being used against them in prosecution cases on hooligan conspiracy charges.

Back in 2011, I interviewed other Stoke City Casuals who asked to remain anonymous, and discussed with them exactly what was terrace culture and how do Stoke-on-Trent's hoolies fit into this subculture? Below are the actual responses which I believe, is a prerequisite to understanding terrace culture from these first source narratives, literally their own words verbatim; what will be fascinating is to compare the general consensus on this whole scene a decade later further on in the book.

Terrace culture has been revealed to be a youth subculture which was interested in two primary aims: fighting and fashion. Coming from a working-class background, the ecstatic feelings from the football and the violence, the surge of masculine pride, often compelled football hooligans to go to the football for many years. The following excerpts are what the Stoke City Casuals responded when questioned on the topic of terrace culture.

Hooligan 1 (H1) 'Terrace culture, it's a way of life, a working-class way of life. Young men, to bond, to form an identity.'

Hooligan 3 (H3) believes that the culture involved:

'The coming together of a group of local lads who spend their money on expensive designer clothing and share a passion for supporting their local football team.'

Hooligan 3 (H3) added, '…it's become a lifestyle rather than just a weekend fixture.'

Hooligan 5 (H5) considers that: 'It's a reason for being, a coming together of like minds.'

The mutual madness, respected backgrounds, reciprocal violence, shared appreciation of clothes…the culture of the terrace Casuals was most certainly becoming noticed, picked upon by the hysterical press, the outraged and confused public and the same cuntish Old Bill.

5|
Don't Believe the Hype

The amount of feverish slang written in the British press, screaming about hooligans, the Saturday bogeymen, is to be taken with extreme caution. The word 'hooliganism' as researched by Bodin & Robène, conjures up visions of extreme behaviours, but instead of just actually defining behaviours, the phrase becomes 'overwhelmed by images, social representations and media constructions which are rather more vague and stereotyped.'

These stereotypes of (football) hooliganism are, like most rumours and whispers, based on some facts. Yes, there was violence, but perhaps not just territorial pissing towards other firms, but maybe as a way of taking power back from the invading mediocre, missionary, middle-class new wave of fans? Bodin & Robène believed that the violence was symbolic of the political status of the class struggle, allowing the hooligans to be the lead protagonists, their own heroes, in this game of life. It can be said that the collective identity of hooligans can be differentiated, not just through their clobber, style and swagger, but by the violence also.

As some of the Stoke Casuals anonymously said (2011):

H4: 'Violence has always been the main reason for becoming a hooligan, the whole culture revolves around Saturday afternoon drinking and late doors fighting. The whole process of buying a new set of clobber, meeting the lads at the boozer and then going the match is really just going through the motions before the 'main event' which usually happens at around 5.45 after the final whistle.'

In agreement, H1 states:

H1: '(Violence) It's the main, definitely the main thing really, the clothes were second to the, you know. Violence in football was there a long time before the fashion became a part of it.'

As we have already seen, the football hooligans' adoption of smart, Casual clothing, is not just a means of evading police attention, but to warn or signal to other hooligans that they are looking for the violence – the clothes being the indicator that those wearing it are up for fighting:

H1: 'It's all about getting in that row, the whole thing about football, you know, being part of the football; your main objective is to have that toe-to-toe row.'

Armstrong and Harris believe that violence is the distinguishing characteristic of the football hooligans' identity, and that due to their generally tougher working-class culture, fighting is 'one of the few sources of excitement, meaning and status.'

H5 certainly seems to follow the above theory, when he defined the attributes of himself and other football hooligans:

H5: (A football hooligan) 'gets a kick out of kicking it off.'

Hooligan 4 (H4) lends weight to the violence theory as he says:

'Violence is an integral part of terrace culture. All the subcultures, that is, the clothes, the companionship, the act of travelling to a match is all geared up to the fact that the firm is geared up to engage in violence with the opposition firm. This is the whole reason that culture on the terraces began.'

However, we know that the violence at football matches has tried to be quashed by the authorities for many years now, which is why perhaps the hooligans I interviewed believe that terrace culture in Stoke was no more. If violence is at the core of any hooligan's character and the violence has been prohibited, then what is to happen to football hooligans and their identity? Do they suddenly stop being who they are? Or do they have to adapt to the changing of the football industry and all the laws and legislations?

H1: 'I think you'll always have that culture side, you know, the actual thing that brought you there, that's gone. The violence side of things, you know, that's what being a football hooligan's about.'

The interviews reveal further just how important it is for these hooligans to wear the Casual clothes:

H4: 'It's still a status thing. Wearing those clothes shows that you're a lad, and people do things for you if they know you're a lad.'

HS: 'You are a Casual at the match, but you are also a Casual 24/7.'

This die-hard, absolute belief in the club has undoubtedly led to the Naughty Forty, then later the Under-5s, and more recently Fine Casual Element's reputation and position in the league of football hooliganism. Ironically, if what the rags say is true, we were actually top five in the Premier League of football Casuals. Pisser!

The Guardian reported back in 2003:

'Football is bracing itself for its most violent season in years as many of Britain's worst hooligans lay plans to attack rival gangs.

'Senior officers believe the hostility between hardcore elements attached to clubs such as Cardiff City, Millwall, Stoke City, Nottingham Forest and West Ham United means clashes are inevitable. The Stoke Young Casuals, who bring up to 600 hooligans to some matches, have already laid plans to confront West Ham and Sunderland supporters, for example.'

Stoke City and other older division clubs were targeted by the media and characterized as being a load of old pissheads on the rampage and a danger to society but (mostly) this mutual aggression was kept to themselves and away from grounds – more for police avoidance than health and safety, but the headlines, along with the horrendously biased reporting of Bradford, Heysel and Hillsborough football stadium disasters, did little to quell the thirst of the media witch hunt for football Casuals. Bodin & Robene found that being blood thirsty spectators of sports has been around for centuries, with the hoi polloi taking great pleasure – and encouraged to do so – as far as back in Roman times at the amphitheaters. If historically and genetically we as humans are turned on/fascinated by gore, then why the media's direct attack on football hooliganism when it is arguably deeply ingrained and programmed into us? Maybe the press and authorities have always reacted and been threatened by youth subcultures; the punks and mods were also targeted, and back in its inception the concept of teenagers itself? Perhaps teenage rebellion and refusal to conform to society made them nervous so they decide to characterize these subcultures as violent, unstable and a general menace to society?

Reporting of football violence had typically slowed down with only the odd sporadic mention of football 'carnage'. One such example was at Stoke's Checkatrade Trophy tie with local nemesis Port Vale in December 2018. We hadn't played Port Vale for yonks, so there was a real sense of excitement as a large volume of us trekked in the dark down the back ways and near the canals to get to Burslem on the quiet. Probably the closest feeling of it being a real game, an old school match with rivalry crisp in the winter air, for a long, long time.

And we weren't disappointed. Faced with hostility and a wall of Old Bill keeping folk back, and the odd group of Vale fans circling like vultures for our Stoke carcasses, it became a little bit lively.

So yeah, flares were lit, atmosphere was crackling, and the toilet windows got put through (I was in close proximity), but all in all a good time was held by everyone! Well, maybe not quite everyone.

Daily Mail, 5th December 2018:

'Lock up these animals: Stoke fans' group calls for jail after night of shame as hooligans went on a rampage after Under 21s match against Port Vale.'

Mary Whitehouse wannabe and general jobsworth Angela Smith, chair of Stoke's Supporters Council then further twists the knife:

'It was disgusting,' she said. 'It was animalistic and I am ashamed to be from Stoke as a result of the actions of a few mindless morons. I think custodial sentences are appropriate, we need to hit these people in the pocket because that is the only way they will learn.

'Banning orders are no good because I don't even think they are Stoke fans. They were just mindless idiots who were hellbent on destroying things.'

Lol!!

If modern day football hooligans can be distinguished by their style and propensity for violence, then surely Stoke-on-Trent's football firm can be differentiated further as leaders of this terrace sub-culture; simply put by Lowles & Nicholls, 'Stokies' just love to fight. As we have already seen, this recipe of extreme violence and cutting-edge clothing in the late eighties and early nineties created the terrace subculture, and it soon became evident in Stoke-on-Trent. Explosive trends in music and fashions were witnessed in Stoke City's eponymous football stadium, the Victoria Ground; renowned for its heavy, violent, passionate ambience. As one young observer recalls of his first time at the ground, it became more like a catwalk than a football match, with the Casual style being displayed like a fashion show. Chester recalled each lad trying to outshine the other with labels such as Lacoste and Adidas, which were rare at the time. Just like many other youth subcultures, those who were there at its birth, and breathed life and soul into its identity, knew of no name for either the culture, or the firm at the time, or indeed of its future importance. What the originators did understand, as do arguably the new generation today, is that the male bonding of violence and style at the match, and of being a football hooligan is unquestionably 'the passion of our culture' as depicted by Lowles and Nicholls. In fact, one hooligan explains this concept further in Chester's *Naughty* by saying that instead of this media hyped up, police patrolled mob, Stoke City's 'firm' was less violent and organised gang, more an association of men who bonded over the love of their team, each other, and a pride in a city no one else wants to know about. This bond, he argues, has got stronger as the club rejects them for the new corporate, family-orientated and aspiring middle-class fans aka the prawn sandwich brigade. Stoke City's football hooligan's ethos has always been to stick and fight together, an unbreakable bond against opposing fans, and later the other elements trying to halt them: the media, the police, the courts, and then the rave and drug scene which would go on to claim many hooligans' lives.

Much of the interviews and literature shows to what extent the proclivity for violence the football hooligans had in Stoke- on-Trent; that violence is the key feature of terrace culture, and since that has been largely quelled, the subculture is dying out. Clothes are indeed a massive part of the hooligan's identity, however, today it is more likely to show an association or solidarity with a time that is no more. The frankness and honesty with which the hooligans' expressed themselves to me, the researcher, highlighted to me a new concept; violence is the driving force of Stoke City's terrace culture, yet without it, it is just a 'culture', a culture that continues to express itself and its status through Casual clobber.

'Be Loyal, Be Proud, Be Stoke' is the by-line to Stoke City Football Club's motto: Vis Unita Fortier (United Strength is Stronger); this mentality is followed not just by the club, but its die-hard fans too, which undoubtedly goes some way to explain the power, identity, endurance and passion of Stoke City's terrace subculture.

6|
Back in the Day, Before the Cliche

Now pay close attention. We're getting to the money shot, past the cliches and lazy reporting of why we're all here: Clobber!

Guillanotti belongs to the school of thought that believes the Casual movement was one of utmost social significance, going on to describe the lads, the advocates of terrace culture, as 'cultural intermediaries' – a term first used by Bourdieu, and applies to those involved in the production, and later sharing, of symbolic belongings. This can certainly be related to the Casuals, who disseminated their unmistakable style at football matches, both home and away, and in social meeting places such as pubs and clubs. Like all fashions, the Casual look evolved over the years, from Lois flares and ubiquitous wedge haircuts, to luxury leisure and sportswear; at first the whole scene was a working class secret, spread and communicated at matches, and also by the younger generation of lads looking to emulate their elders and going to certain shops in Manchester and Liverpool. This unspoken propagation of style from the innovators was ultimately a means to pass the torch to the up-and-coming boys. As Redhead stated, this was an early form of brand or even buzz marketing. The regional styles depended purely on the local resources; compared to today's array of retail choices, the football hooligans in the eighties were limited to a couple of shops in the Northwest, although the Southern Casuals were able to have even more expensive labels available to them, such as Armani,

Ralph Lauren and Aquascutum. Thornton perceived that it meant any lad wanting to look Casual, he had to be both inventive and resourceful, with perhaps the Scousers from Liverpool the best at this; broadening their horizons and often obtaining luxury clothes and watches from abroad when they were supporting their team. This led to a demand in more and more unusual items, in fact the whole process of saving, or procuring, a unique and desired item, or unknown brand before anyone else, was just as much a pleasure as the wearing of the item itself.

A notorious stake in the claim of the birth of Casual culture, going as far back as the late seventies, Liverpool's 'Boot Boys', regular scrappers down at Anfield, were evolving stylistically. Dave Hewitson, owner of 80s Casuals, author of *The Liverpool Boys are in Town* and co-writer of *80s Casuals* – he is basically someone who was there firsthand and pretty much an expert in this – explains to me:

'As the 70s progressed the fashions changed and those Boot Boys started to take on a prehistoric look as a new style emerged. Out went the flared jeans and Doc Marten boots, replaced with narrow Lois jeans and adidas Samba, plus a new hairstyle emerged. The Wedge haircut replacing the crew-cut and feather cut. I'd go into school on the Monday talking to mates about the game, the fights and the fashion. It wasn't long before I was saving up my milk and paper round money for a pair of Samba and Lois jeans. After school I'd stand on street corners with the mates and a lad who'd just left school and was working would turn up in new trainers and clobber every week. This is 1977/78. He was the bollox but I did get an Adidas ST2 Cagoule before him. They appeared in my mums Littlewoods Winter Catalogue in 1977, so I got one ordered quick. Within weeks the other mates were asking would my ma order one for them. That Cagoule was massive on Merseyside over the next 2/3 years.'

7|
The (Brand) Consumption Back Then

Today's attention-zapped, me-me-me, instant gratification needed generation will have no idea what it was like to save up, source and scour wanted items. No internet, no high streets selling sportswear back in greysville UK in the late seventies/early eighties, our intrepid Casuals would have to go trekking across the country, across the channel, or be 'resourceful' – wink, wink, nudge, nudge.

David Elders, co-owner of Original Casuals clothing label recalls:

'Armani, Burberry, Benetton, Iceberg, Ball, very early Next jumpers, Stone Island, Boss, CP, Aquascutum, Daks, Verte Vallee, Chipie, Chevignon, Ciao and loads more – some were legitimately purchased having saved up, others less so (some people did a roaring trade from punting stock nicked from designer shops). Lots of trips around the country to visit the few shops that stocked the (then very limited) numbers that were available.'

Reminiscing about his own brand consumption experiences, Neil Primett, owner of 80s Casuals Classics, a company selling all the old faithful terrace brands (and relaunching other forgotten gems – but more on this later), confides when asked where he went for his clobber:

'London trips mostly and some local sports stores and Hitchin had a decent Market. London was a bit less than an hour away. I recall Chapel Market and pie and mash with a lad from school who had moved up from Arsenal – Finsbury. He had the ski jacket, biggest necklace, sovereigns and biggest hair sprayed wedge fringe. His girlfriend was matching Casual – Farahs, roll necks, Pringle, Lyle knits, sky jackets, cagouls. Brands like Sergio Tacchini seemed to be the biggest and lads would wear full tracks, Lacoste, Farah trousers, Lois jeans and cords were both available local. Kappa went biggest around '84-85 and widely worn – ski jackets to cagouls. Knitwear Lyle & Scott, Pringle and biggest of all but maybe not elite, Pierre Cardin, a fun colourful knit.'

This commitment, this die-hard dedication to traipsing round the country is a common theme throughout and symbolises the commitment to this Casual cause – the holy grail of obtaining something no one else had, the shimmering, shiny, new bit of clobber attracting the group of eagle-eyed magpies, ready to swoop on kleptomaniacally, to take inspo, then fly off to find something even better. After all, these favoured brands faded fast (back then when not looked through by rose-tinted Casual nostalgia), and it was a competition to keep up with the latest trends, the newest brands, the next editions.

Hewitson clarifies:

'Having the most expensive Samba gave kudos and a one upmanship over those kids with the cheaper range. A feeling that would ingrain itself into the culture. The make of jeans changed on a monthly basis with different brands having their 15 minutes in the spotlight. Everything at this point, 1977 to 1980 was available locally. Soon Samba were unfashionable and Stan Smith became the footwear for the trendier smoothie, as one or two were being called. Between '77 to '80 it was only ever Adidas trainers coupled with different makes of jeans, a Slazenger jumper, then a Pringle, a Peter Storm Cagoule or the Adidas ST2 or even a Patrick Cagoule. But the fashion was about to take a turn. Europe beckoned and by 1980 the Adidas on offer in Liverpool had become passe.'

For fuck's sake. So as soon as you'd just spunked your hard-earned/grafted brass, finally tracked down what you wanted, travelled to God knows where, the clobber had already moved on. Left you in the dust. Do keep up.

Looking beyond England's green and pleasant lands became the ultimate goal in this hallowed, much publicised game of one upmanship – and this game was facilitated by the cheap passage of travel provided by the Transalpino travel agency to a flurry of sport-lux infested Euro cities. This penchant for high-end athletic attire sported by these insatiable footy lads was becoming noticed. Subculture magazine extraordinaire and connoisseur of all things firmly on the yoof pulse, The Face magazine proclaimed them the 'Casuals' – they had arrived.

8|
Paninaro, Oh, Oh, Oh

So just what exoticness was occurring on these Transalpino trips abroad? What was this Paninaro style they were bringing back to jaw-dropping affect and making lads drool with jealousy over their effortless styling. In one word, Paninaro culture was swish. Cool as fuck. And the as unnamed yet Casuals appropriated this style, which had its long-lost twin in the UK's mod culture – their commonalities being youth culture, smart attire and a love of scooters as described in Liverpudlian store Transalpino's blog.

We can't talk about terrace culture without talking about the about the Paninaro subculture; the influence of the Paninaro movement without doubt underpins the Casual subculture and how the lads on the terraces dressed. Key looks and brands included Best Company, Moncler, Stone Island, CP Company, stalwarts of Casual dressing even to this day. In the eighties and nineties, eagle-eyed Casuals in the UK would take bits of this style.

Self-proclaimed Casual (Tottenham), tailor and archiver of one of the best Stoney collections I've ever seen, Simon Dowling, says:

'We never saw a whole look but would pick up on individual items through magazines. Some people have really jumped on it recently.'

So, do our Casuals still get inspired by the Paninaro even today? The plot thickens.

Interestingly, even though the Paninaro-inspired Casual movement is still going strong in the UK and abroad, does it still exist in Italy today or have the cool and apathetic Milanese youth today moved on?

Interviewing CP Company's President Lorenzo Osti, son of iconic CP founder Massimo Osti, about the state of Italian Casuals today, I ask him this very question.

Lorenzo: 'In Italy it's totally different. Casual is really small. Really, really small. So, the small part that we have, actually looks to you, Northern UK, as an inspiration, as a uniform, as a brand they carry. But here the same brands are adopted by different cultures. It's more, I want to say fashion related...more lifestyle.'

Me: 'Don't you think it's actually quite ironic then that this now small, Casual group in Italy look to the UK, when obviously we went to Italy to get it in the first place. Some of the Paul & Shark and obviously CP and Stone Island, you know, high-end at the time, Italian brands...and then the fans used to go over there a lot and take them, so it's been a total round trip!'

Lorenzo continues when discussing CP Company's early clientele and how the Paninaro appropriated this style, which the Casuals then reimagined, and now modern Italian Casuals take inspiration from. Full circle, much?!

'Because my father, when my father started CP before Stone Island, I mean, the kind of man he had in mind was very different, let's say, sophisticated, intellectual, left-handed (left wing)...Very close to people he was hanging out with. So, the cultural scene, political scene in Bologna, someone who really, I mean, could appreciate the products...people with knowledge. And that's what happened. They pick it up but then the big boom came from Paninaro.

'That was absolutely a totally different thing. I mean, it was really about the power of the brand, the price of what you get, there was no culture about products. And then the Casuals I think looked at the Paninaro and pick up the brand but again, they transform it again. I mean the connection you have is much more about the culture. And from what I've seen coming to visit your place, there is quite a big understanding of the product and the quality, so again, its…I think it's weird that my father's products follow this very unusual path, passing through subcultures, much different one from the other.'

So, is this proof that Casual culture exists?

It is unquestionable, according to the first edition of the Paninaro Magazine, that people are still purchasing Paninaro/Casual brands and are heavily involved in/affiliated with 'this thing of ours'.

Iconic Casual brands that are held in loving, nostalgic regard include:

Fila, Lois, Bonneville (Navy Arctic), Best Company, Benetton, Ball, Kappa, CP Company, Sergio Tacchini, Ciao, Head, Pod, Maccano, Gabbici, Ellesse, Marc O'Polo, Patrick, Newman, Cerruti 1881, Chipie, C17, Le Coq Sportif, Chevignon, Peter Storm, Ocean Pacific, Adidas Lendl, Lacoste, Diadora, Liberto, Ton Sur Ton, Reebok, Farah, Fred Perry, Next Safari, C&A, Faconnable, El Charro, Taverniti, Admiral, Stone Island, CP, Helly Hansen, Armand Basi, Boss, Lyle & Scott, Aquascutum, Naf Naf, Berghaus, Fiorucci, Paul & Shark, Armani, Dolce & Gabbana, Timberland, Maestrum, Marshall Artist, Pretty Green, Weekend Offender, Burberry, Left Hand, New Balance, Rockport, Prada, Valentino, Clarks, Ralph Lauren, Moncler, Iceberg, Missoni, Henri Lloyd, Evisu, Kenzo, Nigel Cabourn, Plurimus, St95, Napapijri, Belstaff, Barbour, Columbia, Gant, Paul Smith.

9|

From Bowie to Boss, Laaa

But it wasn't just the charm of the Italo aesthetic that drew our earnest young Casual pups in. Influences were also evident from home grown subcultures evolving from the skinheads to the punks to the mods. This was good news for those unable to actually go abroad themselves as another Casual style was emerging.

Hewitson explains:

'By 1985 the Sportswear phase had passed as the older lads passed their gear down to younger siblings or sold it on. The Wade Smith Store had also opened in Liverpool in November of '82 offering all sorts of adidas without the need to travel. The Geography Teacher/Retro Scal (Scally) look took hold with Cord or Tweed Jackets plus M+S Jumpers over a check Shirt and Timberland Moccasins or Hush Puppies on the feet becoming de rigueur in the pubs and clubs as well as the match.'

But don't hold your breath too long. You still had to be rapid as fuck and creatively tuned in to what was going around culturally in order to pull bits of inspiration from all around. Indeed, the Casuals were part of a zeitgeist, each new wave of Casual coincided with a new era of fashion, football, music, politics, culture.

These mediums' influence on the evolution of Casual styles was never more so evident then music icons, David Bowie, Ian Curtis, Paul Weller, Liam Gallagher to name but a few; their style, swagger and clobber playing a key role in the relationship between performer and fans as discussed in MacKenzie's thesis.

Bowie's influence on late seventies pre-Casualites, is particularly striking – and paradoxically from the most un-striking item of clothing from Bowie's *Low* album cover and image from on *The Man who Fell to Earth* – the singer sports a modest duffle coat combined with a wedge haircut. Did the self-proclaimed geography teacher style as mentioned before by Hewitson, actually become influenced further by a muted 'look' from a music icon typically renowned for his flamboyance?!

This simplistic aesthetic of the duffle coat was chosen specifically for its un-uniqueness for Bowie's character in the 1976 film where his alienness/aloofness was key for the film's narrative. But the orange wedge haircut struck a chord with this new subculture – perhaps because of the traditional, outmoded element of the piece, the dandyism was in juxtaposition with the vibrant hair style of the day. This styling resonated deeply and can be traced back historically amongst the working class, underpinning our Casual culture theory of higher-class aspiration which has long been a rooted feeling, going back as far as the 'costermongers, hooligans and scuttlers of Victorian England,' as written about by Mayhew, Pearson, Davies and MacKenzie amongst others. And this 'dandy' look (read British aristocracy but less scruffy, more styled and just OWNED), can still be seen today on certain gents of the older generation still affiliated with the Casual look. Maybe it just ages better, like a fine wine?!

The duffel in question is British made brand Gloverall with a military-purpose background. Due to its popularity, Gloverall was found in outdoor, camping and leisure shops. Hmmm, sound familiar? The pillaging of athletic and sports shops by our lovable roving Scouse footie lads decades later?!

Henri-Lloyd, a label with a strong nautical background, often produced versions of a wool peacoat which is most definitely related to the Gloverall duffel; whilst watching historical programmes featuring nineteenth and twentieth century navy or army personnel, I always see the resemblance to our latter day peacoats, duffels and smocks (like in *The Terror* on BBC2) and think how great they look, often paired with a thick wool knit polo neck jumper which wouldn't look out of place in Simon Dowling's Stone Island collection. A keen eye, attention for detail, and a fondness for clobber that has features associated with leisure/sports/military wear is a concurrent theme when researching Casuals – evident in brands with military/industrial backgrounds such as Burberry, Belstaff and Boss. After all, Hugo Boss designed uniforms for the SS whilst Thomas Burberry provided officers with coats specifically for the trenches, the birth of the everlasting trench coat. Belstaff, a brand with roots in aviation and the navy, was created in my home county of Staffordshire – just up the road in Longton duck. Belstaff is actually one of the brands that all the Stoke Casuals I spoke to still wore now due to its heritage and links with our city.

CP Company is one of the most iconic 'Casual' brands and with the most longevity, appreciation and love within the terrace community. Again, the origin of CP stems from this appropriation of high-class culture by the working class – the extreme functionality, innovation and (again often military style) practicality of these products striking a chord with our young Casuals. Lorenzo Osti explained to me:

'This brand has been successful when it has been able to resonate with the society at that time. In the seventies, there was a big opposition between the young, the fathers and sons, or parents and sons. So, there had been the 1968 the hippy culture. All this generation was really heavily against the previous one or trying to flip the status quo.

'What my father did with CP Company actually was very similar within his field. What he did, he took the garment of that time, actually was the garment of the parents in a way...that garment was particularly stiff. Stiff in two different ways. One, from I mean a fabric perspective so a coat, a new coat really looking new, no? And that was the value, when a family save money to buy a new coat, you want the new coat to look new. All the fabrics a bit like this, really you know, out of the box effect. So, what my father does, he says, I hate that, I want garments that look old, so he starts to garment dye everything and it was very unusual because people went into a nice shop, a coat that was, I don't know, about 700/1000 euros, and it looks old.

'At that time nobody was doing that. Now it's pretty common, we have all the vintage, the fascination of the vintage and old things, but at that time was weird. So, if we flip this the other way...The other way is the garment, and the previous generation were very rigid in their functionality. I mean, you have garments to go to work, you have garments for Sunday, to go to church, garments for hunting, for sport; everything had its own function. He took all this and start to mix it up, taking pockets from hunting jackets and putting it on the coat, and take a military parker and make it something to put over a blazer. So, I think that that generation was questioning their parents and trying to change the status quo and found in the garments something that reflected their attitude to society.'

Lorenzo continues:

'I actually put this as a question to Professor Andrew Groves, I don't know why in the UK, North of UK (Casual clothes) are so popular, and he told me. Again, these people are working class people, familiar with working clothes. One part of it was taking that kind of clothes and elevating with nice fabric...so it was something they understand, it was their own language. It was not like the check cardigan of the upper class or silk scarves, it was garments for them, but elevated and they understood. So probably, again, they have been able to connect with this garment, to get some empathy.'

A working-class game for working-class people. Footy. Football Casuals. We are familiar with these military, industrial and functional clothes. It's our twist, our way of wearing it, owning it, that makes it Casual as fuck.

10|

Music is the Answer (To Your Problems)

In the absence of social media informing you how to eat, sleep, rave, repeat, youth culture absorbed trends from mediums such as Top of the Pops; Bowie, Madonna, Oasis, The Jam, The Pet Shop Boys, Happy Mondays, The Farm, The Stone Roses, to name just a sliver of artists whose style, swagger and sartorial skills, spawned copies nationwide.

Jared Latimer, a key figure in Stoke's Casual retail world and lynchpin in such iconic shops as Review and Terraces, argues:

'In the older days, if you watched early Top of the Pops, the bands that would be wearing designer stuff. They'd be buying stuff from Army and Navy stores or second-hand stores, or something different. So, people wanted to be different, like the bands they were into.'

I recall Paul Heaton on Top of the Pops wearing very early CP. He was a football 'lad' but performing on stage. Heaton is a well-known Sheffield United fan and Casual aficionado, along with his previous band the Housemartins, were one of the first bands that terrace lads could relate to. Heaton himself stated in Proper Magazine that there was a load of football lads at their earlier gigs:

'Yeah, there was quite a bit, especially the further north we went. By the time we got up to Aberdeen circa 1986 it was 90% ASC (Aberdeen Soccer Casuals) in the crowd.'

The eighties and nineties were so creatively rich, so saturated with mint tunes and clobber that led smoothly into the indie pop era which itself ran simultaneously with the notoriety of football Casuals and hooligans, but who has influenced who? Teenagers, the bastions of subcultural styles, have long been influenced by their heroes since the days of Buddy Holly. With key cultural musical markers that have underpinned the Rockers, the Mods, the Punks, the Skins, the Goths, and later the Casuals, do the artists themselves take inspiration from the adoring, thriving yoof around them? Music, fashion, fans; this infinite circle of mutual appropriation, inspiration, adulation. As the modfather Paul Weller himself says:

'When I was growing up, the cultural reference points that defined your character were music, clothes and football.'

Now a legendary style icon himself, he continues the circle of life for clobber inspiration.

Darren aka Oliver Beer (Stoke) believes full heartedly that eighties pop stars and the pop cultural references around them actually influenced and inspired Casual fashion as opposed to the popular belief that the Scousers were the first to find the brands on their Transalpino trips abroad.

'You'd see Duran Duran. You'd see the Pet Shop Boys wearing Armani and Stone Island, and you'd think, that's smart. Because you always want to, if you see someone famous and they look cool, I'll buy that, then you think you'll look smart; sometimes you do, sometimes you don't!'

We only have to think of the legendary Bez sporting just the (CP Company) Mille hood to demonstrate this mutual appropriation of music and football Casual culture.

11|

Northern Monkeys V Southern Fairies; The Influences in the Geographical Divide

With each region having their own Casual nuances and predilections, it's interesting to hear which brands were adopted by particular regions and why. The rivalry and mutual proud chest puffing existed long before the heady heights of the Casual era. Bill Routledge, author of *Northern Monkeys*, succinctly writes:

'Southerners have seemingly always looked down their bent, Roman noses at proletariat, downtrodden scowling northerners.

'The myth is that southerners are the dogs' bollocks, the bee's knees, the cream and everything of worth begins, is established, and ends, in the epicentre of the universe, that is, London.'

Routledge theorises that the cartoonish northern caricature was dispelled by the rise of the 'Casual/dresser' cult; that emanating from the grim up north was this slick movement of dressers, combined with this magical, magnetic, musical mecca…it ain't called Northern **Soul** for nothing.

The concurrence between every single person interviewed that these regional differences exist is entrenched and felt deeply. Coowner of Original Casuals brand David Elders (Hibs) believes that:

'There's always been differences in how different regions embrace different fashions. Probably deep down some psychological reason along the same lines as to why we have local loyalties to teams/regions. Part of setting your stall out as to "who you are" and having an identifiable look to set you apart from others.'

The shapeshifting, fluid movement flowed effortlessly from Teddy Boy to Mod to Northern Soul, to Bowie to Perry to Casual to Madchester, we have discussed Bowie's inimitable influence, the Perry boys were developing very nicely from this – same foppish haircut, same sharp style, this lot were epitomised by the Fred Perry polo shorts they sported. Area? Manchester. Music of choice? Soul. Shop? Stolen from Ivor.

The Stolen from Ivor shop I recall myself in little old Newcastle-under-Lyme in the nineties never struck me as being 'Casual'; I was more than aware of the other North Staffs gems in the guise of Review, Infinities, Gemini, then later Terraces and Pockets that all the lads frequented; badges of honour in the form of the draw string bags with the shops label emblazoned on it. Too cool for school – rocking an Infinites bag for your PE kit – now that felt like the dogs' bollocks. But Stolen from Ivor always seemed a bit shithanger with its stocking of Eclipse jeans and other more 'chav' associated brands.

Clearly, I was late to the Stolen from Ivor party. However, as Steve Lumb, owner of Terrace Cult brand, says:

'They used to do mad shit in there, we used to end up with whatever. It was mad, people used to wear their own thing. Fila was about, then Benetton, a bit of Sergio Tacchini.'

Steve adds: 'It was definitely a football lad thing; I definitely think you could tell who was a football lad and who wasn't a football lad.

'The scousers obviously visited Europe a couple of times and went sort of rampaging through towns seeing gear we'd never dreamed of. So then, obviously if you'd play other firms, you'd see a load of boys from like Chelsea or something and think, 'what's he wearing, what's he wearing?' In them days you couldn't go home and just Google, do you know what I mean? It was a mission to try and find it. Someone would say such and such a shop in town and they got that brand we seen, and everyone would go down and get it, and it was just a part of…you wanted to be the one that stood out.'

So far, so Casual. And one brand that really appears to be a marker and epitome of the North/South divide was Hackett.

12|
Hackett Off

I ask Steve about Hackett and it not really taking off further than the Watford Gap. Agreeing, we have a good 'ol Northern gripe:

Steve: 'I remember, it was about 20 years ago, I remember being in a pub and some guy turning up saying he'd got a load of Hackett gear.'

Me: 'Oh god!'

S: 'Hackett, it was London.'

M: 'It was a southern thing?'

S: 'You'd go to Magaluf with the lads and all the cockneys would be wearing Hackett.'

M: 'With all the collars turned up?! And stuff like that?'

S: 'With number four on and shit…in the North, we've never seen it. So, listen, this guy's turned up, yeah man lets have it, I remember getting a couple of polos off him, sweet. Following week, I've gone into the same pub, the whole fucking boozer's wearing it. And we just looked like knobheads, know what I mean? So, it got binned.'

Hackett did have a moment in the spotlight up North, however. Jared Latimer believes the notorious Donal Macintyre documentary, *Undercover Football Hooligans*, where he infiltrated Chelsea's Headhunter firm, had a lot to do with a surge in Northern Hackett sales.

'I think that pushed Hackett then to the north. But it was definitely a southern thing. And as soon as that came on the TV, obviously it was all about the Terrace culture and everything else. And maybe not in a good way. But it definitely made the northern lads get onto it, just because it was a brand that we didn't really know about up here.'

Well, they do say there's no such thing as bad publicity.

Neil Primett believes these sartorial style variations existed then, and continue to this day:

'There have always been differences, definitely in the '80s and today. On peacock dressing, there's often similarities with south, Essex linking with Liverpool, Glasgow and Scotland, Newcastle, North-East. Manchester and Liverpool can have significant differences.'

I ask these brand owners whether there is significant difference between regions' style evident in physical clobber sales, aside from the infamous one upmanship games played out at the football ground.

Steve from Terrace Cult relates:

'There is a very North/South divide to it, I think. We did, for example, a jersey style polo with a zip. In the north...couldn't give it away; in the south, they lapped it up.

'We've got a massive following in London, Scotland, Barnsley, Birmingham, its little pockets just popping up, so I don't know whether it's just found its way onto the right people.

'In London, well I know the weathers a lot better than the north, but they would wear the shorts and the polo as a twin set. In the north they'd go more with the Pique style polo.'

Me: 'Or a big coat!'

Steve: 'Or big coat and scarf! Haha!'

Me: 'Big coat weather Haha!'

Jared, when he was at Review, says:

'I used to sell clothes to people from Wrexham, say. And they'd buy slightly different stuff to the Stoke lads. I remember, when you were buying things, you wouldn't sell much of them and the Wrexham lads would all want something that none of the Stoke lads would buy.'

Review was in its glory days in the nineties/noughties and, without an online presence, became a magnet for Casuals across the land:

'We were the well-established shop. We'd get a few from Liverpool, Manchester. So, the northern lads would be the main ones, but we did get a few London lads. Usually, people who had moved down from up here originally, and they'd come up with a few of their mates.'

Stoke Casuals themselves have described themselves as a 'mixed bag' (Shelton Casual) and 'like a melting pot' (Oliver Beer); the impact of Liverpool, Manchester and the South (everything sub-Watford Gap) being evident in the fine, stylish dressers of The Potteries. The central location of Stoke helped facilitate the ease in which to shop further afield, but it is indeed a blessing that we had such iconic Casual shops at our fingertips.

With pretty much only football, fighting and fashion for our Casual protagonists in this city, these shops were an interface into this other high-end, high-class world – if they couldn't have that world then at least they could look like they were part of that world. These stores bridged the gap and realised dreams – not the soulless clicking of credit card transactions online but engaging with staff and other customers with the same love of terrace fashion. We bought because we loved. We touched, we smelled, we tried on, we grafted for, a beautiful luxurious piece of fashion, a bit of history.

Jared: 'In the old days, you'd just walk into a couple of your favourite shops in the area, something would stand out to you or something would be shown to you by the staff, because they've been shown it by the people who are selling it.

'When I was buying, when you're actually seeing things and they're (brands) are showing you how it's made, and this, that and the other, then you push that over to the customer.

'Because you're face to face with them, and you can explain the fit of things. You can explain why that shirt is £200 more than that one, because it has been over-dyed or whatever it is. Whereas now, the brand is all they see, they're not getting to touch it or feel it or even try it on.'

It is this seismic change in brand consumption – how we, and especially the Casuals, consume their clobber in this new era. Renowned shops which provided a lifeline and conduit to terrace brands included:

Wade Smith, Flannels, Life, Review, Infinites, Terraces, Pockets, Gemini, Stolen From Ivor, Oi Polloi, Trilby, Palladium, Hurleys, Aspecto, Cruise, Stuarts, Lillywhites. Wellgosh.

13|

When Two Tribes Go to War

The unspoken propagation of style from our early Casual innovators was ultimately a means to pass the torch to the up-and-coming boys. The regional styles depended purely on local resources; compared to today's array of retail choices, the football hooligans in the eighties were limited to a couple of shops in the North-West (see above), although the Southern Casuals were able to have even more expensive labels available to them, such as Armani, Ralph Lauren and Aquascutum. The eighties brands appear to be more Paninaro/Euro-sport lux and appropriated resourcefully and inventively by the North and by the nineties/noughties appear to be becoming more 'Southern' – is this perhaps due to the Casual culture becoming more widespread and accessible, and the South generally being more economically positioned to purchase these increasingly expensive brands?

We know and understand the collective consumerism of certain brands ultimately sets the Casuals' identity as separate from the norm, society, the mainstream (we will discuss if this is still true later). Yet this tribal instinct of belonging with fellow humans, with the same backgrounds and shared interests, becomes even more defined and divisive when looking at the uniform of the rival football firms.

The concurrent theme of wanting to appear wealthy, exclusive, and wearing one-offs to impress not only your own firm, but also the rival hooligans is upheld from earlier interviews:

H2: 'You don't want the other mob to say Stoke are a right bunch of scruffy tramps.'

The clothes are part and parcel of modern terrace culture and are therefore integral to a collective and regional identity.

H2: 'We wear the clothes as part of our identity; the clothes are what we are all about. They are of what we are all about, an extension of who we are. The idea of attending a football match whilst not sporting Casual clothes is just not a possibility.'

So certain brands, image, aura and violence combined can differentiate the different tribes of Casuals. A 'lad' can spot another 'lad' or if they are in fact a shirter masquerading as a 'lad' and pinpoint from where he originates.

Oliver Beer explains:

'When you used to go away, you could spot different firms. You'd know them by the way they dress. The first time I saw someone in a deerstalker and a Burberry scarf, I thought, "you look like a right prick!"' When pressed, the prick in question was West Ham.

Oops.

A younger offshoot of Stoke City's football hooligans, Fine Casual Element, elaborates:

'The North are more up for it and have a row with small numbers, not like southerners who are just all about wearing flat caps and turning up 20 miles away in Stafford for example. They're probably not as bothered up North as long as it's orate; Fila, Peaceful Hooligan...whereas they (Southerners) wanna be flash and wear the dearest stuff.'

Fully getting into his stride, territorial pride starts to kick in:

'No Southerners have ever come to Stoke in my memory apart from Spurs to Stafford and Chelsea to Burslem one year, and we've took it to all of them, some more than once, even Southampton, Brighton, Southend, Colchester, Bristol etc. Not just the London ones, so either they can't sort it to travel, or they think they're too good (for us) and just interested in having it with each other and think they're that good that they only care who is the best in London.'

Football violence in films can also be a means of 'expressing a collective regional identity' describes Rehling. The hyper-macho, souped-up testosterone that is displayed by our snarling, strutting, posturing peacocks at matches (or more accurately pre/post matches), is reflected in the surge of football hooligan films. As a genre, hoolie-porn both conveyed the story of the Casual movement thus far and helped inspire those whose first and early experiences of Casuals were through celluloid.

'Shelton Casual' from Stoke believes Stone Island itself was killed off with films like *Football Factory*. And although they were 'good films' and arguably diluted this stalwart hooligan brand, it also created a renewed interest in the Casuals, with a new up and coming generation clambering for some crumbs of nostalgia and a sense of distant belonging, although the actual fighting replicated in such films, was no longer as prevalent due to Maggie, Sky et al.

He says:

'It's just – it's resurged it. It was dying off anyway, then we had *Football Factory* and it became big again.'

This is the opinion repeated by many of the older, original Casuals who were in the epicentre of the perfect storm that was football, music, clothes and fighting. Yet, the newer generation that was clinging on to the coattails of this subculture sometimes only had myths, legends and films to invite them into the intoxicating world of the terrace Casual.

When I interviewed Matthew Snell, founder of online football community, Casual Client Clothing, about his first dip of the toe into Casual clobber, he says:

'Stone Island was the one to have. And probably still is. Shortly after I first noticed the dress code, *Football Factory* came out in 2004. And that just intensified the interest.'

Exhilarating, intense, climactic – the pinnacle of the mundane, mediocre, middle-of-the-road, mish working week was the violence experienced on match day in all its Casual, clobbered-up glory; these moments captured on film, the visceral passion often relayed better through this medium are, as Rehling explains, to communicate what participants call the buzz they experience when it 'goes off'.

In the voiceover of *It's a Casual Life* (2003), a short film written by former hooligan Dougie Brimson, Jimmy, the narrator, rejects academic 'pricks' and their 'treatises' that hooligans are enacting class warfare, saying all they cared about was 'our manor, our clothes, our mates.' Violence, he tells us, is like no other drug he has done. Hoolie porn films include *Awaydays, Casuals, Football Factory, Green Street* and other virile portrayals of the undiluted, unwavering sense of belonging to your own firm. In fact, director Alan Clarke, the man behind *The Firm*, sums this up perfectly. According to him, there were no shots of actual matches in his film because, 'It's not about football, nothing to do with it. It's about tribes.'

14|

Smooth Operators

Casual films like *The Business* are arguably more stylistic than other, meatier, hooligan films. As such, they are leaders in a sub-genre that both influences millennials that want to be Casuals as well the old-school Casuals that experienced the lifestyle as it was emerging. *The Business*, which spawned a number of watered-down copies, is still regarded as a classic due to its soundtrack, storyline and of course, clobber – who can forget Danny Dyer's iconic tiny eighties Fila shorts?! Um, not me ☺.

Simon Dowling (Tottenham, Stone Island collector extraordinaire) says:

'You gotta weigh up the facts vs entertainment. All very watchable but factually accurate??? Who cares. I love a film about footie and clobber. Throw in some sniff and birds and happy days. *Football Factory* and *The Business* are still my favourites. Good soundtracks as well.'

End of!

The Southern pastel Casual scene appears to be sun dappled, warm and effortlessly draped in Pringle and Fila, as opposed to the cold harsh anorak and Adidas Casuals of the North. Neil Primett owns 80s Casuals Classics which along with stocking 'Casual brands of today' also stocks adored Casual labels such as Farah, Ellesse, Lois and have been instrumental in the relaunch of old favourites such as Patrick.

Primett, who supplies Nick Love-involved films such as *The Business* and future TV series *A Town Called Malice*, explains:

'As much as I like football, I think we were Southerner poser Casuals and drew broader scale influences. All the hairdressers had the George Michael on the wall, he and Andrew Ridgely were brand icons for Fila, Sergio, Diadora and we had sun beds and wanted all the jewellery.

'Nike and Diadora seemed flash and expensive whereas Adidas seemed like an everyman games teacher. Down South, we talk fashion wise about the North as having a tribal mentality and a code that at times might be similar. Words like smoothies, posers, dressers and soul boys went hand in hand with Casuals and I think we really thought girls and boys could be Casuals; being effeminate was no big deal; he/she wore pastel jumpers, Benetton rugby tops, Lois cords and figure-hugging Farah trousers. A white tennis trainer was a must. I don't think it's Southern to adopt the poser look though – it's not Manchester but similarities happen today in Liverpool, Scotland, Newcastle.'

Wham!

15|
End of the (Nova Checked) Line

After a decline of football hooliganism in the late eighties due to the police, media, courts and the rave scene, there was this renaissance of terrace culture in the early nineties, and a renewed passion for violence and the Casual style. There was more choice by now; the internet, more travel and greater retail opportunities meant that certain items could no longer be described as unique. In fact, as Thornton wrote, many fashions became saturated by popularity, and then diluted in credibility. As with all popular subcultures that attract the mainstream, people wanting to buy into the look would copy the labels favoured by the football hooligans leading to disillusionment for the lads, and a brand image disaster for the brands copied. This most famously happened with Burberry. Once a staple of Casual fashion, and almost a symbol for terrace culture in general, the lads adopted Burberry as they had always adapted highly branded clothing, as a means of eluding the police.

Burberry: 'Don't know if we killed it or made it.' (Paul Walters, 2022)

When another subculture – the 'chavs' – joined in and copied the Casuals, Power and Hague researched how the popularity and image of Burberry and its signature check, declined dramatically with both high-end customer and the football hooligan himself. Casuals are quick to discard a label or brand if they feel it is becoming too popular; the brand Stone Island was an iconic label for terrace culture due to its cost and exclusiveness. As one Casual describes to Brown and Harvey, 'the Stone Island label is an ID tag to spot potential lads.' This was true, until the subculture became mainstream, and true football hooligans began abandoning labels that were being worn by (in their eyes) fake fans, the pretenders.

Casuals' haughtiness towards brand bandwagon jumpers such as the robotic purchasing of Stone Island for the match is clear and fixes them a dilemma; do Casuals still want to be known/viewed as 'Casuals' wearing traditional terrace labels such as Stone Island, Burberry and CP, even though Casuals by their very definition and inception are meant to be wearing unique, differentiable and hard to find clobber... How do you do that whilst making it appear and showing to the world you're a Casual?

This is in direct contrast to hooligans who, as Jasper (Mark Chester, Stoke City) recalled, were proud wearing their 'uniform', like part of a platoon and trip off the reputation and connotations associated with being a hoolie.

Despite these two separate mindsets, there is clear parallel between the hoolies and the Casuals, and if hoolies are often tarred with being a chav, does that mean by default there a thin line between chav and Casuals themselves (gulp)? The stereotypical cliché of both is, according to Original Casuals' Davide Elders, that they are 'knuckle-dragging halfwits with no brains or talents' due to both groups' popular and incessant use of Burberry and Stone Island, mindless thuggery and perceived racist connotations.

'Wearing Stone Island to the Christmas family meal in case anyone wants sparking out.' This is a popular meme on social media and is evidence of the general public's overall opinion that anyone wearing Stone Island is associated with football violence – or even worse, tries too hard and wants to be affiliated with it, thinking this is the easiest way of being thought of a 'hooligan'.

'Hooligans were only interested in having a row, the clothes and Casual culture didn't matter to them. Casuals wanted to look the best as well as well as being the best. One upmanship. The hangers on who just wanted to wear the clothes but not get involved in the other side were soon fucked off out of it in the main.' Elders told me.

Similarly, Matthew Snell from Casual Client Clothing says:

'I feel Casual culture and hooliganism are clashing since the Euros final. I say "hooliganism" but really, it's just kids having too much beer and whatever else. I wear a Stone Island soft shell (jacket) for work sometimes and people at work say, "are you wearing that in case someone needs knocking out?" This is the connotation that gets brought with the mindless actions of kids that have watched *Green Street* a few times and their grandma brought them a Stone Island crew neck for Christmas. I wear it because I like it.'

Because I like it. This was a universal answer in every person I asked. The whole Casual psychology was to wear it, own it, work it; not a contrived, forced fashion faux pas. The Casuals were and still now, doing it for themselves. Jared Latimer explains:

'With the Casual, its literally more about how they feel, that they're wearing something that. They're not really fitting into anywhere, they want to look good for themselves.'

Richardson wrote that by claiming to be the more genuine and authentic fan, the Casual is flexing his cultural capital as a means of safeguarding distinctions not only between social classes, but between categories of fans also. Ironically, with heightened media and public interest in terrace culture and its fashions, the very labels the hooligans favoured due to their ability to blend in the crowds, to be looked on as a respectable member of the public due to the expense of the clothes, to project a different image of themselves in order to avoid police and spot other Casuals, was paradoxically now actually making them stand out and be visibly distinguished as football hooligans. Uh oh!

16|
Clone Island

Has the term 'Clone Island' ever been more apt; the uniform for the general masses?

'When you see lads wearing Stone Island overshirts at the match and that, you just think it's a bit chavvy,' says the elusive Shelton (in Stoke) Casual.

Agreeing Oliver Beers says:

'Everyone who wears Stone Island now gives it the big 'un. Back in the day they were lads. It was like a subculture. Your shirters would also be the fighters…they were a little group. And people seem to forget that.'

Shirters, aka supporters who wear strips and club merchandise, are not far evolved from those early boorish fans in the seventies sporting flares with club colours and scarfs. Shirters nowadays are seen as the lowest of the low in the fan hierarchy – commonly found in the family stand, wearing a team strip combined with boot cut jeans, wriggling bored kids and a disapproving look whenever they hear swearing at a football match – shock horror!

But I feel that Stone Island wearers are indeed looked on as shirters now; a diluted hoolie, wannabe, the token 'edge' clobber for the match. Middle aged men who missed out on being a real lad so hope wearing an easily bought Stone Island jacket or jumper gives them a slither of credibility (in the corporate box!) or spice up their marriage with the missus thinking she's downgrading to a bit of rough for the night. Either way, it's fucked.

Why does no one dress opposite of the norm anymore to avoid Old Bill detection and strategically underwhelm/false advertise to the enemy, that they ought to be underestimated and fucking surprise them rather than be pointed out immediately in the uninspiring Stone Island wall of armour aka a shield of glistening overcoats? Why doesn't anyone go in, say, skinny mod suits or just anything different to look stylish but throw police off the scent?! May as well have an arrow pointing saying 'wannabe hoolie' if you wear Stoney at the match today. But this is a product from a very vacuous and uncreative, lazy, socially spoon-fed generation – where's ya originality?!

17|
Symbolic Consumption

The whole Casual love affair with labels meant that football hooligans could spot other lads due to the symbolic indicators of clothes and speech, yet there exists other, more personal reasons for these clothing choices. The threat to what they believe is their territory results in actions of masculine pride, King theorises, and a self-aggrandizement which is reflected in their style of fashion. Hobbs and Robins explain this concept further, as they believe the stylistic decisions by football hooligans are related to: 'the self-imagery and self-promotion of working-class youths through class specific hierarchies of violence and conspicuous consumption.'

The Casuals' trademark smart appearance is also in great contrast to affluent fans and families' choice of wearing replica shirts and team colours; an act which the Casuals regard as un-masculine and extremely fake, and that wearing a Ralph Lauren item of clothing has more identity and allegiance to the club than the array of identikits. This type of fan also likes to be identifiable and distinguishable but uses colours and scarves to do this; an act of their own subculture of consumption, explains Derbalx, Decrop & Cabossart. They go on to conjecture that whereas the Casual (but maybe not so much a modern day, proud-of-the-stereotype hooligan) would aim not to wear anything which could identify him, or his football team, the new middle-class fan will proudly display the team colours to show loyalty and that they are a recognised member of that group of faithful supporters in a bonded communion. These fans are not part of terrace culture and are eyed by the Casuals as inauthentic fans; fans in team colours don't always go to away matches, don't drink, are well behaved and feverishly consume the club's merchandising. It has become more of a corporate past time for this new wave of 'fans' and a chance to show business partners how much money they have, how cool they are for attending a footie match and in general appropriating an entire subculture then diluting it for a further piss take, a kick in the bollox for the working class lads on whom they emulate to a certain extent in terms of bravado and confidence at said match, but most definitely look down upon especially when the going gets tough. Let's face it, if it went off in the box, they'd be scarpering before they'd even had chance to scoff their soggy prawn sandwiches.

Yet for football Casuals, the game was a ritual, a way of life in which they built long-lasting relationships and confirmed their masculinity. The breakdown of the traditional class structure consequently meant that the working-class male's identity was in crisis; now with the middle-class makeover of an historic working-class game, the hooligans and Casuals had to find a way to express themselves, which again, was violence and fashion; something the new fans would not understand or ever be part of.

18|

Consumption Communities

Cova defines the word 'tribe' as: 'a local sense of identification, religiosity, syncretism, group narcissism...the common denominator of which is the community dimension' – in particular tribes that can be held together through their consumption practices. Indeed, this can be applied to terrace culture; a culture which unites men of working-class backgrounds who live for football, fighting and fashion. The act of consumption often involves interaction with families, peers, subcultures or other organisations, writes Holt and later Richardson, and that the consumption choice is frequently made on the ability a brand can provide in terms of social interaction and community participation, the perceived social linking value. King has firmly established that football fandom is a consumption activity, with a community of like-minded men who engage in communicating and advocating their 'beliefs' (or rather their culture and the clothes that represent it), in fanzines firstly and more recently in online communities, fan forums and huge social media pages dedicated to hooligans regionally, nationally and internationally. This post-modern tribe can now congregate online, follow sites, post-match phone-ins and fanzines just as easily as the football stadiums. Terrace culture as a community is strengthened further by expressing their solidarity in opposition to the rival fans; a sense of community which is based on mutual hatred and desire for physical violence.

Football hooligans may appear as though they are part of a brand community; after all, their community is based on a structured set of social relations among admirers of a brand, argues Muniz and O'Guinn. They also share the same rituals and traditions; the clothes they wear on match day, the places and pubs they go to before the game, the fights they have with the rival hooligans. All these experiences are shared, thus activating the belief that they are true members of this community. By wearing the same brands, McAlexander, Schouten and Koenig believe that the hooligans and Casuals become almost disciple like in advocating their tribe's identity; this shared symbolism passed down to the younger generation of lads who in turn spread the 'word' about the clothes and brands.

As we have already seen, however, they are quick to disengage from a brand if the mainstream or undesirables start wearing it too. Burberry and Stone Island are the main examples of this. Certainly, terrace culture is a subculture of consumption, 'a distinctive subgroup of society that self-selects on the basis of a shared commitment to a particular product class, brand, or consumption activity' write Schouten & McAlexander. Furthermore, just like the Harley Davidson bikers in Schouten and McAlexander's eponymous ethnographic study, Casuals identify with a particular style of dress and penchant for violence and through the objects of consumption, identify with other people. Terrace culture is a collective of men who consume the same products in the same way; they are a tribe, a style community perhaps as opposed to a brand community.

Clothes are our way of communicating with the world, we tell our story and character through how we dress. This branded vocabulary only helps build our personal narratives and makes whatever statement we want to make, whether its belonging to a certain group, a shared sense of identity. We are bigger than a brand; we are what we wear, and we are our own brand.

Or for us Casuals, we concur with Liam Gallagher when he said:
'My style comes from football and all this Casual thing.'
Quite.

Part 2:

The Present: The 808 State of Terrace Culture Today

19|

'Death' of Terrace Culture

Even 10 years ago the hoolies and Casuals I asked said terrace culture was dead. What limp, flaccid state is it in in 2022?

The abolishment of the terraces in an arguably hysterical, media-fueled reaction by the police and authorities was at one point said to have 'quietened' football hooliganism and transformed it from a traditional working-class game into a corporate, sanitised hobby for the wealthier classes. When asked about this, and whether terrace culture even exists anymore in, the answer was as follows:

Hooligan 2: 'It's dying.'

Hooligan 1: 'It's not as important as it was 10, 15 years ago.'

The transformation of football in the 1990s has been documented by King and Redhead significantly, and the hooligans in Stoke-on-Trent seem to agree with the main reasons given by the academics.

Hooligan 3: 'In my opinion, terrace culture died with all the removal of the actual terraces from all football stadiums and the introduction of seats.'

This decision from the Football Association to 'clean up its act' (H3), appears to have been taken badly by the hooligans, but there are also several other key factors, such as drugs and growing up, that can be accounted for the decline in the terrace subculture.

H1: 'Yeah, families, all seater stadiums, er drugs as well, er, which you know. The clothes and that became mainstream; part of life instead of a subculture, underground, something that you can identify yourself as being a bit special, different from other people. So that sort of killed some of the identity, and then obviously the police clamped down a lot more, and a lot of hooligans, old school, you know, grew up, settled down.'

H3: 'We started to arrange "rows" away from the stadium using our phones like, only to find the Old Bill also turning up with handheld videos filming the lads in action.'

The empirical data available backs up to some extent the theory that terrace culture is a subculture for the football hooligans, however, the response from the hooligans, that the police, threat of prison and simply growing up played a massive part in the death of the true terrace culture, the disintegration of the atmosphere and sociality of the old non-seating, terraced football grounds. Nevertheless, it is the hooligans' relentless appetite for fighting which made themselves turn away from the culture; they began to 'hunt' for violence away from the ground, making terrace culture fragment further as more and more of the lads split up and looked for violence.

H3: 'With video evidence the Old Bill started to arrest us, like, in dawn raids and that. They hit the lads with football banning orders which meant you aren't allowed to go any football match in the UK. Some had to, like, hand in passports to police when England played away so we couldn't cause trouble abroad, so for me, personally this was the death of terrace culture, and now consider myself an ex-hooligan.'

The other hooligans agreed with this and believed that with the moving of many football team's grounds from the familiar, yet threatening air of the terraced streets, to all-seater soulless slick sport stadia, these transfers also took with it a firm's spirit and terrace culture.

H1: 'Now you've got different little firms that don't come together, do their own thing. Partly because the ground was moved, you don't congregate anymore, you haven't got the pubs like you used to. And once the firm got too big, you couldn't have that bond; just a few of you and you trust each other.'

When asked whether there still exists football hooligans in Stoke-on-Trent and whether it still has a terrace culture anymore there is a resounding, 'No' (H1, H2, H3, H4). However, all believe there remains a leftover, remaining, element of this subculture, as all the hooligans believe that the style and some of the culture is still being perpetuated even today.

That was the general consensus a decade ago. What has been happening to terrace culture and Casual brands since my research in 2011?

Oliver Beer follows on the same theory:

'I think it's still there to a degree. But it's not the way it used to be. Obviously, you've got CCTV cameras everywhere, policing. We used to organize things, didn't have a mobile phone. Your main guys would have the numbers of the other guys – they'd ring up and say, "this is where we're meeting." It's not like that now. So obviously, that's gone. Now you go to a match and every man and his dog has got Stone Island on.'

20|
Credit Card Casuals

The snootiness of which 'original' Casuals loftily hold their opinions of this younger generation is evident in the interviews. With the death of the high street coinciding with the death of the terrace Casual (purportedly), there is a sense of bitterness towards the instant gratification, insta generation.

'Now, every kid with their parent's credit card can jump online and order something to arrive the next day. Hence every twat with jeans that look like they're painted on, is strutting around in Stone Island or CP, completely missing the point. They wear it to look the same as all their mates while we wore it to try to look different from every other fucker.' David Elders from Original Casuals.

'The internet has cheapened a lot of what made the scene what it was. A big part of it was exclusivity. The work that had to go into finding something that you were unlikely to find someone else wearing, that looked different from what everyone else was wearing.'

The uniqueness of a highly desired piece emphasises the whole Casual ethos. Oliver Beer (Stoke Casual) explains:

'I wear the labels I like. No other reason than that. I mean I buy very little Stone Island. I buy a little bit of Moncler. I like stuff like this Plurimus jacket because there's only 99 in the world and that's it, so the chances of you banging into somebody with one of those on slim.

'You're peacocks! At the end of the day, you're a peacock. You go out, you wanna be seen, you wanna look good, and you wanna smack somebody in the mouth!'

The lack of peacocks about and more herd mentality of Stone Island clad sheep clearly correlates to the whole general lack of individuality and creativity since the last free days of the movement.

Where the fuck has youth culture gone? And how has it ended up like this?

21|

Post Subcultural Turn

Way before my 'legendary' master's degree dissertation, *Be Loyal, Be Proud, Be Stoke; the symbolic consumption of clothing of Stoke City's terrace subculture* (for which I received distinction), subcultures were arguably becoming harder to define, distinguish and disseminate due to the changes in society; class boundaries were ever crumbling, equality increasing, and less distinct moral fibre backgrounds. With such seismic shifts in socioeconomics, class, technology and consumerism, was this the beginning of the end of what we would even class a 'subculture' today?

Andy Bennett researched into this and evaluated the notion of what would be known as the post-subcultural turn:

'The term post-subculture was introduced by Steve Redhead in response to what he perceived as an apparent breakdown of previous youth subcultural divisions evident in emergent dance music culture of the late 1980s and early 1990s. The term was significantly refined and developed into a full-fledged conceptual approach by David Muggleton in his book, *Inside Subculture: The postmodern meaning of style*.

Although precise opinions as to the reasons behind this varied between theorists, a general idea held by Muggleton amongst others, is that youth identities and indeed social identities had become more reflexive, fluid and fragmented due to an increasing flow of cultural commodities, images and texts through which more individualised identity projects and notions of self could be fashioned.

Both Muggleton and my absolute fave, the eponymous late Steve Redhead – he who is the ultimate master author and expert on all things football, Casuals, music, fashion – believed that the 'rules' of subcultures had changed to such a degree that there were no longer rules, distinctions or dictations to which youth identities were previously understood on the subcultural theory concept.

Bennett built on this idea by saying: 'Individuals are "held", if not "forced", together in subcultural groups by the fact of class, community, race or gender, neo-tribal theory allows for the function of taste, aesthetics and affectivity as primary drivers for participation in forms of collective youth cultural activity.'

It can be argued, therefore, that nowadays identities and communities can be forged together on the premise of lifestyle choices; a veritable pic n' mix of choice of style, image and ultimate cultural consumption. But whichever school of thought you belong to, it is a truth universally acknowledged that youth subcultures' visibility and power have most decidedly declined post-nineties after the dance and Casual scenes. By human nature we cling together in our neo-tribes, our makeshift families, our rocks in a socially and morally declining world. So, even if subcultures and their definitions cannot so easily be described, there are still some fragments of subcultures we have affiliations with. Even if their power, passion and prowess is nothing but a distant memory (like the height of the Casual movement), members will still dress like their fellow members, with their own slang, dialect and way of life. There is still a glimmer of community left on this ever-increasingly soulless Mother Earth.

Back in the early paranoid days of the Covid pandemic global lockdown, or as I like to recall it, the hazy summer of 2020, I really thought about subcultures, how they have been affected by post-modernisation, and would they survive the pandemic at all. So, just like Carrie Bradshaw, I couldn't help but wonder.

22|

Where Have all the Subcultures Gone?

Am I too old? Or are they too easily being absorbed into mainstream society by aggressive osmosis and a relentless quest and thirst for all things new! now! and throwaway pop culture?

It seems to me that as soon as some things become cool, they immediately become less cool the moment the chattering, Whitehall set jump on it, or the fakes start flying about.

As is well documented, the dilution of the Casual culture (which bled out into the bloated, caricatured football 'hooligans') came about with many copying and affiliating with some of their key brands, notably Burberry and then Stone Island. There definitely exists a scene which people nostalgically hold close to the heart and dismiss anything other than the purity of the first terrace Casuals, but along with the sacrilegious ripping off of brands, or wearing them 'wrong' or at all if you are not a true Casual, and combined with the modernisation of football (crucially no terraces, heavy-handed policing, Sky football, prawn sandwich brigade etc. etc.), this scene is now more of a romantic myth, with many yearning for that lively late eighties/nineties atmosphere; raves, music, fashion, football. The zeitgeist bubble popped. Is that how a subculture dies?

Even programmes such as *Pose* turn from being a gritty introduction to drag ballroom (albeit produced by Gwyneth Paltrow and super producer Brad Falchuk) to being bloated stories. This is possibly due to inflated budgets after initial success. The point is that things inevitably – and sadly – move away from their roots, their true essence, over time.

My knowledge of ballroom culture came from watching iconic documentary *Paris is Burning*, *Pose* (whose soundtrack has an overlap of familial cultural songs that have been adapted as themes in others) and from being a lifelong fan of RuPaul and their (once) groundbreaking series *Drag Race*. I wanted to dig deeper than the pink, pop drag heaven where we witness contestants in their categories flouncing, prancing, voguing in their beautiful dresses with the most perfect painted faces. Indeed, *Drag Race* has become such a success in middle America that many mainstream words emanate from this silky, hidden, vibrant world. On TikTok, little white girls commonly say 'fierce', 'lewk' and 'werk it'.

But this type of cultural appropriation been long been active.

In *Pose*, Billy Porter's character touches on the white middle class pinching of disco/YMCA gay theme by singing it pissed up at football grounds. The use of black rappers on white pop songs to add that urban edge, the coolness, the realness. Madonna is idolised in the LGBTQ community, calling her their 'mother' and 'legendary', yet Madonna is well known for underpinning her pop with almost stolen cultural vibes from the black and gay communities – cultural appropriation at the highest???

Porter uses phrases like 'our greatest asset is our authenticity' – this is in reference to the fall in popularity of ballroom after the dance experienced the dizzying heights of infamy, brought about by the huge popularity of Madonna's *Vogue* single and dance. The craze for all things 'vogue' kinda missed the point. This was cleaned up, white pop vogueing. The absolute irony is of middle-class white people screaming for Vogue, when vogueing itself, and the walking of the categories at the ballrooms, was to try and copy said white folk, often from

Vogue magazine. To have 'white girl shopping at Macy's realness' or 'rich woman having afternoon tea' categories (as an example), was sadly the community's collective aspiration to be accepted, to 'pass' in society, to be as 'real' as the white folk.

Realness is the core of their agenda, their vision, and values. But when the realness is accepted, is it as good, or genuine? When the struggles are real, but then no more, what is there left to creatively rebel against?

Subcultures thrive when they are hidden – do they die when they are seen, when the spotlight is glaring on them? Furthermore, should subcultures stay anchored to where they originate? Is that why I am affiliated with Casual culture so much? We had direct access to the zeitgeist of which subcultures are derived from. It was the music, fashion, political environment, the football. It was just THE time it all went seamlessly hand in hand. It could be argued that most 'notorious' subcultures including Casuals, mods, goths, rockers etc., would not be so pure, so insulated, had social media been involved.

But recently social media has been instrumental and cultural in its own right. There have been definite seismic cultural movements recently. Black Lives Matters has had such an immediate and deep reaction that it is cutting across all cultures, countries and race. Why now? Why not such dramatic calls to arms from the white communities after Watts Riots in the 60s, then later New Jersey? LA Riots was a biggie in terms of notoriety, but was this because of the blanket media coverage?

The BLM Movement seems to be working in tandem with today's digital generation. With outrage at everything and anything and exaggerated, encouraged and echoed by the rapidity and availability of social media, the BLM's unequivocally correct right for justice in police brutality cases and for the black communities to start building futures for themselves, has been harnessed by the power of today's technology and allowed the message to be heard. And brilliantly so.

That is the good, brace yourself for the bad, the double-edged sword of social media. As we have seen, social media has been crucial in the dissemination of key messages and socio-economic calls for change recently. The world could not ignore this one, the fury was red hot. The world sat up and listened. But it needs to for the right reasons. The bandwagon effect and increase in the number of armchair political experts, who then spread their own interpretation of the message, can be dangerous. Social media tricks us into believing we belong. Do we? More importantly, should we?

In today's post-modern online world, there is no central focus; our attention is pulled in so many directions. Brands, celebrities, new crazes, new apps, all vying for our (consumer) attention. With the further decimation of 'real life' and real human contact due to Covid-19 and an unprecedented global lockdown, we had no choice but to cling onto engagement through the various formats of social media. Today's generation live for all things digital – the TikTok movement has taken over even the beigest of mediocre celebrities. There were no gigs, festivals, galleries to attend, to fuel our creative stimulation, to be the venues of the subculture's finest hour. Gigs and football matches were where the Casuals would strut like peacocks in their latest fineries. In the past, the game of one-upmanship was played out at venues, with music, with people.

Is it still too clinical/snowflakey to have subcultures anymore? There are probably many still existing in these crazy times, and new ones rising from the ashes of this period of history. People are getting too scared to let go, let loose, feel free. I am glad I experienced the camaraderie, the passion, the people that make your place and time within a subculture, so important and memorable. I worry for the socially awkward but technically savvy generation that will experience fun and life through the lens of an iPhone.

Stop the world I want to get off. Ah thank fuck it has.

Oxley, R. 2020. Proper Magazine. Issue 35.

23|

Post Fandom: Did Subcultures Die Years Ago Anyway?

So during my naval gazing/soul searching during the pandemic (actually no I wasn't having any life changing epiphanies, just loving the sun, the late nights, no early mornings and the general acceptance of drinking booze as soon as awake, approximately 2pm 😊), I continued my love in with Hebridge, Redhead, Guilianotti et al and found that there is actually some pre-dated work written about the death of youth culture, that post-subcultural turn, which ran parallel with a concept called post fandom. I had always suspected that the pretty much non-existence of any kind of yoof culture had been slowly weakened by the advent of a new world order of political correctness, consumerism and social media. That there had been no strong musical zeitgeists in which to create our perfect storm.

My man Redhead wrote that:

'There is always a connection in practise between particular youth subcultural style and specific forms of music.

'Subcultural styles are seen as unfolding, generationally, from the Teds to the Casuals or from Punk to the present.'

He quotes Jean Baudrillard in his 2000 book, *The End of the Century*:

'I don't know if it's a question of an "end". The word is probably meaningless in any case, because we're no longer so sure that there is such a thing as linearity...History has stopped meaning, referring to anything – whether you call it social space or the real. We have passed into a kind of hyper-real where things are played ad infinitium.'

This constant fluidity of dipping in and out, borrowing bits and pieces of music, fashion and culture has no doubt been speeded up by the advent of technology that connects to everything and everyone. Youth culture was sanitised, less authentic, more commercial. Of course, there were pockets of rebellion in the eighties and nineties – aciiieeeed! – but this came debatably at the very point the death knoll tolled for any kind of raw, caustic, meaningful youth culture, coinciding neatly with the advent of commercialism and consumerism, of which would change the face of youth subcultures forever.

'In the 1950s, 1960s and 1970s pop and music seemed inextricably connected to a never-ending succession of deviant youth subcultures. However, in the Thatcher years of the 1980s youth culture became more of an advertising medium than ever before; it was notable not for opposition, but for its role in selling everything from Levi 501 jeans to spot cream.'

Simon Firth foresaw this, continuing:

'Youth is now just a marketing device and advertiser's fiction.'

Well, he guessed that right.

But how does this lack of culture relate to our Football Casuals? Massively, as this theoretical concept and predictions relate not just to youths and the validity of subcultures today but also to the authenticity of football fandom; the pressures of remaining – or trying to remain – a Terrace Casual when all the terraces were being ripped out to provide the slick new stadiums.

24|

Authenticity: Against Modern Football Part 1

Apparently, it's not just me who is in the school of thought that football is a working-class game for working-class people; this apparently Marxist belief has only been heightened by the absolute commercialism of modern football.

Leon Davis writes:

'The sociology of football, until the 1990s, tacitly assumed that football was a working-class game, however, this position became principally untenable, with the advent of the FA Premier League in 1992. With the new formation, football gained a new consistency – thanks to high-priced entrance fees to stadia; stricter policing; how the ground became manages as a venue; also, the emergence of middle-class surveillance.'

Is nothing sacred!! Why does everything have to be monetised, stripped of genuineness! Why do the middle-class have to take anything ours, authentic (cool), and make it mediocre and mainstream! This was our last respite in this world of false advertising and consumerism! FFS!

This class struggle is also recognised by Millwall fan and author Gary Robson, that it was at these working-class, local football grounds where you learned the values of being a white working class 'deviant' male. This was their coming of age, their true and authentic fandom that was inextricably linked to the ground and their match day rituals with elder, working-class males.

Many believe that the whole concept of football fandom had changed by the nineties and noughties, and why wouldn't it have with so much change and obliteration of the football game and experience? Italia 90s was the crux of this seismic shift (opera at the footy anyone?), leading to the opinion Redhead that, 'we are all post-fans now.' This bourgeoisification of not just football but society in general, the taking away of the terraces, the outpricing of the tickets, the advent of the 'event' experience, the decrease of football hooliganism, has created post-fandom.

'Within post-modern football, there has been a blurring of social classes which has taken the central working-class aspect away from the terraces to the extent that all classes, in a post-modern stadium, integrate,' states Davis. Hmmm, debatable from my experience, but we go again.

Perhaps our Nouveaux Casuals' view of football was/is shaped by historical hoolie folklore combined with this new easy come, easy go consumer world order and their own, new football-lite experience down the match. The 'new generation' are used to being entertained, to being babysat constantly. God forbid they must make up their own half time entertainment to keep their merchandised arses occupied. ADHD'd up to fuck; so bad that matches are now an event with raffles, overpriced and definitely over-processed food. In my belief matches are, a spectacle, nay shadow, of their former selves. But still see you down there, yeah?!

And that's exactly the point. We hate it, we moan, we praise and we grumble, that there is no genuine or authentic football fan experience but we still go! Most of the time! If it's not slatting it down! (Note: Stoke City's Bet365 stadium is on top of a hill, dead hard to get to, miles away from the centre of the traditional working-class streets and backsies, and it is the coldest, wettest place on earth. They sure don't make it easy).

These soulless 'venues' are symbolic of the move of the grounds from the heart of the local working communities to harder to reach (need transport) middle-class leisure hot spots. Under the premise and pressure of the Hillsborough/hooligan (false) connection, authorities and football club management have succeeded in creating vast shells minus the camaraderie of the terraces, restricting, as Davis notes, 'the original fan practises of vastly itinerant celebration and carnivalesque rituals.' Interestingly, our more hard-line European Ultras do have wild and dazzling displays of rituals, including pyrotechnics and coordinated chanting and choreography within their grounds, but more of that later. Within his paper, Davis believes the different categories of fandom really emphasises the authenticity of a fan; for example, with the advent of Sky, pubs showing football, armchair fans, London/Asian-based Manchester United fans, glory-hunters etc., these variations go some way to show post fandom and how levels of authenticity have been diluted by such changes in how we support a team. As football is no longer a regional game; now just a commercialised, privatised enterprise. Paradoxically it can be said that those fans who travel to away games are at the top of the authenticity hierarchy; arguably more passionate, vocal, and clobbered up right. Not as shirters, but to symbolise from which city they are from, or more often than not, what firm they represent by their choice of clobber and the brands they identify with.

25|

Brand Identity; Clobber for the Jilted Generation

The infinite world of consumerism is mind boggling. The vast choice of products and brands is unthinkable to us old school lot, and quite frankly unwanted. If I wanted to buy a mascara for example, where would I start?! Back in the day I would have gone to Boots and found a decent No7 one nestled between the Heather Shimmer lippy and some Sun-In. It did its job, it was sound. When you went on holiday, you bought a waterproof one. End of. Now, every brand and his dog have a mascara line, every watered done C-list Love Islander has a make-up range, and the options of colours, styles and add-ons are limitless. And this is just mascara.

How do brands cut through this noise, how do they appeal to the customer, or more importantly how does it try and 'connect' with the consumer, to win their attention, and then the holy grail of brand loyalty? Does brand loyalty or even brand identity exist anymore?

If we are to follow Bennett's theory that subcultures are not meant to be rigid and stiff but fluid and evolving, that would explain the way in which youths today select their brands. There is not such a strict, unflinching loyalty to brands as arguably the Casuals, which perhaps justifies the longevity of certain Casual brands.

Whichever brand the Football Casual chooses to represent the identity of his tribe, Cova argues that it is in fact the social link towards a community, identity or sense of belonging that is important, rather than the brand itself. The hyper-real, exaggerated world in which we live today has broken down so many of our traditional relationships and communities, that there is a real desire to be part of a group; 'the return of community in our Western societies, a phenomenon usually called neo-tribalism,' Cova explains. This need is even more present in working-class males whose very identities, and the relationships which define them, are fragmented in the post-modern world. Maffesoli also believes that our modern day lives are increasingly marked by our belonging to a group, and our role within that group becomes a basis of our identity. This goes some way to explain the football hooligans' almost primitive desire to be part of a tribe in a rapidly evolving identity. With this subculture, the football hooligans' loyalty and allegiance to their football club becomes so ingrained in their psyche, that the club symbolically becomes part of their identity, discovers Guilianotti, Bonney and Hepworth. The aggressive, physical football game watched can then often be replicated before or after the match. Indeed, violence is such a key characteristic of the hooligans' identity, that often many find the actual pre-arranged fighting more exciting, more blood-pumping, more visceral, than the match itself.

Power and Hague theorise that brands are social implements which help shape our identity, resulting in us having personal relationships with certain brands. Likewise, because status brands are generally perceived as prestigious, exclusive and desired, the Casuals have chosen to consume this fashion as a means of symbolically becoming prestigious, exclusive and desired also. In a society where consumers are driven by a voracious, never-ending craving for status in their lives, the Casual's conspicuous consumption of high-end brands is simply another example of how to enhance an individual's image by communicating this through a whole host of symbolic displays; clothes, hair, attitude and even speech. Casuals have long aimed to show the world that despite their humble beginnings, they too are aspirational and want their self-image to reflect this. In working-class cities wearing such expensive clothing is a way of making a statement; that despite low wages or mundane, soul-destroying and spirit-crushing jobs, a lad can wear sharp smart and costly 'Casual' clothes on match day and be transported from, as Chester himself describes it, feeling like a pauper to a prince dressed in his finest attire.

So, what are the personal relationships with Casuals' and their brands; and why? Many of the key protagonists link their memories of first coming across Casual clobber with being in awe of the elder males, then later a sense of belonging, and arguably now an aching yearning to go back to the time of popping their Casual cherry.

Matt Snell from Casual Client Clothing:

'You would spot an immaculately dressed person in the crowd. Took me weeks to find out the brands they were wearing. I always thought the Casual dress was smart. Looked tidier than everyone else.'

Oliver Beer:

'Back in the early eighties, probably about '85/'86. Saw a lad with a Stone Island jumper on, I liked that and went across and just asked him what it was and where you get it from. He told me, I had a look and thought "smart!"'

Jared Latimer:

'I remember. Jed was the doorman at Freetown. He just stood out. Because he'd got a shaven head, he'd got a Stone Island overshirt, it was probably the first time I'd ever seen Stone Island. And I just thought, "Bloody hell, this dude is a doorman, he's got this cool element to him, everybody seemed to know him. And that sort of pulled me in."'

Shelton Casual:

'I was a Stoke fan and I sort of went Adidas, and then at the game started noticing people wearing different clobber, tops and that. Plus,

I had friends whose older brothers were like, five or six years older than us, they were these so-called Casuals.'

Calandra Menswear's Giovanni Calandra (Hereford):

'I remember watching Millwall and Luton kicking off and just being fascinated by it all and just by what the lads were wearing. Over in Italy my cousins used to read a magazine called Paninaro. I used to look at the photos seeing lads dressed in Stone Island, CP Company, Best Company, Moncler etc. So personally, I got obsessed and fascinated with the Casual brands from an early age. In Hereford you had a lot of lads emerging into the Casual scene from the early eighties into the football and acid house, Balearic scene. In Hereford we had dressers, stylists and youth crews and our lot in the 1990s.'

Transalpino's Jay Montessori:

'I'd say Slazenger V-neck jumper, Farah trousers, Adidas Cag and Adidas Wimbledon trainers. My earliest memory of wanting to be part of something, Scallies as they were known round here. Another brand that got me hooked as a kid would be Kickers.'

Riaz Khan (Leicester):

'As working-class lads we always want to look like we are getting ahead, and clothes are a way to project this. Furthermore, as an Asian, I never belonged to any real subculture. Well, that changed in the spring of 1983 when I saw a group of youths walk past me wearing tennis and golf clothing. I was hooked by the way they looked and the way they seemed to have this bond, a notion of brotherhood, I suppose I always wanted this sense of belonging because at school I was slightly ostracised due to my ethnic background.'

Is it this sense of belonging, this brotherhood which subconsciously keeps our older Casuals loyal to brands such as Stone Island? Although acknowledging its dilution through the mainstream and later urban markets, everyone I spoke to still has this soft spot for Stone Island, CP et al, the stalwarts of Casual couture.

26|

Terrace Culture and the Dawn of the Digital Age

'Life is shit. There is no fucking point to any of it. Not now that we've evolved past the survival stage. Maybe we used to live to hunt to kill to eat to live another day. Now we just kill time in as many sophisticated ways as possible. Pointless jobs. Pointless lives. Work. Television. Football.' (Sampson, *Awaydays*, 1998).

Kevin Sampson – he of naming this cultural phenomenon of Casuals in The Face magazine fame, wrote this cutting piece in influential book, *Awaydays*, the coming-of-age book about a young Tranmere Rovers pup navigating sex, drugs and football thugs. Written in the late nineties but based in the late seventies, this couldn't be more prophetic about the apathy already felt by young white working-class males back even then. With terrace culture encompassing the footy, fights, friendship and fashion, it was the only outlet. We have already heard from the Casuals interviewed that this sense of belonging, and the badges they wore to represent this, was what terrace culture was about. And now we also know that from late nineties onwards, everything basically went to shit in terms of subcultures and their symbolic consumptions – although the affiliations would still stay loyal, and our older generation will stay have a sense of brand loyalty.

But what about our young lot, the up-and-coming Nouveaux Casual pups with such a vast array of luxe products at their fingertips; do they still purchase a brand with at least some degree of history; can they match the brand loyalty of their elders?

In a post-modern approach to market research in a global pandemic, and a fresh addition to the ethnographical style of my book, the mixture of academic papers and first-hand narratives, I decided to ask some Casual fan sites on Instagram to ask their followers some of my questions. Like a scythe, this bite sized approach to sift answers to direct questions and from a cross section of society, it definitely sorted the wheat from the chaff in terms of getting succinct information for my research from those who either identify themselves as Casual or at the very least are interested in it.

'Spose this social media and instant response stuff can come in useful after all?!

I asked a series of questions through Casual Client Clothing (85k followers, UK based online community for Casuals. All answers are sent from an Instagram story with just their Instagram handle – no info on age/city/team at this stage. Some are savage!

What do you think of terrace culture today?

'Renting Stone Island and watching the game through your phone.' (justicegraeme)

'Full of idiots, young lads with stinking attitudes and snide gear.' (jimmartin6348)

'Much more wide spread from UK into other parts of the globe even Asia which I think is great.' (sumilo24)

'Too much hype I guess.' (lozhkin.casual)

'It's a bit mainstream.' (scottygallacher)

'Plastic.' (dan_parry_ll31)

'It just shows how iconic the 80s/90s was because still wearing the same.' (atkinson72x)

'Very mainstream. Lots wearing who would not know what a terrace is.' (dolydd25)

'Nowhere near as fun as the 90s, but then I was young, free and went every week then.' (turnbulltawks)

'It's more of a hype rather than a choice nowadays.' (simonborys)

'Getting back to the 80s in my opinion.' (lads_exclusive).

And as casualbynature_ltd succinctly puts: 'Sanitised.'

What got you interested in terrace culture and when?

'Late 90s music inspired us and we looked up to the older lads who were living it up.' (justicegraeme)

'When I visited Manchester in 2018 and saw how people in the pub were dressed.' (sumilo24).

'15 at football with older lads.' (c.a_clothing20).

'Belonging to something and from a young age, gives you a sense of identity.' (Kenny_fckin_powers).

'First game Stoke v Cardiff.' (lads_exclusive).

For social media savvy millennials, these football, fashion and fighting pages are of a second nature and their primary source of interaction and engagement for the youth 'culture' of today. But what about our older Casual fossilites – do they get this format, and does it help perpetuate the legend of Casual culture, and indeed inform and teach our younger ones?

Apparently, they aren't as switched off as possibly perceived, with many using old style forums years ago which were the blueprint to the social media sites and online communities of today and a means of keeping track of the what's what and the who's who of the football Casuals world. Whether they like them or not however is a difference of opinion:

Simon Dowling (Tottenham):

'I always found them nerdy and too cliquey. I really just enjoy wearing it rather than talking about zips and buttons etc. There are plenty more knowledgeable chaps out there about the fabrics and details etc.'

Which seamlessly moves on to the opinion of one such knowledgeable chap:

Oliver Beer (Stoke):

'I used to be on 80s Casuals which was like a forum/chat room. That was set up by a guy called Jean Na, who did the Massimo Osti book – he massively helped Lorenzo on that one. That was his baby. He's a strange one 'cos he came into as, he liked the clothes, but he had no idea of the background...and he did it purely as a fashion thing and took it off in the chat room. He was good, he built up an amazing collection, but he is a multi, multi-millionaire.'

Paul Walters (Stoke/N40):

'I love online communities to reminisce. Love it. Love hearing the old stories, hearing all the older lot talk about the times. It's a way of keeping in touch with other lads/firms.' Does it mention the old school puffer jackets with umbrellas carried as weapons, Paul? 😊

Riaz Kahn (Leicester):

'Online communities play an integral part in keeping this culture alive. To be honest, it is dead to an extent, with lonely lads reminiscing about the bygone days of how it was before CCTV and banning orders (I personally believe the House/Rave scene in 88/89 killed it off). Online groups, especially on Facebook, have managed to keep this culture going with stories and pictures of the clobber we used to wear. Furthermore, in the bygone days there were lads who really couldn't afford to purchase the clothes that were in fashion during the 80's but now due to these same lads earning money from work, businesses etc they can buy certain items of clothing that they missed out on. That is also the same for those who wore the clothes but could not acquire a certain trackie top, trainers or even a t shirt. We are reliving our youth!'

As Bear Grylls says: 'improvise, adapt and overcome.' And this is exactly what the Casuals have done. Some who I spoke to are not just using these pages to reminisce, more and more are becoming au fait and adapting with these modern times, setting up to monetise their own football Casual sites with others using social media as a tool to promote their terrace inspired brands.

Matt Snell (Blackburn Rovers) founder of Casual Client Clothing explains:

'Initially I joined Instagram with a personal page back in 2014. I noticed a huge community of Casual lads on there. There was a small handful pages doing a similar thing, so I thought I'd have a bash and create my own community. I initially wanted to sell via the page and managed to sell a few Stone Island bits but then the profits went in an Ibizan summer, never to be seen again.'

Goals!

His Dutch counterpart, Casual Ultra (SC Cambuur, 86k followers) adds when asked of the importance of online communities in terms of how we perceive and purchase brands:

'I think the involvement of Twitter, Facebook and Instagram pages are a big part of how we perceive and purchase (new) brands. I remember I started with the promotion of Marshall Artist back in the days when they just had a restart. With pages over 300k of followers promoting a brand or a company where to buy these brands, it could give a certain brand a boost and become very popular. A good example are Weekend Offender and Marshall Artist, both of whom grew up by profiling themselves online on social media.'

Asked why he set the page up in the first place:

'I started the page because I made some compilations of the Ultras/hooligans footage that happened during the weekend. So, I needed a place to share it. That's why I started my Twitter back in the days (and of course Facebook and Insta followed later).'

27|

#JointheCult

Steve Lumb, die hard Man City fan, commentator and owner of the brand Terrace Cult, gets it; the belonging, the background and the need to utilise social media, but in an authentic, non-contrived way, to engage with his customers who are predominantly football Casuals.

'Terrace Cult is Terrace Culture but it's Terrace Cult because it is a cult, you're part of a cult, feel part of a cult. That's what I mean #JointheCult. You get up in the morning, put your Adidas trainers on, you make sure you've got the right clobber on, and you've got a bit of pride in what you're wearing, and you're out to the football or whatever.'

Brands or shops affiliated with this culture must have the bollox, the background and the right credentials to even have such sweeping statements of football association. Jared Latimer recalls the background of Casual clobber mecca Terraces in Hanley, Stoke-on-Trent. The shop was the brainchild of known footballer Mike Macari, who came to Jared at fellow clobber shop Review for advice in brands and customers:

'He got a shop, still didn't have a name for it. So I said, "most lads I deal with, they're all football lads, so I'd call it Terraces" – and the name stuck.'

The gravitas of real Casuals running brands and shops only highlights the rest of the shysters out there, that these brands are targeted directly to those who know, and if you don't know, now you know...

Steve explains Terrace Cult's social media strategy:

'I've tried not to flood Facebook groups with Terrace Cult, I never do, I don't flood them. And I don't try and push it on people all the time. We stick to our own social medias, and we wanna see if people share it on their accounts. I don't look at it for feedback, we're just trying to find our own niche in this market.'

In a consumers' world of shiny marketing, incessant glossy advertising, and general brand noise, I find the direct sales approach a massive turn off, so a brand that targets its key customers with its shared core ethos, works for me.

Apparently, this approach is also a thumbs up for CP Company themselves.

President of CP Company, Lorenzo Osti, spoke to me about this more egalitarian and authentic way in which to showcase, not promote as such, their clobber. Not turning their back on any subcultures but allowing them to adapt and appropriate as they saw fit.

Lorenzo: 'We leave the people to adopt the brand freely. So, that's the way it worked with Casuals, they adopted, we never targeted. When we made the (Cinquanta, 50th anniversary) exhibition in the North, part of the comment was, "hey, why in the North and not in the South?" Come on, we have to start somewhere!'

Me: 'Haha! I've heard this, I've heard other people saying this. Some Southerners were really pissed off. And we were like, at least us Northerners can have something for once, like let us have something first, I mean, come on! We started the movement!'

L: 'Exactly haha. So that's fun, it's not a big deal. But again, it's part of the previous question you made, if we target someone? No, we never target anybody. I think the good strategy is, do what you are good in doing, ok us doing garments, and then stay open to be adopted but not target anyone.'

We discussed their more gender fluid approach to consumers in both product and marketing. Talking about CP clobber:

L: 'Eighty per cent are men but twenty per cent are women and that shows that, I mean, the garments are the garments, that's what we do. Men can be adopted by men, by women, by young people, by old people, by subculture...we're fine. And I think this is the most honest way because when you target someone, you are using marketing, you are treating people like a consumer in a more commercial and exploiting way.'

M: 'Absolutely.'

L: 'And we don't want to do this, no? I think people realise when you are trying to sell something to them.'

M: 'Yeah, they can see through it now, I think. Especially newer generations see so much through advertising campaigns, you know, they can see through it. And I don't think it's kind of ethical to spend so much money on these advertising campaigns now, which people can see through anyway. It kind of goes against everything I was taught in marketing, but if people wanna buy a brand, they'll buy it because of what it's connected to them, not because of the marketing campaign.'

L: 'Yeah, I think the reality it's a bit in the middle. Meaning I agree with what you say, but to be honest, it's just a different, more sophisticated way of marketing haha.'

And that's why ladies and gents, he's the President of CP Company. Recognising the current market for non-labelling labelling. And then nailed it. Selling to us without us even knowing. That is in indeed top-notch marketing. Bravo.

28|
Nouveaux Casuals

Social media is an integral part of a brand's marketing strategy. After all, it is both accessible and cheap. With 2.77 billion internet users around the world, this new unlimited era has totally redefined how companies interact and engage with their customers, according to Ebrahim. A brand's social media presence is the windows to its soul; how a company portrays itself online can underpin its total success. Kim and Ko identified five brand building blocks: interaction, entertainment, trendiness, customization and word of mouth. All are key aspects that create consumer behaviour, and more importantly, brand loyalty.

We know that our original football Casuals have trust in certain brands, those with a backstory, a battle-scarred narrative which makes their brand impression and memory their own and personal to them. But what of the younger generation, whose only memories of terrace culture and its symbolic consumption of clothing is through social media? Whether that be through fan sites and pages with old timers reminiscing about the good old days, or being sold a dream by brands, therefore forcing a consumer behavioural pattern, being spoon fed a half-baked story intended to create a brand loyalty, to a brand they are meant to trust? Are the millennials, Gen-Z and Gen-Alpha that naive to not see this? Do they not have the passion and creativity to create their own stories, their own memories? Perhaps they can't in this diluted, clinical world of ours and that sadly the only living they do now is through an online avatar.

Now it cannot be assumed that those asked online are young (nouveaux/wannabe) Casuals, but the response is extremely interesting to read…

Asking followers of Casual Client Clothing, 2022:

How do you hear about new brands and products?

'Instagram.' (19bamk88)
'Social media/selling sites.' (charlieausten5)
'Internet.' (alfyyoung55)
'Internet and lads.' (theodort_ws)
'Instagram, You Tube, Facebook.' (liambuchan1873)
'Social media or friends.' (lucasbeergstrm)
'Socials, word of mouth, oi polloi pegs and independent retailers.' (prettycasualsmocks)
'Word of mouth from the lads or you see the odd garment at games.' (benobodyshero3)

What platform or where do you buy your clothing?

'Store only CASH!' (19bamk88)
'Either from the main supplier or eBay/Vinted/Depop.' (charlieausten5)
'koza_menswear brothers page.' (alfyyoung55)
'Casual shops or website of the brand.' (theodort_ws)
'Flannels, Cruise, Instagram, Facebook.' (liambuchan1873)
'From Swedish or English stores.' (lucasbeergstrm)
'The modfather, 80s Casual classics.' (the_dorset_spur)
'Instagram, flea Bay, independent retailers, vintage/charity shops.' (prettyCasualsmocks)

'Local shops, sometimes online.' (benobodyshero3)

And now the big reveal – let's see if age/geography has any correlating factors in these responses which were sliced randomly from dozens of answers:

Age and location?

'33, Amsterdam.' (19bamk88)

'17, South West.' (charlieausten5)

'15, Dunfermline, Scotland.' (alfyyoung55)

'19, France.' (theodort_ws)

'24, Aberdeen, Scotland.' (liambuchan1873)

'56 years young, originally in London but now in Poole.' (the_dorset_spur_)

'30, Plymouth,' (prettycasualsmocks)

'35, Scotland.' (benobodyshero3)

It comes as no big surprise that brands – and certainly the smaller and more independent ones, will use these fan sites to promote their clobber as this is primarily the marketplace for the new generation; they source information and then purchase from a mix of social media and or brand websites, or even a shop! An actual physical shop!

Steve from Terrace Cult strategises: 'I think using the Casual pages to advertise is of great interest to the brand, we are literally certain that our products will be getting out to our target audience; sometimes big ad campaigns can cost a lot and you're unsure whether your target audience will see it. Using these kind of football and fashion pages ensures you get your products in front of the right people. We use a few pages, and it works well for us.'

This arguably targets our die-hard genuine Casuals and football hooligans, but what about the later generations? If they have no nostalgic ties to a subculture, why do they still purchase Casual clobber?

29|

Brand Loyalty in Millennials; Consumer Behaviour Now

Our Gen-Z, and now scarily Gen-Alpha, babies are a savvy lot; they have been born into the digital age. They are so IT-literate, but with arguably less life skills (not that they're required so much these days). They will never remember the days of just three TV channels-with no remote. Or *Grange Hill*. Or *Top of the Pops*. Or gigs where no ID is needed. Or festivals where no fucker wears flowers in her hair. Or a loyalty and particular allegiance to a brand without a real reason to. They know their consumer shit.

'Only 1 in 5 millennials describe themselves as loyal to specific brands and that loyalty isn't easily earned. Millennials can see through marketing claims and will question if your brand delivers on its promise. Loyalty is built on several factors, like reliability, the product's quality and positive interactions with their customer service.' This checklist comes courtesy of the Digsite website.[1]

For our switched-on millennials, it takes more for a brand to take their heart. Digsite writes also that the brand must jump through hoops for consumer loyalty, incorporating:

---

[1] www.digsite.com/blog/millennials/six-essential-brand-qualities-building-millennial-loyalty

'Heritage, Health Benefits, Efficacy Claims, Transparency, Aesthetics, Social Media and Online Support.'

Sounds like a massive ball ache. But is this what the latter generations, the actual teens/tweens and everything in between think?

Apparently, some don't think that much into it. The young lads interviewed were impressively impassive to trends and more modern consumer behaviour, citing male figures, football and music as their primary influences of Casual culture.

Aidan Tregay, 22, Burnley, owner of up and coming brand, Project North:

'My uncle was the first person who grabbed my attention to fashion. I remember like he came down in Stone Island and it was the first time I had seen the logo; it just captured my eyes – the distinctive button and patch I hadn't seen before on any other brands and is what caught my eye. That is what I feel makes a brand, that touch of exclusivity. My first Casual outfit came about when I was watching *The Firm* by Nick Love which captivated me with the distinctive retro 80s Fila and Ellesse track top. I was obsessed, I needed these, the 3 stripes to Trim Trabbs, old school Munchens, the whole vibe and feel I just fell in love with.'

Harry Butler, 20, Leeds Utd:

'I wear Casual clobber because I go to Leeds United frequently and from a young age, I saw what people would wear at the game and in the pub before the game and I took this and began to replicate this. I also saw lots of the eighties and nineties films and lots of people in these wore Casual clobber, so I began to take an interest. I also take lots of interest in football culture especially in the old school firms, how they used to operate, what they wore, and how that was associated with each firm.'

Matt Williams, 17, adds:

'It's smarter than everything else other lads my age are wearing. Quality on the clobber makes you feel a cut above when you got it on, and a lot of the gear has got history behind them. A couple of years ago, I watched *The Firm* (Nick Love) with the old man, loved the way they dressed and got talking about Casual culture. Went out the week after and got myself a Fila Settanta track and a pair of Trimm Trabs.'

So, dressing 'Casual' even though there is no 'Casual' scene? They believe there still is to a certain extent, continuing to wear Casual brands, to wave the flag for terrace culture, to dress impeccably, not just for the match, but to branch this Casual brand identity out further afield, to make it a lifestyle:

Dan Butler, 20, Leeds:

'I wear Casual clobber because of the environment I have grown up in as I regularly go to football matches and attend live music events with indie music being key to this. I will always continue to wear the brands I do as it is my sense of identity against others who follow the crowd.'

This attitude is refreshingly familiar. Whether it's a deep loyalty or a milder allegiance, it's not just the stereotypical terrace cult brands they are into; these lads are favouring classics-80s Casuals classics such as:

- Adidas
- Sergio Tacchini
- Fila
- Diadora
- Lacoste
- Pretty Green
- Barbour
- Lyle and Scott
- Weekend Offender

- Reebok
- Marshall Artist
- Ma. Strum
- Lois

And of course, the behemoths:
- Stone Island
- CP Company

There does appear to be a resurgence of popularity for the eighties clobber and a general heritage revival; there is no other company that does this better in terms of brands, success and popularity than 80s Casual Classics (clue is in the name 😊).

30|

80s Casual (Classics)

Passion and authenticity have always driven Casuals. We have seen how this is reimagined through Casuals' own start up brands or retail spaces. Neil Primett (Liverpool), owner of the eponymous 80s Casual Classics, has been involved with this subculture for many years and is now arguably helping bring eighties Casual clobber to the Nouveaux Casuals whilst also bridging the gap between original hoolies and their eighties labels.

Primett tells me how and why he got into it all:

'I do think it's from sport and the sport passion. To be good at football and running, you had to have decent spec gear – footy boots by Puma Dalglish, Patrick Keegans. Puma GV trainers were mind blowing. Runners were Nike and looked the part down the Youth Club with Farahs. My mate's dad was a member of a country club with tennis, squash and swimming pool etc.; that was quite some place for me living with my mum and brother in a two-bed house. My business began by selling clothes as a passion, whilst also being a small-town music promoter with a Camden-esque style store with some mixed retro and vintage gear.'

Primett was clearly onto something; finger firmly on the pulse of a movement, a resurgence for Casual clobber unwittingly heightened by the presence of Casual films in the noughties.

'So here I was, in retail and a music promoter with two stores in Bedfordshire and Hertfordshire, when I got offered a heritage revival of Sergio (Tacchini) and then weeks later Fila. At the time we were having a retro vibe student/Oasis type store and, having been an eighties Casual myself, I jumped at it.

'Bedford is a small town, but it soon became apparent the appeal and appetite was countrywide, and then *The Business* film got the eBay world chasing revival and "vintage" became the in word. Be it true vintage or a revival, Fila launched the brand called Fila Vintage and the two worlds became one, new and used! Soon we took our local business online via eBay and I guess the rest is history! Honestly, eBay became so big, people travelled miles to Bedford. We started to buy up all stocks of niche limited brands and then eventually launched our website.'

With these two worlds colliding of old and new/faux vintage, it takes someone extremely knowledgeable of old-skool Casual clobber to be able to relaunch it and drag it into the millennium.

The Stato of eighties brands, Primett's understanding of Casual clobber and its minutiae continues:

'Farahs, roll necks, Pringle, Lyle knits, ski jackets, cagouls. Brands like Sergio Tacchini seemed to be the biggest and lads would wear full tracksuits. Lacoste, Farah trousers, Lois jeans and cords were all available local. Kappa went biggest around '84-85 and was widely worn. Lyle & Scott, Pringle and biggest of all-but maybe not elite – was Pierre Cardin, a fun colourful knit.'

There's a poster boy for the Nouveaux Casuals, the faux vintage millennial and sponsored by 80s Casual Classics, Jude Moore. He has the Gen-Y DNA of retro Casual nostalgia combined with slick social media platforms.

Moore's attraction?

Primett: 'I think it's because his look could be defined by thug or pretty boy. Jude Moore defines the pretty boy posey lad and hits the spot as to why we sell. He crosses over to the North; Scottish and Welsh young lads want to be him. Also, the Danny Dyer Essex boy look is not limited to the South. Parts of Scotland always seem more aligned with London, than say Manchester. Liverpool also. Newcastle has that Geordie Shore type thing going on. They all want to pose without it being too male bravado.'

Eighties Casual Classics have adopted Moore and the relationship works well. Describing Primett as a 'Boss!' in all sense of the word, he tells me about the Casual style of his that is influencing a newer generation.

Me: 'Would you describe yourself a poster boy for younger Casuals?'

Jude Moore (Arsenal/West Ham): 'I think there's a good few! But I think with the success of some of my TikTok's, I've definitely brought over a new generation and people who've never seen the clobber before. They've transitioned from being all about the roadman look and now dressing up and looking smart on a daily.'

Citing Aquascutum, Fila and Gabbici as favourite brands, Moore certainly owns his look. Mixing pretty boy charm with a Southern roguish appeal, Moore just gets it and gets what it's about:

'I first saw it when I was about ten/eleven years old and my uncle was a fully-fledged Casual. I love the clobber. I'll always have a pair of Gazelles, Lois jeans and a little bit of Fila. It's just smart Casual and looks the bollox. Don't get me wrong, in the winter I wear a tracksuit here and there, but I do love dressing up, sticking my Pringle on, me cords and having it large.'

Is Moore the patron saint of the new breed of Casuals who are more knowledgeable about their labels than simply dragging their neanderthal knuckles towards the nearest Stone Island? Can the

Nouveaux cut it with the same panache as Moore? Or does this new crossbreed have its own identity, pilfering from Casuals and Roadmen alike? Whereas once there was believed to be a thin line between Casual/football hoolie/chav, is there now an arguably thinner line between pastel, double badged Stoneys and Love Island wannabees? Please, God, noooo!

31|

Doing it for the Gram

Are we all a bunch of preening, prancing peacocks? We know the Casuals were/still are, but it appears that image is literally everything for Generation Alpha, a highly superficial image that is. The attention spans of gnats, kids are being bombarded with noisy, aggressive snapshots of celebrities, brands and INFLUENCERS URGH online, 24/7. The introduction of the hideous TikTok only heightens this limitation in concentrating on anything; the dances and jigs or whatever have a soundtrack of a song that lasts all of about 15 seconds, never reaching its pinnacle, a climax or even the bridge of a song. Any modern-day marketeer worth their salt has now jumped on the bandwagon of this undeniably vast social media platform, although not I'm sure how much successful engagement is going to be procured from chronicling Sue from accounts' dinner time dance in some generic corporate office? Depressingly, I heard that nowadays, if an album is even downloaded in its entirety (as opposed to cherry picking solely the charted hits on Spotify), people don't listen past track four. What the actual fuck. TiKToK and Instagram – the new 'sub' culture amalgamated into one social online dump.

Online accessibility has created a creative vacuum, a place for vacuousness and inauthenticity. No exclusivity, no one-upmanship, no balls to dare to be different. Only to be like sheep wearing shiny Stone

Island overshirts 'cos it looks cooler than Boohoo Man, they've seen a few Towie lads wearing it and its expensive enough to brag on the 'gram.

David Elders, Hibs and Original Casuals says:

'This Instagram lot just want to have something recognisable, like a Stone Island badge or a CP watchfinder on something. I'd say their main trend is simply looking like cunts lol.'

These 'cunts' can get Stone Island or CP or any other brand whenever they want simply by scrolling on their phone. The availability to be able to purchase something that was once so prestigious, so exclusive, expensive and sought after is mind boggling.

Oliver Beer nails it with this comment: 'It's almost like catalogue culture.'

So now we have Catalogue Casuals! They order off a vast online catalogue where they can copy and imitate to their hearts content – blithely buying shit without knowing its proper history, which in my opinion, is total sacrilege.

Jared Latimer (Terraces) believes that they are aware of brands with a history, but to an extent:

'I think people are sort of grasping onto something now. The younger ones are. They want to be part of something that has already been there, already been created. And in a way I feel sorry for them, because they're being pushed brands which haven't got any history of terrace culture whatsoever.'

I don't. I don't feel sorry for them. I might seem scathing, I'm not; only critical of the superfluous world our children are meant to live in – their sartorial interests and consumer behaviour already mapped out for them in a pre-pubescent algorithm.

And whichever brands they have been robotically programmed into liking, if they can't afford the full shebang, or don't want to

Klarna it, there is an option to RENT a garment; rent as in borrow, take a few pics, #getthebadgein, then sack it off!

Jared: 'They just want, want, want, and get what they can afford…Like this culture of renting clothing, which is sort of becoming a newish thing. To rent something to just put on your Instagram.'

Me: 'That has actually just killed me inside. I didn't know people did that.'

Jared: 'Selfridges do it. You can rent a top, a piece of Stone Island, from Selfridges now. You can investigate that. I'm sure they still do it.'

Me: 'That's kind of soul-destroying isn't it.'

The instacranks are inspired by music videos (or mini music 'clips' on TikTok bloody Tak), footballers, influencers and Z-list celebs, smitten by their luxury cars, bags and brands – their wealth. They want to wear the coveted clobber and create this fake charade of a lifestyle for themselves without having to work hard or graft for it.

This conspicuous consumption is underpinned by many varying factors and is even more accessible than ever before for. Dhaliwal, Singh and Paul write that:

'Contemporary luxury consumers are now not limited to the privileged and elite only and downward extension has fueled the growth of the luxury sector.' So more of us peasants can now break into the elusive world of high-end brands, and we do this because, 'they provide status elevation, socio-psychological benefits, emotional value, social identification and mass prestige.'

So, we can all show off, all give it the big un in a sweet, blinged up, harmony. Pandora's Dressing Up Box has democratically and officially been opened.

32|

If Everybody Looked the Same; the Dilution of the Brands

The TikTok generation are pussies. Pass it on!
'Everybody has got the same phone, the same haircut. I think people are afraid to stand out, because it's so easy to get slagged on social media, Facebook, everything else. So, people just fit in, because they don't want to have a bit of abuse.' Jared Latimer, Terraces.

I get abuse online in some shape or form on a regular basis, but who gives a fuck?! Seriously? Do you care what some crank says about you? No one has any bottle these days – to either dare to be different, or to deal (aka simply ignore) any 'unkind' comments. Get a grip.

The shallowness and vanity of today's youth culture could be forgiven if there was even an ounce of creativity in their 'looks', rather than watered down, mum's own brand, Tesco value versions. Today's generation are force-fed brands and what they are meant to aspire to, so you can't really blame some for wanting to have an affiliation with something with an actual authentic legitimacy, an enduring, long-lasting, popular and genuine tribe, the Casuals. But Casual culture and its brands have been diluted to such an extent, that some young lads think it's acceptable to wear Stone Island – DOUBLED UP. Or a polo shirt NOT buttoned up to the top!! Someone call Old Bill (😊)! And don't pander to them for fucks sake!

'Without any doubt, the two brands which have had their "specialness" diluted the most would be Stone Island and CP Company. Ironically though, these are still two of the brands which continue to come out with some of the best, most original and iconic pieces to this day. It's about seeing past the stuff which is squarely aimed at the Instagram massives out there and finding those pieces that are original.' That's the opinion of David Elders, from Original Casuals.

Steve Lumb from Terrace Cult adds:

'I think there's a turn. This is why the market's turning; I think the young lads these days, looking at these brands, are thinking; "hold on a min, Stone Island was a uniform, it was what you worked a month for to buy a jumper. You walked out the house, you felt part of something." Now Drake's rapping crying about his bird with a fuckin pink Stone Island jumper on, do you know what I mean?'

Ah yes Drake. Canadian born rapper-lite warbler with a shedload of autotune and a penchant (and massive pendant!) for Stone Island.

The vitriol towards Drake and other hip-hop stars coming from the Casual community is loud, vocal, unsurprising and totally acceptable. It also stems from the fact that the higher-end Casual brands are sponsoring said hip hop stars and targeting a more 'urban' market in general. The elephant in the proverbial room being that there is a clear irony in brands wanting to move away from the archetypical hooligan/football violence culture, yet have public affiliations and marketing campaigns with rap stars with allegedly questionable backgrounds, whose music can be thought of as actually promoting violence and/or drug culture.

Jared explains:

'Rap culture, really, is not just a small bit of violence on a Saturday afternoon, its violence, drugs, guns, anything. But originally, a few lads knocking hell out of each other, realistically, isn't that bad of a thing.'

In a further paradoxical twist, Stone Island was once believed to have had racist connotations. Jared adds:

'When I first started selling Stone Island, it was almost like a racist thing. Because it was such a strong football thing, and obviously there definitely has been, and still are, racist elements to hooliganism. Some wouldn't go near it because they felt it like it was a racist symbol.'

Oliver Beer agrees and recollects:

'When we first started wearing Stone Island, we went away, might have been Liverpool or somewhere like that, and they were like, "Are you National Front?" We were like, "No, why?" And they were like, "Them badges on your arm, they're National Front." They hadn't seen anything like it.'

But, as mentioned earlier, it must be hard to construct clobber befitting of your subculture, especially if there is only a barren and lacklustre music/festival/fashion scene. What is there to aspire to when there is nothing dominating the airwaves apart from mumble grumble rap where the artists are from big cities or the States, not relatable local stars whose lyrics speak directly to you. But once again, youngsters will imitate what they believe to be cool, and in line with a type of society they live in; watered down rap, wank pop, CP Goggle hats and Gucci man bags, all perpetuated by a pretension of wealth and lifestyle, with wannabe influencers, YouTubers, TikTokers and reality stars heading up this lazy generation – believing doing fuck all apart from some make up tutorials, a shithanger dance, a naval gazing vlog or (worst case scenario) shotting bits of weed will get them their 'Benz.

'You get the new generation and see the rappers and aspire to it, or they might see lads down the match, cos young boys emulating the Stone Island thing, even though it's gone, there's no connection there, but they wear it because they think it's the right thing,' says Oliver Beer.

Aidan Tregay, 22, Burnley, owner of new label Project North comments:

'The younger generation of today all want the best brand to show off and the music industry is one of the biggest influencers. I feel that plays a part, there's a lot of rap about and grime all over which is usually people in tracksuits, man bags, big Canada Goose coats and brands like Hoodrich, so I feel their behaviour of buying is from that, but not everybody likes the same so it just depends on what attracts you to a brand.'

Let me be clear, mimicking a style from a musical 'hero' is of course a teenage norm and an absolutely correct rite of passage. But to just copy directionless, rudderless, with no idea of what it's all about, what the references are, that is just sheep mentality. Blindly jumping off the sartorial cliff cos some mumble rapping TikTok star said so.

'People see someone, they want to wear the exact same thing as that person is wearing, instead of something similar yet different. Say Liam Gallagher, he gets a jacket, people literally ring us up for the exact jacket. Fair enough, he's your idol, but you don't want to be like a lookalike. That's the way I think things have changed. People want to copy off people, instead of coming up with their own ideas. You can still fit into a culture, but it doesn't mean you have to be completely uniform.' That is the option of Jared Latimer from Terraces.

The exposure brands such as CP and Stone Island have now is due to this more recent scion of music adopting them is not unnoticed. By us.

Matt Snell (Casual Client Clothing) believes that the trend is also due to the emerging Major League Soccer in America:

'Their football is years behind everyone else, but the fans really are trying to make their mark and there is plenty of money washing around. Tifos, flares and banners show they try to recreate Europe and South America so the clothing won't be far behind. Also, with

Americans being exposed to more Stone Island through Drake and other outlets, I can see it happening.'

Told, you, that fucking Drake again! Take your bedazzled Stone Island medallion and sling it!!

It appears now that appropriators have become the 'appropriatees' – that the labels the Casuals adopted have become increasingly popular.

Riaz Kahn notes: 'These brands will never mention how the Casual culture enabled these labels to become more mainstream. If the Casuals never wore these labels, where do you think they would be now? Credit where credit is due!'

Jared Latimer: 'CP, Stone Island; those brands trying to get away from Terrace Culture. And whether they like it or not, that culture is a massive per cent of their business.'

Jay Montessori: 'Would Stone Island etc. exist without street kids and youth culture…all stagnated with no originality. 800 quid to look like each other.'

After interviewing Lorenzo Osti, of CP Company, I feel reassured that us Casuals have not been banished or excluded from the label's background, history and notoriety now that he has become in charge of the company.

Lorenzo: 'In the past, honestly, there was a kind of opinion to hide this relationship because it was perceived as negative. It's not like this for me. I mean the reason we came to Darwen in Blackburn (for the Cinquanta CP Company 50th anniversary), was to make the biggest exhibition we ever made, to celebrate this community.

'So, not only am I aware, but I'm also proud and I'm grateful for this fanbase that have really kept the brand alive for many years where, when nobody else was doing that. In Italy and the rest of the world, CP disappeared for more than 20 years, and the only sales were in the

North of England. And so, I'm extremely grateful. And then honestly Roo, I met a lot of lovely people.'

33|

I've Got 99 Problems but A Coat Ain't One

When speaking to Lorenzo, it was easy to see how much respect he has for the Casual community, a mutual respect for authenticity from both brand and consumer, and whereas Stone Island has arguably turned its back on the terrace culture narrative, focusing on the luxury high-end urban market instead, Lorenzo ardently insists that CP Company will stay true to its roots:

'We want to stay close to people who really have affection and loyalty to the brand. So, people who run communities online, for us they are very important. We don't want to do catwalks, to talk to the luxury world, we want to talk with people who get passionate. So that place, that market, that community, is very important.

'The point is, it's not easy to really interact as a brand. Because if you're stepping in as a brand, it doesn't work. It's something from the bottom so, I mean, we more or less leave it like it is. We are pleased, we look at it, we take suggestion, but we do not step in, we do not want to advertise, or push because I don't think it would work, it must be very authentic, no?'

Fellow Italian label Plurimus is just as committed to their customers and appreciative of their continued brand loyalty. Plurimus (which is Latin for 'Many from One') has its roots firmly entrenched within

Casual culture, and by speaking with the sole owner and designer Fabio Cavina, it will remain positively in its future.

Cavina is in direct contact with his customers through the magic of online communities which is how he came to establish the brand in the first place.

'In the eighties, I had this fascination with some brands...Paninaro brands. I think at the end of the eighties, it kind of disappeared and for basically about fifteen years, I didn't look into it anymore. And then in the early noughties, there was no social media but there were forums. And I started getting involved with some forums. Most of them were UK based. There were all these people collecting jackets from the eighties and the nineties and they knew a lot of things about the brands that I used to like in the eighties and about stuff from Massimo Osti, so basically, that's how my passion came back.'

Arguably Cavina was drawn back into Casual culture due to nostalgic forums reminiscing about old brands and old times, thank God as it helped create Plurimus! And even now, Cavina talks about the importance of social media in connecting and engaging with his followers:

'I talk to them through social media, which is basically two forms. One is Facebook, on Facebook there is a group, which I did not create. Two friends of mine, one from Germany and one from Scotland, basically they created this group and its closed, it's not an open Facebook group, you need to be invited by someone. The thing is, they want to keep it limited because they say if they get too many people, they'll have a problem getting the jacket if they want to get the jacket. So that is one platform.

'The other is Instagram, but I'm not that active on it. I always try to make it for people, to involve those following the page and I try to select the best pictures. So again, it's something I do myself, I don't have like a media expert. And then there is also the possibility to subscribe to our newsletter through my website. So, if you subscribe, as soon as the new garment is presented, you will get an email. And that's how it works. Online communities are fundamental. I haven't been on a forum for a very long time, because I guess Facebook then Instagram, have replaced most of the forums. I think the forums were very important for me because basically they supply me with a lot of information from people who were very similar to me in terms of background, taste, what they were wearing. Social media has been my means of promotion for the past three years, not because I don't want to do advertising, but because my customers, I'm very active with them. I'm advertising Plurimus in a very genuine and effective way. I think without social media I would have a problem communicating the brand the way I do.'

Cavina's modern approach and attitude to social media, and the relationship and direct contact he has with customers, allows him more control of how his brand is perceived. This then gives him the privilege of insider information of what the customers want exactly – a kind of mass focus group. The connection the customers have with Cavina allows them to feel valued, special and their Casual rights have not been violated, or in fact that they have picked up a brand that respects the football Casual heritage:

'Even now when sometimes people write to me on Facebook, and they say, "ah I've heard your brand is for the Casuals." I think, what I'm doing is basically like product research, and I'm aware that the majority of my customers are lads you know, football lads, but that is fine with me. But I didn't start Plurimus only thinking of football lads, I started Plurimus because of the product, and the heritage, which is, you know, very strong locally, and just following my passion, and doing the things that I would like to wear as a customer, as someone who has always worn jackets.'

The love-in Cavina has with both Casuals and his brand is clear to see; he's refreshingly not arsed about becoming a money spinning, mega brand such as Stone Island; although arguably Plurimus' quality and technological innovations in its clobber are just as high in standards and is also becoming just as mech a cult classic favoured by original football Casuals.

'I think what they feel, and what they are recognise in me is that I'm very similar to them. And I have the same passion that they have, and I always try to do the best I can when I start to work on a new garment. And as I aways say, this doesn't prevent mistakes, but even when I make mistakes, my customers recognise my passion. And that has always helped me, and the brand and I think what they really like about this project is that it's actually, it was created by fashion, and not like, you know, let's make a business plan and try to make as much money as possible.'

Cavina totally goes against the fashion grain in all aspects of his 'second baby'. He staunchly refuses to be dictated to by showrooms, retailers and even the fashion seasons.

'I think when I started Plurimus, I was coming from an experience with another brand and we were like developing collections and showing collections to showrooms, and we were doing things back then, the best way possible with a lot of pressure and everything. But when I started Plurimus I thought I want to take the standard model and try to focus on things that didn't work for me. Other things that I worked for their dimension, for their philosophy, I just changed them. And I took the standard model and reversed it, turned it upside down.'

This stubbornness and refusal to conform to the fashion norm, this raging against the machine, a naughty school kid doffing his cap, or more likely putting his fingers up to school and the authorities; the laissez faire, free spirited, almost hippy mentality, makes him stand out as the rebel of Casual couture.

Like Alexander McQueen who felt the artistic pain of the rat race of the fashion industry, the incessant focus on financial success and of being the most sought after and publicised of the luxury brands, is no doubt suffocating. Fashion houses pressuring designers to peddle out collection after collection, rinsing every last drop of creativity out of our knackered artistes, and then there's the cruise lines to wheel out ffs!

Both visionaries, renegades, a fuck the system-mentality in their own fashion fields. Cavina, the saviour of Casual culture, producer of the most Casual-esque clobber we've seen for a while will not be bullied or hurried into making his Plurimus brand a part of the mainstream fashion industry:

'I don't want to do collections, I don't want to work with the showroom because prices get inflated, they get crazy. The brand is very young, and people don't know it yet. I need to be able to talk, to communicate to the customers, I need them to like my products. Remove the theatres, remove the consultants.'

His ethos of taking it slow, keeping it real and keeping it limited, is most certainly working:

'The 99 concept started when I was doing the first T shirts a couple of years ago. Back then, I was doing the same, I had 99 pieces, and to me, 99 has always been a number which expresses the will of a person, trying to achieve perfection but in the end, you can't achieve perfection as a human being, so 99 is like; I do my best, I might not get there but I'll get as close as possible.

'I kept it and brought it back when I started Plurimus, because as I said I wanted to keep it limited. I think people like the feeling to have a number of these which is quite limited. I tell them, if I make more, you could order but I think that's wrong, cos I think what people really like about being so limited, is the feeling of managing to get something very exclusive in a world where you can get basically everything; but I think people like there's only 99 pieces in the world.'

In other words, a Casual's wet dream!

34|

Wake Me Up Before You Go Go; Smart Marketing for the Woke Generation

If Plurimus' underground style of rebellious, yet curiously simplistic marketing strikes a chord with our older dressers, what kind of advertising do our sensitive, self-aware and sustainable friendly Gen-Zs and Gen-Alphas respond to?

Let's ask one!

Aidan Tregay, 22, Burnley:

'The ad campaigns, I always find really interesting; how are they going to portray the brand's image to people and then take inspiration and try to implement them in mine. I feel that I do care who wears these brands as it's almost a uniform and group of people you are associated with and how you wear it.'

These Nouveaux Casuals have some high purchasing power, a disposable income that delights retailers. But do big brand campaigns inspire the younger generation to buy? Does it provoke some brand aspiration or is the old world of mega campaigns over in general? The youths I spoke to continue to be influenced by Liam Gallagher and other bands and musical icons, so has the evolution of marketing in fact gone full circle and more authentic guerrilla tactics need to be used instead or do we trust the young pups to make their own minds up?

Harry Butler, 20, Manchester:

'If I see a musician or band for example Liam Gallagher or The Sherlocks wearing a brand or a piece of clobber, I will research it and buy it.'

Dan Butler, 20, Leeds:

'If I was to see one of my favourite artists or sportsmen advertising a certain brand or product, it will influence my decision on if I choose to purchase the product.'

Matt Williams, 17, Swansea:

'I'm always interested in the new stuff coming out. Would like to see some more younger lads wearing the brands but it is nice standing out from the crowd. Also, not everyone can pull off a pink Sergio!'

Do brands even need to do any traditional marketing with this young market who are wised up to obvious selling techniques and instead getting their influences off friends, family and foe (TikTok)? But of course, all labels market their brand, to display the core identity and values of themselves. Brands can harness the importance of online communities and infiltrate into the psyche this way. Stone Island appears to be choosing the urban, streetwear market, with its choice of styling, models, collaborations and rap affiliations.

Back in May 2016, Maria Cristina Pavarini interviewed Stone Island President, Carlo Rivetti, for The Spin Off magazine. It coincided with Stone Island's third collaboration with street label Supreme and in the article, Rivetti discusses the brand's involvement with this market, believing it's more of a natural progression due to the mutual focus on technical innovation:

'Stone Island is a sportswear brand defined by textile research, great care for functions of use and a strong male aesthetic. The streetwear market – an increasingly growing and always evolving international movement strongly attracted by product value – has recently started adopting us, so it's not the result of a particular marketing strategy.'

He understands Stone Island has a savvy, switched on new fanbase:

'All over the world, young consumers are strongly attracted to high-research products. We owe this in part to the sneaker-culture, though there is much more to it...The digital world has given us a higher profile among younger generations.'

This profile has become more high-end and successful in a linear development that has come in part from social media and the latest urbanites who have appropriated Stone Island and made it into an almost new brand, far away from the cold English terraces where arguably its public profile was first born. The collaborations with street brands and relationships with street stars has unquestionably helped Stone Island conquer the vast North American luxury goods territory:

'In Canada and the US, we've been distributed through about 40 select multibrand stores for some time. I had positive signals over the last two years from North America, so we decided time was ripe to explain how we create and build Stone Island projects and our unique products to a continent that still doesn't know much about us.'

Well, the continent most certainly knows about the brand now, with rappers even staking a claim in the discovery of such a cool new brand.

'Rappers like A$AP Nast, Travis Scott and Drake all wore garments with the iconic compass tag on the left sleeve and Stone Island became less of a subcultural thing, and more of a cultural thing. Celebrities argued over who discovered Stoney first and the rise of UK grime music amplified the brand's importance even more.' This opinion coming from Tarik Halil in Culted.

Now I'm not going to regurgitate the same old tripe about how this hip-hop appropriation has spoilt Stone Island (it has), but there are articles discussing it around the world:

'Why Drake and Streetwear are ruining Stone Island for Football Fans,' Aleks Eror, 2017, Highsnobiety,

And opinions such as these from Casual Ultra...

'It's disgusting to see people like Drake wearing Stone Island.'
And:
'Is there anything worse? I mean it ain't too bad when he's wearing it but it's just all of them sore lot (fan boys) that follow him. If they start knocking about in it, it'll be done.' The Chaps Club, a page on Instagram states.

It's not rocket science to see that people believe it to be a major factor in the 'decline' of the label's identity within the Casual community. We just don't like anyone else at all wearing our clobber, even though it wasn't ours to start with, alright?! ☺

Rivetti talks about the streetwear market that has adopted Stone Island, but what of those who adopted the brand many years ago? Lorenzo Osti believes that Stone Island's move into the high-end sportswear market leaves a space for CP Company to become the brand du jour for Casuals, appreciating their brand loyalty, and not shunning the terrace community:

'Stone Island is much bigger than CP at the moment. It wasn't like that, of course we need to differentiate at the same time. The more they go into the luxury world, and they walk away from the original community, that is the world we want to step in. So, the same reason why we went to Darwen (Cinquanta 50th anniversary exhibition), why the same reason? We want to stay close to people who really have affection and loyalty to the brand. People who run communities online, for us they are very important. We don't want to do catwalks, to talk to the luxury world, we want to talk with people who get passionate. So that place, that market, that community, is very important.'

When it comes to actual advertising aesthetics currently utilised by Stone Island, Osti continues:

'Stone Island models look more like mannequins...so I think here (at CP Company) it's a different strategy. We want, first, to personalise. I mean, we have a connection to the people, we want to have this connection and then we want to have regular people. We don't want to have models. We will do the campaign for the next seasons with just regular people. Authentic people in love with the brand, but not models, nothing like that.'

CP's strategy appears to be spearheaded by Osti himself who throughout the interview was very clear in the brand's acceptance and appreciation of football Casuals' adoption and loyalty of the brand, rewarding them by not taking the piss out of them, nor forgetting their grassroots support and most certainly not ignoring their love for the brand with isolating urban marketing campaigns.

The inclusive strategy adopted by Lorenzo and co is most certainly very modern, woke even?

Jared Latimer believes so:

'I do think it's a bit of woke culture in there, brands don't want to be seen to be stuck with one type of culture. So, I don't necessarily think they're pulling away from cultures, I think they're just widening the search. But like any groups of people or any tribes of people, when they see something they have been affiliated with, then being affiliated with somebody else, it dilutes a bit, and it puts you off the brand a little bit.

'I've got no problem with pop culture grabbing hold of things. But you just feel like saying, "get your own bloody stuff," don't you?'

Yes. I do.

35|

Vive La (Consumer) Resistance

Cultural consumption underpins this entire book, but why does it do our head in so much when our precious subcultures are commodified, and the brands appear to sell out and people are copying our stuff?! Do the subcultures and their group identity remain the same and, more importantly, will the Casual and terrace subcultures?

Purity, authenticity and originality are all cornerstones of subcultural capital; many subcultures go culturally bankrupt once their style has been nicked and adopted by the mainstream. When things have gone from underground to mainstream, even things like TV programmes, when they go from no one knowing about it, to watercooler gossip at work, to a total caricature of itself when everyone has jumped on the bandwagon; I mean you know it's gone to shit when your mum and dad know about it. And, as per, once the powers that be see how successful a trend has become, they automatically see pound signs in their eyes, wanting to squeeze every ounce of realness and creativity out of a subculture by commodifying and copying the fuck out of it.

In a fascinating study on subcultures taking control and preserving their identity, Schiele and Venkatesh write that:

'Mainstreaming by the commercial marketplace assimilates the symbols and practices of a subcultural community into dominant norms.'

Schiele and Venkatesh use the subculture of Japanese youth consumers, the Harajuku, as examples, discussing how their extreme style and fashion has been 'mimicked' and 'mainstreamed' by Gwen Stefani, thus rendering their subcultural equity as weak, less authentic, and having 'negative effects on the group they target.' Of course, Stefani is not the only American accused of cultural appropriation, more and more celebrities are accused of this, along with blackfishing.

But to what of Casuals' thoughts on their original terrace style being mimicked?

Neil Primett, tactfully:

'Whatever someone says, If I was copying someone who looked great – why not, if someone was to copy me would I be bothered not at all just don't do it down the local on the same night!'

David Elders, not so tactfully:

'Everything gets copied eventually. I suppose the difference is blatant plagiarism compared to merely taking inspiration from and putting your own twist on. For those on "our" side of the fence, (or of a more "vintage" age lol), it's the same as it ever was; trying to find new brands, styles, designs and fabrics to stand out and be different, whereas the young team seem to miss the original point, and all want to look the same.'

Riaz Khan muses:

'About the young ones copying. We know fashion repeats itself. The Mods revival came fifteen years after the Mods hit the street back in the 60s. Also, the Teddy Boys came about again in the late 70s. So, it was inevitable that the Casual culture has had a comeback.'

But will their game be as strong? Will they still be game as a badger?

Riaz Kahn continues:

'The youngsters see the strength of the one-upmanship amongst the older generation; they see this and try to compete but for some reason they cannot pull it off. The look will change as that's what the whole ethos of being a Casual was back in the day. We were dynamic, always changing our look but still holding onto the designer labels.'

There will always be differences, the subcultural mimicking can never be the same and replicated exactly. There will be subtle nuances and discreet references that the Nouveaux just won't be aware of due to the generational differences. By putting on an original spin, an invisible marking of their territory, they are 'reclaiming authenticity', just like the Harajuku:

'When the mainstream appropriates their fashion, the Harajuku reported that outsiders copy the overall idea but usually leave out specific details. The authentic members thus put more emphasis on the importance of details and symbols that appear slight to outsiders but serve as a non-verbal communication tool to convey to fellow members. Items such as jewellery, buttons, and other accessories have been made specifically for group members, and these resources are shared exclusively within the community. When a symbolic item has been mimicked by the mainstream, the group changes these symbols.' This analysis comes from Schiele and Venkatesh.

David Elders explains how the older Casuals are different:

'I think a lot of the time-just as back in the day – we aim for more subtle looks. Less blatant. The young lot seem to have names and brands everywhere, as big as possible. Everything has to have that label on it. Whereas a lot of the thing was/is to try and find stuff that looks the part and makes other like-minded souls wonder what it is rather than it being obvious.'

In fact, it is these subtleties, this nonchalance, the effortless way in which the Casuals would put outfits together, OWN wearing the labels rather than let a brash garish brand own and then overpower them. This is Casual. Or as the Italians put it, and explained to me by Riaz, 'Sprezzatura' means putting on a piece of clothing and not needing to make any effort. This is something the mainstream cannot do.

Me: 'I've always dressed for myself. It's just how you wear it. It's how you walk, how you own it. Some people wear it for the sake of wearing it.'

Oliver Beer: 'I've always mixed and matched.'

M: 'You can spot someone who's had money from Mummy and Daddy to buy expensive Stone Island, and you can tell someone who's grafted for it. And they wear it differently.'

Oliver: 'And they wear it well. Simple as that.'

Riaz Khan agrees that the older Casuals' means of reclaiming authenticity – and arguably authority – is by sourcing out newer (Casual labels), the more expensive versions, or vintage.

'The only problem with the culture is the "clone". Every bleeder dresses very similar! So, there are labels out there that the young 'uns haven't caught wind of yet like Hawkwood Mercantile, Uniform Bridge, Adidas Spezial etc. Also with Stone Island, I try to wear Ghost or Shadow. Even I go for the vintage Stone Island stuff. CP is the same. Go for the collabs and stuff.'

36|

The Vintage Connection

Vintage is the last fling for older Casuals wanting that unique, rare clobber fix, but it also appears to be having a renaissance in popularity in the young 'uns an' all. Upselling/vintage/recycling or preowned garments are part of a trend that appears to be facilitated by sites such as eBay, ASOS Marketplace, Depop and a smattering of reselling sites specialising in classic Casual couture. With more and more vintage procurers of terrace fashion sprouting up online, will this keep the fire burning in the pits of our stomachs or will this also become a line of authenticity that eventually gets thrashed and/or Gen-Z beat us to the online bidding?!

This is the point about vintage though, from the decent reselling groups, there are rare holy grails on there that are collectors' items for a reason. But there is also a lot of chaff and crap to sort from the wheat, like online jumble sales, you must rummage to find the gems.

Online page The Chaps Club and I asked its followers:

Who buys vintage/pre-owned clobber? If so why, and what labels?

Our survey said:

'No better feeling wearing classic Sergio, Fila, Ellesse to the football.' (luke_cawte)

'Better quality if that makes sense.' (visuals.by.benjamin)

'Sergio Tacchini – it's mint!' (samjmaes.04)

'Modern remakes are rubbish. Bad material, modern, wank fit and made to look modern and cheap…Plus original clothing has that feel of being in the trenches. It's unique and gives you the look of someone who knows what they're on about.' (olivablitza)

Casual Client Clothing followers added when asked why:

'Cheaper and better for the environment.' (charlieausten5)

'Price, no longer available to buy…prefer vintage to new sometimes.' (emmawhufc)

'To get grails that sold out years ago.' (sirjaxonthefirst)

'Insane pricing today and way better quality on vintage.' (bigmikecolonia).

'Vintage Stone Island in particular is miles better than the new stuff.' (clobber_fanatic)

These huge fan pages are not only promoting bands and independent shops but also the vintage resellers, helping their followers find the best clobber. Casual Client Clothing founder, Matt Snell, explains:

'I pride myself on helping the community find cheaper items than buying from the high street and finding legit resellers. I speak to a lot of resellers regularly and always promote them as I know they are trustworthy and won't scam anyone. Far too many people out to make a quick buck from the hype around the clothing at the minute.

'I have managed to get people their money back from scamming resellers in the past so obviously the page and the other community pages I know and speak to regularly and the 400,000 people have enough clout to do it. If I say someone is a scammer a lot of people will see it and hopefully put them out of business.'

The camaraderie continues:

'The causal community is one of the best. No nastiness, no bitching, just others bigging others up, but I have seen a lot of people turning to the money grabbing side of it recently. I feel more and more people are coming round to the idea of buying via Instagram and buying via resellers. It needs to be a trustworthy process for people to part with their hard-earned cash but doing it this way can save 50% and more on the high street.'

Original Casuals adopt and appropriate clobber with heritage, with a story, hence the popularity in vintage garments and resellers. Scratch under the surface of the turquoise Stone Island overcoat, Casuals want outfits with more depth, more history, uniqueness and just generally cooler appeal. This method of sourcing one-off pieces can be demonstrative of the older Casuals' reclaiming power and status in the pecking order of Casual culture.

Kyle Dixon, (Chelsea), became a vintage clothes reseller, setting up Archivio Clothing during lockdown. He talks to me about the vintage market:

'We all know there's a magnitude of resellers who are all prospering when they do the basics well. I think the high RRP is always a driving factor as well. The rarity of items that are becoming harder to get also show why turning to vintage sites is a good way to look unique. I say unique, you feel unique; in reality hundreds of people are hunting the same pieces, just not all can get them. I think being able to share a good rapport with buyers and sellers also builds relationships.'

Kyle also believes the quality of certain high-end brands withstands the test of time – physically and visually – despite the hefty price tag which people argue is totally worth it for its longevity:

'Brands that have high price tags and are seen to be popular will always have people wanting them, the creativity of Massimo Osti and all that still carries through to what we have today. The imagination, creativity and rarity are some key reasons. Additionally, great investments and a brand that has always renovated with the times. Look at the 1982 teal capes, and now look at the nylon metals, smocks, overshirts act they are always at the front foot smashing out fashion pieces.

The number of badges you see bouncing around everywhere you go now is crazy!'

Oliver Beer adds: 'It's like, I'm looking at stuff that's 40 years old. And I'm thinking, "I want that!" I mean, how many people have worn that? Could have been hundreds of people. But you're like, "I like that," and give it a wash! It's gone full circle!'

I just don't know how we have the audacity to be so touchy and territorial about the Nouveaux and the clones copying the Casual aesthetic when we are still buying up all the original Italian heritage labels!

As Neil Summers puts it, 'There are probably loads of Italian playboys going, "What are those dickheads doing wearing our – ?" Yes. But that's life, isn't it? It's the same with music, isn't it? Everyone going on about Kate Bush. "Oh, these kids getting into Kate Bush." It's like, "Well, they're kids, aren't they?"'

Ah yes, the Kate Bush affect, which is another example of things going full circle even as we speak; The Times writes about how Gen Z fell for Kate Bush; the generation listening to Kate Bush's Running up that Hill 37 years after it was first released (and became number one in July 2022). The song is still as spine tingling as ever and thanks to the medium of hit Netflix show Stranger Things, it has been brought to their attention. At least they are listening to it though. At least it's something decent for this new audience.

Nostalgia, and looking back to the future, has always been behind 'new' trends. And the nineties do appear to be 'in' at the moment judging by the stealing of iconic nineties looks, make up and making that deal with God. So, by default, getting the Casual look, is most definitely fashionable now anyway due to its unmistakeable nineties connotations and (mis) understanding of that was when Casual culture was in its zenith, that nineties Casual clobber was the pinnacle of the movement.

Simon Dowling explains:

'The nostalgia thing is huge. Especially on my Armani pieces. That eighties/nineties eagle is…(love heart emoji!). The fact that oversized nineties style is in helps a lot. It means the pieces have more current style relevance.'

It is testament to the quality of these brands that they do stand the test of time and become appropriated by the next generation.

'It's just how long they stay at the top for. But they'll all come back round. Obviously, Burberry in the nineties went through a terrible time of being a chavvy and cheapened brand. But now it has come back. Because they're put their prices up, the quality is a bit better than it used to be. Obviously, to a lot of younger people, it's a new thing again,' says Jared Latimer.

Burberry – you have absolved your sins and wiped the board clean to a fresh generation; ignorance is indeed bliss.

But just as the newbies are assuming the Casual look by its caricatured appearance and taking the labels at face value, so do they of other trends and looks that they have pilfered; filtered versions of the subcultures they once were.

Neil Summers: 'My daughter, probably a year-and-a-half ago, she was wearing flares, smiley t-shirts and bucket hats. She was 11 then. A book came out on Spike Island, so I went to her, "Have a look at that," and it blew her mind. She was like, "This is ace. Who's Joe Bloggs?" "Don't worry about Joe Bloggs. Just skip over that."'

Me: 'Everything just goes full circle.'

N: 'It does, doesn't it? A cycle.'

Me: 'Gen-Z often don't know their references from it. How mad is that? So, like you say, your daughter is wearing flares and a bucket hat and a smiley face, but where does she get that influence from?'

N: 'Yes, definitely. Which I think, back in the late 'eighties, when we all started wearing flares, we knew about the Beatles and Jimi Hendrix…'

Me: 'You could say that they're wearing them but, to me, it's blindly. They don't know why they're wearing it, whereas we all did.'

N: 'They're wearing it because some kid on Snapchat or YouTube is wearing it.'

And there you go. We have all gone full circle, the affinity for Casual culture continues and flows, ebbing between generations. Borrowing styles, tastes in music and putting our own societal spin on the proceedings. We are all copying from each other, nicking ideas and styles, in fashion's triumphant, everlasting, ever-evolving circle.

'Youth culture now really looks back and embraces the past but keeps it contemporary, not sticking to one particular style,' argues Alexander McQueen.

37|

'Daduals' and Mini Mes

What do our young fledging lads think of the elders in the tribe? We know that they are directly influenced by male Casual culture within the family/extended family/musical icons, but are they sneaped that the more they emulate their heroes, the heroes then sack it off and look for more originality in their clobber to get away from the aspirational Casual looks of the Nouveaux?

There appears to be mixed bag of views on older Casuals, aka 'Daduals' (great term coined by Matt Snell/Casual Client Clothing):

'Great to still see them dressed Casual.' (19bamk88)

'I am the older generation and I'm keeping it going baby.' (the_dorset_spur_)

'Tremendous.' (danieldjscullion)

'Cool. I think it's the inspiration for the current style of people involved with football Casuals.' (charlieausten5)

'Best dressed people out there.' (liambuchan1873)

'The older generation started the movement, so I don't see what the problem is?' (mattriley267)

'The creators of the band between football and clothing.' (lucasbeergstrm)

'Always game, it never leaves you.' (benobodyshero3)

'Too stuck in their ways.' (sirjaxonthefirst)

'Don't understand, they've had their day.' (aidan.murdoch)

'Love their enthusiasm, should realise fashion changes.' (prettyCasualsmocks).

Aidan Tregay, Burnley, (Project North) respectfully states:

'I love it, the old boys will never change. They pass their style onto the new Casuals in the football culture. I remember when I was a young lad I would always look up to the older lot and want to dress like them so in a way it's like a repetitive cycle.'

But is the generational gap now more of a generational crevice in terms of brand consumption and brand loyalty? The older Casuals are getting older (and more stubborn?!), the younger 'Casuals' are getting (even more technically) wiser. There appears to be a difference in opinion of either distancing oneself completely from the stereotypical Nouveaux Casual look or holding on to terrace culture as much as possible by dressing the even younger generation in Casual clobber. There appears to be a big demand for kids' designer Casual clothing, with mini-mes spotted with their 'daduals' at football games up and down the country – and with matches catering for these goggle clad sproglets with family stands and big fuck off furry mascots, why shouldn't they?

Neil Summers:

'I've got two kids and I never, ever tell them what to wear. I'm not into that mini-me thing where you make your kid dress what you want to wear. Like, obviously, my kids have both had CP jackets, but again, I try and make them listen to the music I like. They don't, but I think it's good to let your kids find their own look.'

Matt Banks, Digital Marketing, Terraces:

'I've never known and seen so many youngsters nowadays wearing high-end Casual gear. Some of our top selling kids brands like C.P. Company, Napapijri and Weekend Offender do really well online and instore. Kids are recognising more and more what their mate's new jacket is, or what they see on social media being worn by the latest artists – and they want it! Parents are happy to pay a little bit more for that quality, as they'll know it will last longer as they've probably had similar styles in adult sizes!'

Jared Latimer, Terraces:

'It's not as big as you think to be honest, especially in your average working-class town. My missus has two kids and I like to buy them clobber, but I also like them standing out in not so well-known brands. I dressed in designer brands from about age twelve but was told to pay half. I think it's tricky for junior stuff because too cheap cheapens the brand, but too much for something worn twice is crazy.'

But if we can afford to pamper our entitled little brats, then is it not our choice to do so, or is this further example of diluting the brand? I myself am guilty of it, but more in the sense that it is a working-class way to dress your children in their Sunday best, to represent your family, even if you literally have fuck all. Which is the same as our peacocking Casuals' mentality; therefore, is it a massive surprise that we want our children to be the same whilst out and about and impeccably dressed?

Jay Montessori certainly thinks so:

'As a buyer for Tessuti, I had access to cheap samples of great kids' brands when going to appointments. So usually, you could put your name on the sample being used to pre-sell the collection and get it 50% off cost price to us (so dirt cheap) once the selling season was done. I would buy lots of them to keep for my kids, Paul & Shark, Stone Island and CP Company in particular.

'They sat in drawers until they fitted Luca (who had very little interest), then Vinny (who outgrew them at some pace) and then finally passes down to Franco the baby. Some were such good quality that it's even been passed to my eldest grandson.

'Vinny was the only one who loved the match and went to Tranmere with me for years; I took great pride in my boy being renowned for his turn out as a kid.'

Lorenzo and I also discussed this tradition of passing on the Casual baton:

Me: 'I think CP Company has become so entrenched in our culture, just like Stone Island is, you see kids like all round the neighbourhoods and stuff, all wearing the goggle hats, cos they might not be able to afford something else, but everyone's got the goggle hat. And it's still they want to be affiliated with this football culture because football Casuals round here and in the North and middle of England, have been held in quite high esteem, you know. And obviously it's not the same anymore, that modern football has totally changed it, but our areas still kind of cling onto it, because when there's nothing else in the area, when its economically challenged, you know, to go out wearing these expensive labels shows something. And I think it shows that we're still proud of being able to do that.'

Lorenzo: 'It makes sense, it makes sense completely. I spoke about that with Gary Aspden, he told me exactly the same. A kind of proudness, proud. Being able to walk around with this garment, when you show you've made it.'

Neil Summers: 'I think it is a working-class thing. I think there will always be that bloke who hasn't got a pot to piss in but will somehow find a way to wear a really expensive jacket that makes him feel better. If he gets a nod off someone that's like…I did it the other day. I've moved house and I put my coats in a storage unit at the bottom of the garden. I've got a (Stone Island) Ice Jacket and I put it on, because I just wanted to know where it was. I put this Ice Jacket on and walked out into the sunshine and it changed colour and I went, "Fucking brilliant," and then put it back. I don't know what's wrong with me.'

What is wrong with us all?!

38|

Brand Longevity; Where Has all the Faconnable Gone?!

We still trip off these Casual labels, whether new, vintage or nouveau vintage. Once hard to source, Neil Primett and his team at 80s Casual Classics stock online and in store some blinders like the brands mentioned previously, such as Lois, Fila, Sergio Tacchini, which are most definitely hitting the G-spot for the more 'Casual' of the Nouveaux Casuals. But 80s Casual Classics are also driving the resurgence and actual brand revival and relaunch of some long-lost classics such as Patrick.

Patrick has been in relative obscurity since it's heady days as an original 80s Casual brand being worn by footballers and hoolies alike. There had been flurries of activity through dealings of Patrick cagoules on eBay, very sought after, elusive, and if you managed to get one, you had struck Casual gold.

Fast forward to 2022 and Patrick is back by dope demand; 80s Casual Classics have brought it back (I was lucky enough to be sent two cagoules on its release – the red and navy one and the eponymous turquoise blue which I sported for the Knebworth gigs – ideal for the Great British Summer festival weather; either baking hot or slatting it down). It goes without saying it has been a roaring success.

Why us? Why not us? Owner Neil Primett explains further why his 80s Casual Classics were instrumental in Patrick's relaunch. He discusses the background to their relationship:

'Patrick had been an associate brand with Le Coq Sportif at the now defunct JJB Sports, so kind of like an in-house brand in the nineties/early noughties. It had a brief period doing rugby products for Sports Direct in the UK and the opportunity came up to start afresh here as a heritage revival and I was approached as the partner.

'I guess the success of Benetton and the fact I lived in my favourite Patrick boots in '80-81, even having Kevin Keegan's Southampton away kit for school, they knew I was well placed to champion the brand! Enough Casual pages were shouting about the cagoule, and, along with renowned vintage, back in the day photos and discussions that their favourite footy boots/trainers were Patrick, I soon saw the brand still had appeal.

'For a standalone launch on 80s Casual Classics, it was far bigger than Benetton and possibly easier to fit into football and festival music cultures as modern day relevant. The reality of all my launches is scaling the size of support and opportunity to grow – however the true champions are the nostalgia and passion from the lads.'

Another favoured label, Benetton, especially the eponymous rugby shirts, are hugely popular once more after being brought back from the black markets of eBay to the easy click world of online Casual clobber sites. A lot of eighties, nineties and noughties brands are relevant, evident and popular throughout the decades. Some come back to life after a hiatus. Some don't. Are there any Casual classic brands that don't stand the test of time, that don't have a longevity or a devoted band of brand admirers? And why don't they?!

Riaz Kahn (Leicester) surmises:

'Mass producing has had an effect on some of the labels, it became easier to buy and access. Labels like Lacoste, not many people wear it and feel like they are wearing something unique. Labels like Fila, Ellesse etc. were very popular in the early eighties and there was a slight revival of these labels after Nick Love's films *The Firm* and *The Business*, but that exclusivity wasn't there like it was many years ago. I feel this could happen to CP as now we see it on the racks in JD Sports. But CP will always bring out an exclusive range which will keep it popular.'

Asking Jay Montessori (Tranmere) about eighties brands' longevity, why some succeed and why others are left by the sartorial wayside, he says:

'Most of them that have re launched will never hit the previous heights in my opinion. Fiorucci, Pop 84, Best Company etc.…Fila has had limited success off the back of Nick (Love's) films. Ball Jeans has even been re-launched badly. There are still a few rocks unturned but would only go the same way. We used to all be desperate for these things to be brought back in the early noughties on the old 80s Casuals forum but in truth it's all been fucked, and most older lads would agree…be careful what you wish for and all that.'

A warning indeed and a sentiment mirrored by Fabio Cavina, owner and designer of exclusive Italian label becoming increasingly enamoured by older Casuals, Plurimus:

'It's always difficult to recreate the same magic.' Read that again.

These brands being relaunched from back in the day may be hitting a bit of the Casual G-spot but are relaunches ever the same if the magic and the times simply cannot be recreated again. Does the ease of purchase make it the same, or a replica? And are these terrace-lite but character and cock heavy, credible brands going to keep the torch burning for Casual culture?

Best Company, a staunch Paninaro favourite, is prevalent on vintage clobber sites but there has been no actual brand relaunch to become a more profitable faux vintage.

Jared Latimer believes its due to the inimitable and highly distinguishable Olmes Carretti-designed loud and garish designs for the company that could be the reason:

'Best Company's big and embroidered sweatshirts were the most wanted at the time but looked so dated, so quick.'

Personally, I believe that the vibrant colours and designs, symbolic of the late eighties and early nineties, are just too fun for the sober, serious, Stone Island snowflakes of today. Best Company's iconic designs would definitely set you apart from the crowd – and as we all know, wasn't that the point in the first place?

But timing is everything and a brand must fit into the epicentre of the zeitgeist or the heritage revival at the right place at the right time. Primett explains:

'I think again the slight fringe brands like Best Company and Chevignon, we tried a comeback, but I don't think there was enough of a UK approach and understanding, and maybe the brand suffers more as it landed within a period of post Casual/fashion trends where everything was moving too fast.'

And what about prime eighties knitwear brands such as Pringle, Pierre Cardin, Lyle & Scott?

'I feel it hasn't had a comeback-maybe it won't at the minute- whilst knitwear got sunk by sweatshirts etc. so Scottish knit brands like Pringle, which I had owned myself, struggle. It's also not helped by being owned by a Japanese company who have little interest in U.K. heritage and prices at £500 etc. and I'm not even sure if Lyle and Scott would want to embrace the elements again that made them a key Casual brand.'

Interestingly, another quintessential English brand, Aquascutum, a personal favourite of mine and huge in the late nineties and early noughties, has become defunct. Bought by a Japanese company, and then passed through many hands, the company has gone into administration numerous times. Where did it all go wrong?! The Aquascutum checked scarf and cap are absolutely iconic of the Casual revival in the indie era, and emblematic of Casual culture for the nineties' generation. As popular as Burberry! They were as historical as Burberry! The upper class wore it the same as Burberry! We appropriated from them just like we did with Burberry!

Back in 2012, *The Guardian* writer Lauren Cochrane pondered this total dichotomic derailment, this completely (unfair!) dilemma in, *Tale of the Two Macs*:

'Five rows of brown buttons. Check. Buckled sleeves. Check. Storm flaps and belt. Check. Checked lining…Oh, this is getting silly. You get the point. These two beige macs – trench coats if you're talking fashion – look remarkably alike. And yet this week the British company that makes the one on the left – Aquascutum – has gone into administration, while the British company that makes the one on the right, Burberry, has announced expected profits for 2011 of £372m.'

Cochrane finished the article by writing about the history of both English brands; we have already investigated the rise and fall of Burberry; but Burberry rose again after the CHAV/Westbrook/Hoolie (PR) debacles. They appointed key creative directors, modernised the business and foresaw the importance of the emerging Asian markets; Burberry owned their licence in Asia, Aquascutum did not. But Aquascutum is beloved by Casuals because of its quintessential English background? Surely this will save the label? Apparently not:

'Heritage is a double-edged sword,' says Martin Raymond, editor-in-chief of trend agency, The Future Laboratory. 'Aquascutum is still talking about cavalry officers and bad British weather. Burberry has cleverly harnessed its heritage to innovation and edginess.' This came from *The Guardian* in 2012.

Aquascutum was one of the earliest brands stocked in the fledgling Terraces in Hanley, Stoke-on-Trent. I have extremely fond memories of watching/casing all the lads at the match wearing the variations of the Aquascutum caps and/or scarf wrapped round the face. Jared Latimer agrees and adds:

'Aquascutum was a great brand but took off in the shadow of Burberry, but when they both filled the market and got copied and faked, the arse fell out of them both. Luckily for Burberry they learnt to stay top end and have become popular again. It's a strange thing that high-end prices that are arguably not value for money but keeps brands on top of their game. And English brands are always in demand in Asia because they seem exotic and different, the same way as Italian clothes and Japanese denim is to us.'

I always liked Faconnable as a brand, which was also stocked in Terraces. A clean, French, unassuming, low key late nineties label, the garments were well tailored, Casual enough, and crucially, wasn't thrapped by the masses. It is still available but more for euro-luxe down in St Maxime.

So, what did happen to fucking Faconnable?!

Jared tells me: 'I think it's just one of those odd things that happen, nothing wrong with the product. It just didn't take off.'

Oh, right sound, just an anomaly. But I want it back! Let's appropriate it again!

These images of Aquascutum, Faconnable, Gant, Burberry, Napapijri, Stone Island and CP Company invoke feelings and emotions that are imprinted in me in such a visceral way. The match was where I grew up, felt alive, came alive, met people, met boys, then MET boys 😊. The whole of the late nineties when I was coming of age has such a deep impression on my psyche, on my core, my soul. Is this the same for you? Did the music of your era, combined with the clothes, the culture, the lads, the parties, the finding that sense of self, ever leave you? Because I think this indelible print has scarred me in such a way that it has affected most of my decisions, my actions, my CLOBBER, my choice in men (sorry Mum), even until this day? I'm writing a book about it right now ffs! If clothes are used to present ourselves to the world, then what am I presenting? An undeniable, unexplainable, unquestionable desire and attachment to nineties/noughties Casual culture? Do I need to see someone?! Am I generational?!

Something happened to me in this era, a magical time that breathed life into my very being, but was it just because I was growing up? Even 'basic' pop music from this era transports me immediately back in time. Yes, I do listen to Absolute 90s, yeah, I do watch *The Royle Family* and *Absolutely Fabulous* with such a pang of nostalgia it makes me want to weep! However, this is not because I am stuck, narrow minded, like a typical back water town resident, it's just because I have yet to find such clobber and music that make my soul sing!

And if this means I'm labelled then fucking good! What's wrong with being labelled? Why wouldn't you want to be labelled? Doesn't that give you a sense of identity rather than just a nothingness, that humans by their very nature will want to know who you actually are, what you represent and how you represent it? Straddling one foot in the past and one in the grave, everything back then was fucking mint! Na na na na naaa naaaaaaa! And round our way the birds are minging! Music and clobber for the jilted generation indeed.

'I think we just need to accept that the 90's was our peak as a species' – unknown user on social media.

39|

Silk Slut; Social Media & the Evolution of Marketing

And in the beginning of brand marketing there was the newsletter. Old skool or what? And that's a method Fabio Cavina still uses at Plurimus (and most labels too, but this, along with direct contact through social media messages, is his only marketing activity); a perfectly quaint, and extremely efficient way, of informing your customers of a new product. Fabio tells me:

'Basically, social media has been my means of promotion for the past three years, not because I don't want to do advertising, but because of my customers, I'm very active with them. I'm advertising Plurimus in a very genuine and effective way. Because if you see a friend of yours who probably has like 200 jackets, because he's a collector, and you see the brand, and he says it's extremely limited, it's made in Italy...I think without social media I would have a problem communicating the brand the way I do.'

They've seen the brand on some Casual. They like the brand, they go to the website, they want to know more about the product, they want to be kept informed of when they can get their mucky paws on it. They sign up. End of.

Cavina, at the helm of Plurimus, the lone wolf, is simplistic in his marketing activities as he wants to cut out the whole business noise –

which will ultimately, and maybe for him unrequitedly, become deafening due to the cult success of his Casually adored brand:

'I never worked on a business plan, I never thought, "Ok I'll be doing this in three years or five years, where is the brand going to be." Even now I'm constantly pulled between taking the next step, which would mean in my opinion, going through standard distribution chain and try to look for retailers. My ideal would be keeping the same model, basically keep doing everything (as it is). Expand the range, but then, I've been doing everything by myself. Of course, I have my suppliers, but I have no staff, so I take care of all the sides of this project, and if I wanted to take it to the next level, I would need somebody to help me, which is probably something that you can avoid, but at the same time is a struggle for me, because I like to keep control of everything.'

Due to its huge success, let's hope Fabio can keep hold of his baby and not be taken down that business (main) stream and keep the Plurimus brand undiluted, un-thrashed and with no worry of Daniella Westbrook being kitted out in full Plurimus regalia with matching handbag and pushchair.

Always pushing the boundaries, in the mid-late nineties, Stone Island was slightly more advanced in their marketing, sending buyers and retailers their collections through CD-ROMs (Gen-Z, you lot had best Google this). Jared explains:

'Stone Island have always been just ahead of the game at dyeing techniques and fabrics and everything else. So, originally you got a CD Rom. And you couldn't buy off it, it was just a way of putting it in a computer, and you could look at a jacket and spin it around and change the colours. Like you can obviously on all the internet now. But in those days, it was just a dead good marketing tool.'

Like everything in the past, even the adverts used to be better. They were provocative: Silk Cut, Calvin Klein…Levi 501 Jeans adverts were salivated over and anticipated due to the banging tunes, iconography and general coolness of them. Now even Yorkie's ads 'It's not for girls' has no place in this woke and 'civilised' society, having had its slogan replaced by 'Man fuel for man stuff' back in 2012. Sanitised advertising regulations continue to this day with even Pretty Little Thing's knuckles been wrapped for 'objectifying women' in the promo photo of a model in mom jeans slightly unzipped with hands across her top, as reported by Manchester News in June 2022. I mean, the clue is in the name of the jeans!

The clear evolution of marketing campaigns and brands from before correlates with the evolution of society today (devolution of humour if you ask me). Obviously, social media is a massive part of how they're getting their new products out, especially to this media-savvy generation, who want it instantly and they want it now.

Aidan Tregay, Project North owner, uses all formats of social media and gives me a tutorial on TikTok and Snap Chat; am I griping away simply because I don't know how to use it and just dead old?!

'I am on TikTok, and I love it, you can really hit it big with the right music you choose at the right time. The variety of hashtags to use to link your product to the right people is vital to get maximum exposure as a lot of the younger Casuals use it. The app opens the market up for you. And technology and apps are everyday norm for our generation, everyone is on it. I use Snapchat too but only just recently started with that but again it's a good way of expanding the brand.'

Apparently, it takes more than some Tacchini trackies to be the young Casual king; social media is a must to be showcasing brands and showing off the garms. Jude Moore explains:

'It's important to keep in touch with my fans and let them know about the latest trends, gear and just in general let them know what I've got going on.'

Depressingly, he informs me about the relevant platforms which brands must use in social media today from the yoof perspective:

'TikTok is definitely the new platform to use. Instagram has lost its originality a little and Snapchat I haven't used for a while. I see terrace culture doing well (on social media), but the momentum needs to keep it up on there. There are always people who haven't seen it, so it always needs marketing so people, new people, see the latest trends. The platforms are just as important as having a shop on the local high street.'

My old school pal, and grandson of England and Stoke City legend Gordon Banks, heads up digital marketing at Terraces so I ask him what they are doing for their marketing strategy. Are they upping the ante with social media channels whilst still retaining a strong retail presence; what's their stance on the newer platforms such as Snap Chat and TikTok?

Matt Banks: 'We promote Terraces on Facebook (164k followers), Instagram (41k followers), and Twitter (18.6k followers) as well as our email newsletter. If you sign up with us or follow us on socials you'll find some belting deals from loads of our brands, and also you can be first to find out when our new arrivals have dropped.

'I think someone did the odd TikTok the other year, but we struggle for time due to numbers. We've more work on lol. It's manic!'

Neil Primett of 80s Casual Classics, believes this is the future, this is where it happens and, like Terraces, also have a huge social media presence:

'With over 1 million followers on Facebook, Instagram and other communities on social, I do think there is a new subculture. People will give an opinion, educate and share their finds. Limited releases are still popular, and people are keen to do their own thing even if it means they are peacocking for others to follow.'

Ebrahim writes that this space for exchanging and educating opinions (on brands) along with receiving up to date, tailored information can almost certainly create more equity in a consumer's brand loyalty:

'People going online are looking to share their experience, build relations and discuss ideas with others. The social network theory postulates that human behaviours are embedded in these online interpersonal relations, therefore it is likely that the behaviours of members are influenced by social network practices.'

Brands must utilise social media to provide the driving factors to build not just brand loyalty, but attitudinal loyalty which is described in Ebrahim's research as: 'psychological predispositions including attitudes, preferences and commitment toward a brand.' Both forms of consumer loyalty are researched in this study, which theorises that there are three key social media marketing activities that have a holistic impact:

'Trendiness, customization and word of mouth. From the consumer point of view, users are engaged in the online platforms to get tailored services and obtain latest information while they share their experiences and other recommendations.' This holy trinity of social media marketing 'enhances brand loyalty…loyal customers with positive attitudes holding revisiting intentions toward an online platform are triggered by updated, trendy and information-based media.'

But as we have discussed throughout, it is this mutual trust, for Casuals, that builds their brand loyalty and drives their consumer behaviour towards certain (Casual) brands. Ebrahim study agrees:

'Consumers need to trust the digital content; trust is subsequently developed through their various experiences in social media. Consequently, trust is a key factor in creating positive brand associations and long-term relationships.'

Brands, please don't take the piss basically. We can see through it unless it is authentic activities, not collaborations, relations and affiliations just for the sake of it. Or as Primett puts it:

'I rate real people bigging up brands, it releases the company hype, the placement can be a bit bullshit. The internet plays a huge part in consumption. To me if a celebrity wears a brand, he must earn his stripes as being true like anyone else otherwise it's just fake placement.'

But do some labels have to arguably work harder to encapsulate Casuals' brand loyalty through their social media marketing activities due to the Casuals typically being of an older generation that are perhaps not arsed about certain platforms. For the Nouveaux Casuals it's a no brainer, but the chasing of brand loyalty in the digital age can be said to weaken the elusiveness and mystery of the brand, which is what attracted the original Casuals to a brand in the first place.

40|

Luxe Brands; Living the Dream or Social Media 'Mare

This can be said the same too for all luxury brands, not just the higher end of the Casual clobber spectrum. Oliveira and Fernandes write from researching Chandon, Seo and Buchanan-Oliver et al:

'The digital landscape poses a dilemma to luxury brands...social media's versatile, democratic and unpredictable nature may dilute their dream value and damage the perception of luxury itself. Initially reluctant to adopt an online presence, luxury brands were late adopters of social media, where they face the challenge of maintaining their elite status while enabling unlimited consumer interactivity and access to broad masses around the world.'

They add:

'Luxury brands were initially reluctant to adopt an online presence given potential hazards to their core values of exclusivity, scarcity, authenticity and uniqueness.'

The problem luxury brands face is the threat of dilution of the brand, whilst also remaining relevant in the digital age. We have seen the weakening of terrace culture through the commodification of its labels and identities and mainstream simply washes out the strength of a subculture through the adoptions of their style, brands, slang and music. But the advent of the internet age has made everything access all areas, so easily available. Too easy. Boring. The one upmanship that the football Casuals are renowned for is hardly a one-sided game now that every fucker and his dog can flex their sartorial and financial muscles with ease. But the social media game is a necessary evil, even if it goes against what the brand – and its staunch devotees-believe in. New markets, new targets, new goalposts:

'In an age of fast changing trends and increased digitization, brands cannot ignore that they operate in an online world that has completely changed the way postmodern consumers interact with them and therefore calls for a total review of how brands should be managed. This may be particularly true for luxury brands, where a younger generation of tech-savvy luxury consumers, estimated to account for 45% of the global market by 2025, led to a notable shift in consumer perceptions and consumption habits,' Oliviera and Fernandes theorise.

There is a middle ground however, where luxury labels can still be digitally lusted after by the hoi polloi from its haughty positioning online, by choosing the perfect compromise, Instagram. The sleek escapist and aspirational branding and advertising is the perfect combination for the image-based platform with the hazy affects where people can (pretend to) be whatever they want to be.

But wait! Don't the techno wizards see through all the dreamy guff that is marketed to them? This generation are, of course, wise to the fantastical campaigns, but through their own choice they still select to aspire to it, a skewed sense of brand loyalty (or more accurately brand aspiration). They want to engage with the online activities of a luxury label, whether they can afford it or not. Oliviera and Fernandes conclude that this holy grail of consumer behaviour indicates the strength of a brand:

'Consumers that feel more involved and identify themselves with their favourite luxury brand, because it reflects its personality and central beliefs and/or a social status the consumer wishes to convey to others, are more likely to engage with that same brand on Instagram.

Consumers with high levels of involvement are more likely to experience engagement...(even though most) luxury brands' fans are unable to afford them, and thus may use social media as an ideal tool to engage with their inaccessible symbols of status and showcase it to others.'

It is a common theme then, that consumers often want to portray their image as that of high-end, to represent themselves in a way that they hope others to perceive them as being aspirational and wealthy. But if the science behind the theory is right, then ought I engage more with my followers for my 'brand?' Should I respond to the DM fiends to get their 'brand' loyalty, so they keep coming back to me, their affection not being swallowed up by some other insta-razz?!

The hypotheses generated from a number of these studies are most definitely conducted in a correct, scientific and qualitative manner, but can genuine, heartfelt and considered answers be assumed from such black and white monotone questions and surveys, particularly when dealing with people and their emotions towards things so intrinsic to their personality as clobber? My research is not clinically tested, nor am I pretending this is a work of ethnographic genius; a lot of these interviews are with friends and acquaintances taking place down the pub (with the flowing of beer to loosen the lips). But it should give a true and genuine insight into clobber – Casual clobber – today.

41|

Fast Fashion; Check out my Discount Code Boohoo.Com/Rooey25

It is a truth defo universally acknowledged (within certain communities at least), that nothing beats consuming your favourite brands in your favourite shops; the tingling combined senses of touch, sight and smell completely pisses on the damp squib, anti-climactic feeling when you scroll then click, receive the confirmation order email and spend the next couple of days tracking Hermes and hoping you'll be in for when they deliver your order to your designated safe place.

We want our custom to feel valued, we expect to be treated special, and why shouldn't we if we're about to spunk about 700 quid on a new piece? Every decent clobber shop has an owner, the face of the company that knows his customers, their taste, size and budget. Oliver Beer explains:

'If I want something online, I'll go to the Terraces site, Paul & Shark site, whatever, and I'll buy it. It's easy to buy, but I much prefer to go into a shop, try it on, get buttered up by Carl from Review: "Darren, you look really good in that." Yeah, have that, for a thousand quid, and think, "yeah, I look the bollox. But online it's depersonalised."'

Giovanni Calandras caters for these clobber connoisseurs at his own menswear store:

'The type of customer who shops in store are people who want a customer experience, enjoy quality products and those who would like to try a product on because different brands have different size scales and breaks. Also, those who want advice from professional, experienced and knowledgeable sales staff who are passionate about what they do.'

Terraces still put a big emphasis on their retail spaces and are developing other branches in conjunction with their hugely successful online sales. Digital Marketing Manager Matt Banks, tells me:

'Online does dominate in terms of sales, we've grown so much over the last 10 years since I've worked here. But we do very well in-store as well. There's nothing like having a bricks-and-mortar store where you can go in and try on clothes. We have two sale outlet stores where you can find some cracking offers the same as you'd see online in our sale outlet. Our main Terraces HQ store in Hanley is centred in the heart of the Cultural and Business district, the shop covers 2 floors and approximately 8000 square feet.'

Jared Latimer:

'In the old days, you'd just walk into a couple of your favourite shops in the area, something would stand out to you, or something would be shown to you by the staff, because they've been shown it by the people selling it.'

Adding as a retailer himself:

'Maybe that's one of the big differences as well. Maybe that's why it's not so much about the manufacturing and the quality and the fabric anymore. Because when I was buying, when you're seeing things and they're showing you how it's made, and this, that and the other, then you push that over to the customer.

'Because you're face-to-face with them, you can explain the fit of things. You can explain why that shirt is £200 more than that one, because it has been over-dyed or whatever it is. Whereas now, the brand is all they see, they're not getting to touch or feel it or even try it on, half the time.'

Riaz Khan adds:

'There's nothing like going into a shop and trying on that new garment and posing in the mirror. It's a shame that big companies are taking over the smaller clothing shops (Mike Ashley bought out Well Gosh in Leicester, a shop that has been independent for 30 years or so); it loses that individuality and just conforms to society.'

Fast fashion, the advent of the internet, conglomerate retail parks, fucking Boohoo.com, Primark... how are you meant to have any loyalty to this mass produced pish that lasts about two washes and/or you're bored and just chuck it?

Riaz Khan, when asked his opinion on this, says:

'It's wank Roo. Throw away clothing, adding to the landfill, it's not sustainable unlike the labels from Massimo Osti we have from years ago that have lasted. The internet is good as you can surf and get a bargain, there's also no pressure from buying, especially when you have the shop keeper hovering over you expecting a sale.' (Not the legendary Carl from Review I hasten to add ☺.)

Review, Infinites and Terraces are all iconic clobber shops based in the Stoke vicinity; Terraces is still owned independently by James Turner (Stoke), Review has become Pockets, Infinites was bought out by Scotts Menswear as was Tessuti, which are now part of JD Sports.

The theme of smaller businesses being gobbled up by the big bad corporate wolf is personified in notorious Sports Direct and football team dabbler/destroyer, Mike Ashley.

'Mike Ashley, he basically owns and is fucking up the fashion industry. He is on a mission to put all independents out of business, he also owns a part of Four Marketing the company that imports Stone Island and CP Company, so he has the power to decide who gets the brands.' This is the opinion of Jared Latimer from Terraces.

Neil Summers, agency boss, creative and social commentator says that Ashley also owns a stake in Flannels and House of Fraser; a stranglehold on the stores that house our precious brands. Ashley's peevishness is both worrying and childish: 'He just tends to use them to piss off his rivals at JD, He also put Paul & Shark and CP in Sports Direct, proper dickhead.'

What the actual fuck!! This is sacrilege! Diluting the brand? More like fucking it over, violating it and kicking it to the curb. The final nail in the coffin for what Casual labels represented...exclusivity, NOT (as the general woke trend is) inclusivity. Sports Direct is where you go to get some gym trainers (still Adidas) and your kid a football. NOT being able to pick up a Mille Miglia jacket ffs!

Mike Ashley's threats to society continue. As the adage goes, quality over quantity. But we are living in a disposable world, a society where a lad wearing a vest on Love Island will promote his new 'edit' code: boohoomanwannabehoolie10, long thrown out and replaced by the latest crank on there. Ashley's Frasers Group has bought Missguided out of administration, another fast fashion business. Targeted at Gen-Z and ex-Love Islanders, Missguided has suffered the consequences for its clothing's live fast die young mentality.

National World writes: 'A failed experiment with physical stores and questions about the sustainability of fast fashion appeared to create issues for the brand.'

Oliver Beer: 'I'm a postie, so I see people every day with parcels from Boohoo and whatever. They will literally wear something once or twice, then it's gone. And it's so bad for the planet, perhaps we, as hooligans, we're actually saving the planet bit by bit by keeping old stuff going!'

Interestingly though, just like the death of the high street (RIP), is fast fashion going the same way? Our woke kids are extremely environmentally aware and are now favouring the more sustainable of brands. Lorenzo Osti also believes that they are wanting clothes with more depth and quality, a heritage that poses more to them than some sweatshop-tortured garment:

'I believe that after the movement of fast fashion, today young kids, they want something more meaningful, with a story, with some value in it. Not just something to pick up, dress it, drop it. Because fast fashion is a commodity, and now I think they're looking again for something more meaningful. And this garment they found in our wardrobes; they have meanings. First of all, you have this personal attachment and so it probably intentionally or unintentionally can pass this on to them, and you can tell them the story. I think this garment in their eyes, are full of fascination, no? For the history.'

Ever the barometer of civilised society (!), even *Love Island* has gone green; the show has fucked off previous partners Missguided and I Saw it First and is now being partnered with eBay. This clearly demonstrates the change in attitude towards fast fashion, and like we mentioned before, Gen-Zs want their labels to be holier than thou, making them work hard for any type of loyalty (symbolic of *Love Island* itself, no?!).

In 2022, *iNews* reported: 'The move is a reflection of new research which revealed 20 per cent of Brits buy more second-hand items than two years ago, and that 18-34 olds have the highest average percentage of second-hand clothes in their wardrobes at 22 per cent…With the second-hand market set to grow 127 per cent by 2026, it could be argued that Missguided's downfall is simply part of a wider consumer wake up call. The fact that Top Shop went into administration in 2020 and H&M is set to close 240 stores corroborates this concept.'

Did they interview any Casuals, or even age befitting Nouveaux Casuals, for this research? Because most of us lot hold onto our clobber like hoarders!

Let's see what some of Casual Client Clothing's followers had to say when I asked them how long they hold onto their clobber for?

'Years and years, oldest jacket I ever got was 12 years.' (19bamk88)

'Forever.' (the_dorset_spur_)

'Forever.' (danieldjscullion)

'Until it's literally unwearable, but I keep my clothing in really good nick.' (Charlieausten5)

'For years.' (Lucasbeergstm)

'Until it doesn't fit me.' (alfyyoung55)

And my two personal faves:

'Grails forever, other stuff 5 years max.' (sirjaxonthefirst)

'Revival never goes out of style.' (benobodyshero3)

No more questions your Honour, I rest my case!

42|

Stop, Collaborate and Listen

Collaborations are everywhere and have varying levels of success. Here are some of the better ones; David Bowie and Queen, Aerosmith and Run DMC, Everything but the Girl and Todd Terry, Robert de Niro and Warburtons... the list goes on!

For this book's intentions we will focus on co-branding, with brand collaborations in the clobber industry becoming an increasingly popular way in which to keep relevant. Indeed, Oeppen and Jamal observe:

'Co-branding is a strategy that has gained significant popularity within the fashion industry, in particular with luxury brands and mass-market retailers.' This frenetic noisy world in which we live can be silenced by brand differentiation, which then often leads to a staunch brand loyalty.

Kim, Ko, Mi-ah Lee, Mattila and Kim found in their study that:

'The fashion consumers' needs have been seeking for diverse benefits from products such as uniqueness, rarity and utility ... Consumers want more than just a product which expresses an individual's characteristics and image, especially from a fashion product.

'Thus, a differentiated branding strategy is necessary for a fashion brand to fulfil consumer needs and to achieve competitiveness with regard to fast changing diversified consumption sensibilities and market trends.'

This is mint for certain brands, say more sportswear/apparel brands, who want to jump onto the luxury goods bandwagon, gaining instant credibility in this market through their new brand allegiance. The friends with benefits relationships are mutual; the democratisation of high-end labels means that their consumer audience is not so much stuffy WASPS any longer, but anyone wanting to appropriate the luxury label from whichever subculture they are from. Everyone a winner?

'Co-branding is a strategy that allows valuable brand assets to be leveraged and combined with other brand names to form a strategic alliance in which, from a financial point of view, the brand value of both is greater than individual parts,' write Rao and Ruekert.

Not quite as easy as that. These brand partnerships will only be fruitful so long as both brands are favoured by the consumer and is seen as a genuine, as opposed to contrived, collaboration. Yet again, the savvy consumer will know if their brand's identity and strategies are authentic.

Wu and Chalip theorise from their research that:

'Consumers' judgments about co-branding may depend on their degree of brand familiarity and prior attitudes toward each parent brand. The more familiar consumers are with a brand and the more they like the brand, the more they will like the brand with which it is partnered. Thus, a strong brand with high brand equity is critical to securing a successful match-up perception in a co-branding alliance.'

The marrying of brands is certainly perilous in terms of turning off brand purists, but also for the luxury labels co-branding with more mass-market brands such as sportswear brands, risking that pesky brand dilution and exclusivity once again.

'Fashion brands face the challenge of extending their markets while also retaining brand image. This challenge of using co-branding to attract a wider audience at a lower price point while also maintaining an existing market and avoiding brand image dilution was seen as the most important factor for luxury brands when considering downscale co-branding as a strategy,' Oeppen and Jamal believe.

There seems to be loads popping up in recent times, especially the sportswear/luxury label combo, Adidas x Stella McCartney, Puma x Alexander McQueen, North Face x Gucci and Supreme x Stone Island:

'In the case of co-branding, when sportswear brands and fashion designer brands are combined and shown on the same shirt, consumers' perceptions of apparel attributes might change. In theory, the attributes they associate with the fashion brand and those they associate with the sportswear brand should be joined together, which should be advantageous to both as the range and depth of brand associations is enhanced,' Wu and Chalip argue.

Was Stone Island ever going to be favoured by the Casuals doing these collaborations and co-branding exercises when they are not keen on the dilution of the brand anyway, never mind going in with Supreme and New Balance for the arty designs as loved by techno geeks, hipsters, hip hoppers and the rich as fuck Asian market? Nope. So, in terms of Casual culture, what, if any, collaborations do we like? Is it the way forward for our Casual brands to survive or is it the final nail in the coffin for them to cannibalise themselves, spitting out the scraps of any brand integrity?

Jared Latimer observes:

'It's just an extra string in the bow. I think it's good for both brands, if they do a quality job of it.'

He warns:

'I definitely think they need to be careful who they affiliate with, because sometimes you might do a project with a company that, all of a sudden it goes really downhill, and then it's sort of pulling you down.'

Uh Oh.

Jay Montessori sits on the fence as per 😊 :

'I can't stand them at a high-level Roo; have confidence in your product and stick by it. Some of the Stone Island and CP and Adidas ones are ridiculous. I can understand the smaller brands lapping them up if given the opportunity as it's good exposure, but why collab with brands less prestigious than your own? Makes no sense.'

Riaz Kahn firmly believes that collabs, if done correctly, may hold the key to brand longevity: 'More collaborations and an injection of new designers have kept both CP and Stone Island strong. I believe it will continue for many years. Any Stone Island Tela Stella or CP Company Mille Miglia will be future classics along with some of the collabs that have appeared; CP x Adidas Spezial and CP x Barbour for example.'

Oliver Beer: 'I'm not really a fan of the collaborations but saying that the CP x Barbour jacket is very nice. I think the whole point of the collabs is to introduce younger buyers who would not usually buy Stone Island or CP Company. Some very hit and miss collections!'

The Chaps Club: 'To be fair, I'm never majorly into them. Best one recently was CP x Adidas Spezial. I think Spezial have had the best ones. The Barbour Collab was good.'

David Elders: 'To be honest, I think it's rare it works. CP x Barbour was pretty good though. A lot of the time it seems more done with the actual kit secondary to putting two names and logos together on some advertising.'

There is a clear favourite, CP Company x Barbour. This is no doubt because of the brand synergies of both labels being associated with Casual culture; heritage, credibility and much-loved design attributes.

Neil Summers:

'I put those two brands together.'

Say what?! I've known Neil for a couple of years now, he's sound as, finger firmly on all things clobber's pulse, and unfortunately for him attended Stockport County games (albeit not for long as he wasn't into footie, not surprising if they're your local team). Involved in digital content for many brands, big and small, we discussed collaborations in depth.

Neil: 'You should judge them all differently on their own merits, collabs. They should make sense, really, or completely blow your mind.

'The Barbour thing is like, I introduced them to each other, because I'm kind of mates with both sides. I just thought in my head, "Imagine a Bedale with goggles." Fucking brilliant. Fucking amazing. That's kind of what they did, isn't it?'

When asked what other brands he thinks should collaborate:

Neil: 'I don't know. It's a weird one, isn't it, collabs? I'm working with a brand at the minute who are a very young starting out brand and thinking about collabs for them. I always think you should do a collab with someone who makes something you can never make. Like a footwear brand if you're a coat brand, which ties back into the Sebago thing, I guess.

'It's like Barbour. I used to have a brand called Hikerdelic, and we did a collab with Barbour, which I still can't believe happened. But I think people do it because from a design perspective they want to keep things exciting and work with new people and do something a bit different.'

This theory is backed up in Wang, Shen and Lui:

'Goworek argued that fashion designers not only frequently collaborated with manufacturers to improve technical knowledge, but also integrated with fashion buyers to increase their awareness of fashion trends and market information. Design collaboration is thus beneficial, as knowledge about aesthetic, technological, temporal, and financial constraints can be shared among fashion designers, textile designers, and fashion buyer.'

Collabs can be so much more than an 'edit' by an influencer choosing their favourite pieces from a fast-fashion online retailer that will most likely be forgotten about by the time the next ITVBe celeb gets more airtime. Shared resources, skills, marketing and brand equity by affiliation are all benefits of co-branding. As well as creating this unique product, it can spark a bit of magic that would not have happened had the two brands not disseminated their work between themselves to leverage something brilliant and new. Fabio Cavina explains his thoughts on collaborations from his experience as owner and designer at Plurimus:

'I have always thought that collabs make sense when the result gives birth to a result that would have not been possible without the input of the two brands. For instance, when I did the Northlander with the Swedish guys from Our Culture, they provided a camo pattern inspired by Scandinavian borders and I had British Millerain do a fabric with it. Then I used the fabric to design a set; a jacket, inner/overshirt and bag). This was the result of two different brands coming together. It made sense as we were both collaborating and each part was supplying something different, adding the two factors, the result was something special for us, kind of $1+1=3$ if you will.

'I have been offered to do other collaborations during the years but honestly, I could not find the same sense and avoided doing them. I find that most collaborations are done to gain exposure nowadays, but they lack the soul. This is my thought about them.'

Fellow Italian designer Olmes Carretti, he of Best Company bright vibrant 80s design infamy, tells me his plans of a brand-new collaboration with a Norwegian sweater company, combining clean, stark Norse symmetrical design with a visceral, distinctly Italo flavour:

Olmes; 'The collection will debut at the end of September (2022). The label is brand new: O.A.D by Olmes Carretti. Its target is women and men; a Nordic cultural inspiration with materials including mohair, alpaca, cashmere, yak and Norwegian wool.'

With fifty years in the industry, working alongside others of his generation, Massimo Osti, Filippo Alpi, Guido Pellegrini and other prominent Italian designers, Olmes' creativity was perfect for the eighties style. And half a century later, here he is, still producing garments in innovative and imaginative designs to new audience across the world. His experience therefore is second to none. When asked why this moment to launch this Italo-Nordic collab, Olmes explains:

'The company established in 1853, Devold, with which I had already designed since 2004 for three years. From that collaboration three different sweaters were born that are still on sale and have become iconic worldwide: 'Swalbard,' 'Norsjo,' and 'Alnes.' Today, this is a new, very modern and innovative project in the knitwear area.'

It goes without saying this collab has soul; it also goes without saying that I have asked for one of the legendary sweaters. Another match made in co-branding heaven is the Liam Gallagher x Adidas Spezial launch of the LG2 SPZL, which is an amalgamation of vintage Adidas trainers favoured by Gallagher amongst others; his 'brand' totally aligning with THE footwear brand of choice for football Casuals. Along with Olmes' sweaters, as I write this, the demand for these trabs is feverish and only another 9 days until public sale.

Hyperbeast, an online magazine whose name has been reappropriated itself from an actual insult to too cool for school media agency, writes:

'Gallagher is a die-hard adidas fan, especially when it comes to Spezial. Seldom seen wearing anything but Adidas and Stone Island, the musician has honed his unequivocal style which now heavily influences the LG2 SPZL. For the sneaker, Gallagher looks into the archives to create something that's immediately timeless, celebrating things close to the artist's heart such as heritage, music, culture, and the intersection of this particular trio. It's the natural successor to his original Adidas Spezial collaboration from 2019, but brings a cleaner aesthetic fit for all occasions.'

An unsurprising yet still sickly collab recently comes from the rapper Travis Scott's Cactus Jack x Dior collaboration which is arguably a result of his Kardashian Konnection; Kim Jones (Dior) is a friend of the family. Nepo baby! But, as another global fashion and lifestyle 'zine, High Snobiety, writes just days before the scheduled release of July 2022:

'The internet is mad about Travis Scott's Cactus Jack x Dior collaboration, but not for the reason you might think. The team-up, shelved in the wake of the Astroworld tragedy, is back on the table and slated for release on July 13th. Breaking with Scott's previous steps back into the spotlight (those Utopia billboards, the Coachella afterparty performances), the renewed collaboration isn't igniting debate on whether or not the rapper's return comes too soon after 10 Astroworld attendees died in a crowd surge – instead, Scott and Dior are being accused of appropriating skate culture.'

No shit!!

They continue: 'The duo's footwear collection is a range of sneakers very clearly inspired by skate shoes. On Instagram, the kicks have garnered comparisons to Airwalks of the nineties and Pharrell's Ice Cream offerings of the mid-noughties. Critics are also pointing out the likeness between Cactus Jack x Dior's logo and the emblem used by Piss Drunx, a Cali skate crew that rose to infamy in the early noughts.'

'More luxury brands appropriating skate culture,' one comment on Highsnobiety's Instagram reads. 'So everyone just making early 2000 skate shoes, another user wrote.'

Welcome to our world, skater bois. Perhaps this could be another book for a skater g1rl to write in defence of her beloved subculture?

As for some of the others? In my humble opinion:

Nigel Cabourn x Henri-Lloyd (decent but one of many amongst his millions of collabs – don't spread yourself too thin Nige!).

Fiorucci x Napapijri – I like! I have!

Michael Kors x Ellesse – Unsure.

Supreme x SI – Fuck no.

CP x Barbour – Obvs yes.

CP x Armani – Subtle yet disappeared too quietly.

Adidas x Balenciaga – Looks like a night on the Garys down Shelley's back in the day.

Wu and Chalip's findings demonstrated that co-branding is not a straightforward path to enhance product value. Indeed, it can be downright harmful, at least at first. The challenge, therefore, is to identify the means to combine brands in ways that appeal to consumers, and to develop marketing tactics that create and nurture synergy between partner brands.

It's not rocket science. Collabs can be a way of keeping ahead of the pack, the Nouveaux and the mainstream, the ultimate game of one-upmanship with scarce limited editions. And if you are to do a brand collaboration then it must be a genuine pairing, brands with similar brand values so that when they do come together, both bring something to the table, and create something new and desirable- without diluting either party. It's got to be quality and not a contrived partnership, nor sacrificing their individual brand equity for the sake of it. Give us something exclusive, limited and decent enough that will set us apart from those pesky kids!

And don't even get me started on acquisitions…

43|

An Oud; RIP Casual Culture (for good this time)

Waking up to the news in late 2020 that Moncler has unexpectedly acquired Stone Island in a deal worth $1 billion dollars, my heart sunk.

That's all folks! This is the very end of the post-nineties Casual era. The final nail in the coffin for what Stone Island was once associated with; now watch an influx of even more fiendish counterfeits.

Why??? No! Gutted!

Despite this deal being a hushed, surprising one, it doesn't shock me when you think of these two big brands, the behemoths of today's Casual clothing scene joining forces to take a monopoly of the luxe-sports market, and the ever important (now strengthened) presence in the Asian markets.

As we know, Casual culture has been on its arse for some time now... its death contributed by many, well known factors; Maggie, Sky, the evolution of football into a middle class, shirter's dream. But many of us still live with the ghosts of Casuals and its many affiliations still in working class cities today.

From my own perspective, I will always love Stone Island and its connotations unique to me. Growing up in the glory days of iconic nineties Stone Island clobber, my collection started then.

I understood and appreciated Carlo Rivetti's continual quest for technological innovation in the garments colour, material and design, for that is what Stone Island is renowned for, the quality and superiority of the clothes. But when they started bringing out all the mad crocodile shit, and seeing 'lads' doubling up in it, it made me feel uneasy. Then with the Supreme x Stone Island collections created for 'urban' markets, it was becoming clear of the direction Stone Island was taking... and it was one far removed from the terraces. Seeing Drake swaying that hideous vejazzled Stone Island pendant round his neck was akin to the tolling of the death knell for the brand synonymous with Casual culture.

Stone Island has shied away from its associations with football, and certainly does not sing it from the rooftops. Hooligans and the nineties Casual scene being grossly caricatured about their love for the brand, has made Stone Island look like a slightly embarrassed relative of an unruly child, quietly shifting away from the noise.

Moncler has also grown exponentially, firstly by Italian youth subculture the Paninaro, the luxury brands market (after rising from being a popular ski resort label), later in the urban hip hop market which is then adapted by the frenetic fans in Asia whose thirst for luxury brands knows no bounds.

When WAGS and hip-hop stars start to wear it, to me PERSONALLY, it dilutes the brand's identity, or more specifically, what the brand's identity means and resonates uniquely to me.

It can be argued that this is a very short-sighted and small-minded perspective to take, that fashion and culture should be more inclusive and fluid and adapted by all. But I don't want it to! I don't want my favourite labels to be taken and diluted by other subcultures, and even worse taken to the mainstream! Stone Island is my brand, my memories, my youth. And now it has gone.

For many years it is toe-curling to see how people think they are Casuals just by putting on Stone Island or Moncler. You cannot just drape yourself in your Selfridges purchases and think you're the bollox. You must 'wear' and own wearing the clobber, and be a real lad to wear it, but in today's narcissistic generation, how can any of them ever be real lads when there is nothing there anymore?

Football culture has changed beyond recognition too, even more so in this Covid wasteland; add that to the ghastly prima donna, 'me me me' snowflake culture, and anyone born post 2000s will never experience the real terrace culture, just a watered down, mum's own brand, Towie-loving version.

"Beyond fashion, beyond luxury" was the joint philosophy being peddled today with the news of the acquisition. We have now lost our beloved Stone Island to the soulless corporations. Thank you for the amazing times, some amazing pieces and never before have I been so grateful for my collection. Started in the eighties. Ended in 2020. Final kick in the metaphorical bollocks for a particularly shit year.

Let us keep the vintage dealers in business now and let the reality stars double up with the shiny, loud, brash Moncler and technically savvy Stone Island. You may have our brands, but you will never take our memories…"

Oxley, R. (2020). Proper Magazine.

44|

#Getthebadgein

Writing this book throughout the summer of 2022, Stone Island and its legacy/infamy appears to be on everyone's lips once again. The Face Magazine's piece, *How getting the Stone Island badge in became a way of life*, which along with mentioning celebrity fans also writes about how there are many accounts with fans, 'desperately attempting to angle the badge into photos, symbolising they aren't to be messed with.' One such page, 'Get the Badge In' with accompanying hashtag for folk to tag themselves into, #getthebadgein, was a pisser at first, a mockery of Stone Island's notorious football hooligan phase. But, as per everything that gets popular and mainstreamed (we know the drill), the fun and magic has gone out of it because a load of chavs and their snide Stoneys are popping up there, wearing it without seeing the piss taking patter that preceded it. This exasperation of the absolute flagging of the horse of Stone Island's brand integrity led for many followers' caustic comments:

'Stone Island and CP Company are up there with McKenzie and Lonsdale now.'

'I've got a very large collection of Stone Island and CP. The quality and special treatments are unreal. The only fault is with these brands, is that it's getting chav wear as there is so much snide gear out there.'

'It's as trashy as Burberry was in the 2000s.'

'More afraid of Hoodrich now.'

Even Labour leader Sir Kier Starmer was (inadvertently) getting in on the act and getting the badge in when he was posted on Glenn Kitson's tart, acerbic and just dead ace Instagram page wearing a Stone Island polo with Glenn commenting: 'When you got PMQs at 1 and Millwall at 3.' (Glenn Kitson, Instagram, 2022.)

More accounts and memes have been spawned mocking the Stone Island's parodied past, the brand being watered down once again by these rent-a-mob wannabe cranks who genuinely think wearing some basic/snide Stone Island will make them feel hard as fuck. Despite me wanting to keep having a nose at these prepubescent schooligans flexing in Ricki Lakes just like you would curiosities at a circus, by the end of September I reported the page for posting unauthorised pictures of me in Stone Island. When I voiced this online privacy illegality, I was barred from commenting myself! This page really is the epitome of the downfall of Stone Island, and someone needs to make it stop. 5 minutes of fame you really do not want. Urgh.

Counterfeits (more commonly known as snides) are just an abhorrent side effect of the brand's influence, a result of them being a victim of their own success. They say imitation is the sincerest form of flattery; apparently it is also an indicator of success for Stone Island, along with other luxury brands. The Graduate Store writes:

'Very often, well-known brands are prone to counterfeiting. In order to limit as much as possible the spread of fake Stone Island, the Italian brand endows its creations with a unique authentication number. Although Stone Island products are made in a unique way and are difficult to imitate, it is necessary for any amateur of the brand to know how to spot a fake Stone Island, in order to avoid any disappointment.

'Stone Island is distinguished above all by its authenticity. Although it is in the spotlight, the Italian brand has always been able to maintain its identity, namely that of creating technical, innovative and non-conformist products. Stone Island garments are not designed for a particular sector, it is above all universal. Everyone is free to make their own interpretation and create their own link with the brand.'

I would rather wear an unbranded garment rather than bowl round in something fake. It just wouldn't sit right with my soul, and why risk the public humiliation off the brand geeks who can spot a snide a mile off? This question of why even bother was posed to fans of 'Get the Badge In' on Facebook with yet more cutting comments:

'They want to feel hard but, on a budget.'

'If I can't afford it, I simply wouldn't bother. Fakes just look awful, and I don't care if it's a decent fake I would still know.'

'Because the money saved goes on knuckle dusters and sniff.'

'For the same reason buy fake Rolex.'

'Barry Island.'

'Can't afford, save up. Don't buy the badge, buy the brand, the materials, design, history. Nothing worse than fake shit, even if the no-mark thinks it looks ok – same with moody tarts on a night out with shit plastic Gucci and Louis Vuitton handbags.'

You tell them!

This world is fake. Fake lives. Prosthetic fake faces. Fake-ness has been normalised. Labels have had to deal with knock offs for years; people wanting to have a branded item, to have that feeling of self-empowerment whether it has been faked or not. There have been brand marketing strategies in place in order to control this with some labels purposely 'diluting' a bit of their brand by creating a diffusion line or enter a co-branded relationship. The advantage of this is that it can make a product cheaper, and theoretically, this can make a counterfeit version less tempting.

45|

#Takethebadgeoff?

Minimalist dresser, fashion icon, NYC socialite and eventual wife of JFK Jr, Caroline Bessette-Kennedy was a definite influence for a big part of the nineties. The decade's effortless cool was reflected in her taste in brands: Prada, Dries van Noten, Yohji Yamamoto and other classic, non-showy, flashy brands (bet she would have tripped off Faconnable 😊). I vaguely recall reading that she would even take off the labels on her high-end sportswear she would wear to the gym. Classy.

This desire to let the clothes do the talking and not a garish label is typical Bessette-Kennedy. But what of our peacocks who's very being and psyche are intrinsically linked to showing off, to flaunt wealth as opposed to hiding it? Do any of our original lot take the badge off anywhere for any circumstances, so as not be seen wearing Stone Island due to its badged up hoolie connotations?

Jared Latimer: 'I'd rather leave the premises. Would you (take it off)?'

Me: 'Would I fuck!'

Jay Montessori: 'No as it's pretentious snobbery in my opinion. Yes, some divs wear Stone Island but you can spot them a mile off. It's not about what you wear so much as how you carry it off.'

Oliver Beer: 'I have done. I wore a Stone Island mac for a friend's dad's funeral and took the badge off. Apart from that I always wear it. A badge doesn't maketh a man (or woman).'

David Elders: 'Yeah sometimes. Have done in the past. Lovely heavy knit black full-length zip. Looked better without.'

When pressed further if he had taken it off due to embarrassment of its hooligan past and associations. Elders responds: 'Nah. Those who know, know. And the rest's opinions don't matter.'

Riaz Khan: 'Nope. There was a time when the Casuals took off the badge but that didn't last long. Peeps were taking them off to avoid detection from Old Bill and entering clubs in the noughties.'

Indeed, just before the beginning of the Millennium, many of our lads were forced to take the badge off when frequenting the local watering holes as it was assumed that these badge wearing Casuals would start smashing the place up. Ironic really when the small town had such a major Stone Island retailer positioned there (in the shop called Review), yet locals were not allowed to wear their new pieces. Jared recalls that around '96/'97, one doorman told him to take the goggles out of his CP hood and at the same time police were collecting Stone Island badges at scuffles down the match at Stoke. Sounds almost like the colonists with their trophies of Indian scalps; prizes for being one up over the footie Casuals themselves. Well done. Yawn.

Even earlier than that there were occasions when they weren't even allowed to wear trainers to bars or clubs so instead of having to trudge all the way home, many pulled their socks over their trainers in the ultimate disguise! Can you imagine nowadays having to camouflage their wild Yeezys or Balenciagas?!

The trend varies however when I asked the younger generation if they would take off the badge:

Aidan Tregay: 'Yeah, I would. I've seen a few people do this and in fact myself have worn it without the badge. I feel it's different and I like different.'

Matt Snell: 'Personally I would, only on a technical jacket or big statement piece. Because the badge isn't what you're buying it for.'

The Chaps Club: 'To be fair, I have taken the badge off a couple of times on my black jumper. Was for a more smarter event but mainly because Noel Gallagher said it was cool to do so.'

Does this perhaps reflect the younger ones' brand loyalty, that they are quick to take off the fabled badge whereas our original lot wouldn't. Stone Island may be ridiculed, but only they can ridicule its mentality. Indeed the 'Get the Badge In' phase has become a parody of a parody and is cringeworthy in the epic humour fails.

The proudful boasting of what are clearly counterfeit Stone Island garments makes my toes curl. Bought off some moody 'reseller' or from somewhere like Cheetham Hill, fake clobber is just so sadly prevalent and always has been. Jared recalls from the late nineties when they (Review) were selling Stone Island and caught wind of some blaggers in town trying to do the same.

'We rang Stone Island up and were like, "You haven't given an account to them?" and they were like, "No…" We were obviously telling them about it. But that was in the days when you had to cut the label out because it had the tracking code in. We used to get leaflets from Stone Island with every local area that had a counterfeit goods office. So, if we saw any shop the idea was that you rang that number and they would literally go to the shop straightaway. But that lasted for about six months, because there was so much counterfeit with those brands.'

Snides will never disappear, despite even the Old Bill trying to crack down on it. In December 2021, Operation's Magpie and

Cranium (very creative and apt operation names I thought), attempted to reign in Manchester's Cheetham Hill counterfeit heaven.

'As part of the crackdown over the last 10 days, tens of thousands of items including clothing, perfume, jewellery and accessories have been seized and an investigation alongside partners continues.'

Inspector William Jennings-Wharton, of Cheetham Neighbourhood team, said: 'This is all part of our continued work to tackle organised crime taking place in Cheetham Hill and I want to reassure the local community that we are listening to their concerns and this week's action is all part of our continued crackdown.

'Counterfeit goods and drug dealing will not be tolerated and all of these raids – which are a result of months of hard work – are a huge step in really driving a wedge in organised crime in the area.

'These desired items may look good and are cheap, but they are funding a wider picture that involves money laundering, organised crime and cheap labour. The profits from such businesses can be used to fund other serious crime, and often with that comes violence which can have a devastating ripple effect on communities and nearby legitimate businesses.'

This conspicuous consumption, this need to validate one's social status by wearing labels, yet ironically wearing fakes, is huge. Even when you go abroad, there are 'lucky luckys' selling knock offs to tourists who want to come back with a branded garment/bag/pair of sunglasses. And these substandard fakes are certainly getting better and are miles off from the 'Lactose', 'Dolce & Banana', 'Adidos,' 'Clone Island' and 'Superme' from the recent past.

46|

Covid-19 Sucks

The depersonalisation of the internet, the lack of (face to face) social interaction and engagement has only been exaggerated by the global pandemic of Covid-19. But the key questions are, how do we perceive and purchase brands in these post-pandemic days; do we still actively and conspicuously consume high-end brands? Is that why there's an increase in counterfeit goods? More importantly, how have our Casuals survived Covid?!

This book, as we know by now, is investigating the current state of terrace culture, whether it even exists at all anymore during these difficult Covid times and if the Casuals have adapted their lifestyle and consumer habits to survive and stand the test of time and huge social changes.

Covid-19 and its ensuing world lockdown has been unprecedented in modern times. At first it appeared that it was nature's way of getting our constant 24/7 world to just... stop. To breathe. Polluted skies cleared, murky rivers became inhabited again, the unrelenting societal noise of being on the go constantly was finally hushed.

'Running everywhere in such a speed

'Til they find there's no need...'

The Beatles weren't wrong. We got back to basics. We stopped fucking about in our oh-so-important commuting to and from work. We chilled in the garden. We were still connected by technology

(God forbid we couldn't have another pointless meeting about a meeting on Teams).

Davari, Iyer, Guzman and Veloutsou believe that even in times of recession, or global financial uncertainty due to huge influential factors like Covid, 'consumers need to escape and impulsiveness are positively associated with luxury brand purchase intentions.' They added: 'consumers are selective splurgers. Driven by a need to escape and feel better about themselves, consumers indulge in luxuries during a recession as a coping mechanism.'

You would naturally assume however that luxury brands would be the first thing to cut down on when the population is tightening its belts, relying on furlough and only spunking money on the actual outings we were allowed to go on; B & M and Rishi's Eat out to Help Out (I mean, you couldn't make that shit up). But it appears that us humans are not that complex. Insecure and needing our egos to be stroked, our high-end brand obsessions 'are driven by several factors that may be internal such as symbolic value, experimental value, vanity, self, and conspicuous consumption, need for status and social desirability.' This insight coming from Devari et al.

Us delicate little flowers need these labels to reflect a sense of self, even if we are locked down and have nowhere to even peacock our new clothes. It is, and always has been in my opinion, a sense of escapism, to break free from the humdrum banality of our lives, and even more so in times of a recession or global pandemic. And even though we might feel guilty indulging on non-essential, non-practical products, we power through. We splurge. We move again. We see the fog descending, clouding all judgements on whether its rational to buy an 800 quid Plurimus jacket. Well logically, if you can even get your hands on one anyway due to its rarity, then it makes sense that you buy it, right? Zero self-control for luxury purchase intentions. Fuck it!

47|
Apocalypse (N)ow!

This mentality is shared with consumers across the globe; the world has never been so paranoid, anxious and fearful that we were all going to die, not since the brink of the Cold War. So 'fuck it!' resonated and echoed throughout cities across the globe whilst continuing online shopping, not knowing whether we would survive this forthcoming apocalypse as predicted by the media foaming at the mouth with hysterical daily death statistics.

Steve Lumb, Terrace Cult:

'I think people are scared of the money situation, got families and that. You know, you could go out and spend £500 on a jumper cos you knew you had a roofing job coming off the week after. So, you'd bung a little bit on it and get some money back. Now, they don't know where their next bread and butters coming from, you gotta be careful.'

The hatches were battened down. Gloves and masks adorned if you had to make an essential shop. The wiping down and sanitising of everything. This was like some wank B-Movie with the only saving grace that we did have a digital window into the world, a means to stay connected. But did we still consume in this atmosphere of heightened tension?

Our fearless Casuals seem totally unaffected psychologically, trapped only in the physical constraints that lockdown brought on them and their shopping habits. But that's 'cos they wear Stone Island, yeah?! Not bovvered about no pandemic ☺.

Oliver Beer told me: 'I pretty much stayed the same. Hours trolling through eBay etc. to try and find stuff I've not had before. I kept in touch mostly via Facebook, apart from when they kept banning me.'

Riaz Kahn similarly: 'I sold loads of stuff as I realised I had too much that I didn't even wear! Trainers, trackies, jumpers and jackets.'

Matt Williams: 'I got way more active online with people and really got my collection going in lockdown, defo something new every week to have something to look forward to. Addicted to it now haha.'

What did I tell you about our rambunctious and determined Casuals – they improvise, adapt, overcome!! Lockdown Schmockdown! Being online became a lifeline, what else was there to do apart from binge Netflix box sets or get up to do that Joe Wicks 9am workout (did not happen in my household or make that ridiculous banana bread – was that even real?!). Our entrepreneurial lads utilised this time by swapping stories, memories and clobber, and even creating their own football fan pages.

Kyle Dixon from Archivio Clothing tells me: 'The page took off during lockdown when no one had anything better to do then spend furlough money on items they more than likely would not have otherwise. Also, with the closure of pubs and football, more time was spent on Instagram shopping which allowed for my business to grow.'

Likewise with Casual Client Clothing, Matt Snell agrees: 'During Covid, many sellers saw a boom in sales due to people having more disposable income because they couldn't spend it going out. New sellers popped up daily (average guys trying to make a bit of money during the pandemic), then disappeared quicker than they started once everything opened again.'

Everyone had to get their hustle on through lockdown, which meant an unsurprising increase in shysters.

Matt adds: 'Far too many people out to make a quick buck from the hype around the clothing at the minute. I have managed to get people their money back from scamming resellers in the past, so obviously the page and the other community pages I know and speak to regularly and the 400,000 people have enough clout to do it. If I say someone is a scammer a lot of people will see it and hopefully put them out of business.'

There are always opportunists trying to weasel their way into the action, to jump on the bandwagon and dilute, not just the brand with a shed load of snides, but a weakening of the chink in the armor of the online Casual communities.

These unbreakable online communities are crucial to the Casuals' conspicuous consumption of brands; they have an important emotional undertone, as they are a means of keeping in touch with actual people, and with those that share these values, affiliations and brand loyalty.

TV presenter and passionate clobber enthusiast John Fendley – 'Fenners' – has met fellow clothes lovers/resellers/swappers through online communities.

Fenners: 'There's a lot of lads on Instagram, and I follow all of them, I put notifications on, they can post it on their stories. You have a chat. I mean, I've met so many people through doing this that, you know, it's great. And I haven't met a lot of them in person, but a lot of them have befriended and come down the show, you know, really great-likeminded as well. I think for a lot of people it's a good outlet. For people's mental health as well, I think it's really good. It's a massive subculture.'

Lifejacket is an online page Fenners has set up to trade vintage pieces but has ultimately become a digital lifeline to some due to the underlying communal aspect of the 'jacket fraternity' writes Paninaro Magazine:

'I want to use Lifejacket to help (with male mental health issues). I'd like to organise events like, 'An Evening with...' people I love and admire such as Paul Heaton, Stephen Graham, and we'd talk about jackets, clothes, trainers, music and football, as well as men's mental health. If you have guys like them putting the spotlight on mental health to three hundred lads in their nice coats, they might relate.'

Fenners and I discussed further the importance of opening up to fellow minded counterparts online, the escapism it can bring to an overworked mind, the bonding over clobber consumption; these communities have most certainly been a 'lifejacket' for those trying to stay afloat in a world where human contact had in certain cases ceased.

Fenners: 'I found myself just trying to get away from stuff by chatting to people online. Like, chatting to my mate out in Italy, or chatting to whoever it was, you know, talking about stuff, or "Have you ever had one of these?" I spent a lot of time doing that. And that's what kind of led me to start Lifejacket with a view to growing that into something a lot bigger than it is at the moment and something very different to what it is now.

'I was certainly doing it before Covid, but during Covid as well, I find it very therapeutic. Something (clobber wise) comes in, and it needs something, you have a look at it, and you wash it, and you steam it, and then you might need to fix the zip, or something. And what I do as well is I sell stuff for other people, who maybe haven't got a massive following etc.

'So, I've got a mate who, you know, he says he struggles to sell some stuff, but he's got an incredible amount of stuff. So, what I'll do is I'll take a box of stuff off him, he'll send it, or I'll go and collect it. And he's got a ridiculous collection of CP, Stone Island, Boneville, Armani, everything. Just a great store. So, then I'll get it, and then I'll photograph it, and then I'll list it on Lifejacket and then I'll send him the money. And that's it.

'And I don't do it to make money, you know? It makes me feel good that I can help him out. And I also get to see all his amazing things, all these amazing clothes coming through. And occasionally, I'll go, "What do you want for that, mate?" And he'll go, "I tell you what, I want £150 for it, but you can have it for £90." And it's good, we've got a nice little working relationship. And it's not a commercial thing, it's just a nice – and I feel good about doing it, because I'm helping him out.

'And that's, to answer your question, that's something that wouldn't have happened if the pandemic hadn't started, maybe, or I hadn't been active on social media.'

Throughout Covid there have been such pockets of ingenuity and creativity, to help and reach out to our fellow men, not games of one-upmanship, but examples of all-upmanship. And if men are typically more reluctant to talk to loved ones when struggling internally, then what better way than to indirectly form relationships through the mutual connection of clobber and this shared brand identity. If anyone is going to understand you, surely it's someone who you have been conversing with over the love of some vintage Marina?

48|

How Brands Survived Covid; Survival of the Slickest

We hustled, ducked and dived and tried our best to survive physically and psychologically during Covid times. Throughout the pandemic, high-end brands were also concerned about the fragility of the brand, that without any retail, any fashion shows, travel and events, their profits would also decline along with brand integrity and equity.

Kearney's Luxury Study 2021-22 investigated this: 'consumers changed their purchasing behaviours, stores closed under lockdown regulations, and international travel was dramatically curtailed.

'Yet the luxury goods market has demonstrated its resilience in the face of widespread pandemic-related disruption, with many leading brands seeing their sales figures rebounding relatively rapidly to pre-pandemic levels, and in some cases, even surpassing them.'

So, the big boys bounced back.

The Kearney explains:

'Trust played a crucial role throughout the pandemic. According to our study, most consumers consider the large, renowned luxury brands to be more trustworthy. Trust in local, niche brands is highest among older generations in China followed by Millennials in the United States and Germany. Large, renowned luxury brands can also expect continued sales growth.'

Brands know how to get into our heads, to pull at our heartstrings, to generate the holy grail of brand loyalty, and they surely rolled up their sleeves in preparation for this new consumer landscape.

Rolling Stone Magazine's Brandon Ginsberg writes:

'Life-altering events – much like the one we're currently experiencing – will always produce significant changes. One of the pandemic's biggest impacts so far has been its influence on consumer buying behaviours. Many consumers have switched their preferences and now favour online shopping, with 53 percent of people reporting that their purchasing habits have permanently changed as a result of the pandemic.

'The challenge for retailers and luxury brands is ensuring that their customers experience the same level of service online as they've come to expect from brick-and-mortar stores. Part of that means finding the right balance between brand experience and ease of shopping.

'We can all agree that the Covid-19 pandemic has been life-changing, but that doesn't mean that its impacts have all been terrible. The brands that refocused their efforts on e-commerce were able to not only survive in these unprecedented times but also stand at the forefront of transformation in the fashion industry. Thanks to e-commerce, the retail industry can come out on the other side of this pandemic, maybe brighter than ever.'

Thus, the pandemic gave both luxury brands and more independent labels time to reflect and reorganise. Original Casuals explained: 'It let us focus more on our own internal processes and organisation, make improvements in how we work.'

At Plurimus HQ in Bologna, Fabio Cavina tells me: 'I was a bit worried but, in the end, Covid did not really affect my project, I was doing everything online before anyway, so I could not really see any big difference. I was lucky, I guess! I would say that things got much more affected by Brexit to be honest, as it has caused price increases and a lot of bureaucracy with exporting goods.'

This stagnant combination of both Covid and Brexit has undoubtedly left a stale environment, a no-man's land where subcultures are unsure of where next to turn. Have they thrived under the seismic global changes through more online activity, or has it left many feeling like we have hit a cultural brick wall?

49|

Get the (Post) Covid Look; Hooligan Rennaissance Classics

The fashion tribe of the Casuals is resourceful if nothing else, constructively sorting shit out, or honing their branding skills in some cases:

'In lockdown is where I really pushed the brand. I learnt photoshop and how to design on it. So, every day I'd wake up and spend all day and night designing, then as the months got longer, I applied for university to study fashion for which I passed the application.' Aidan Tregay who set up Project North during the Covid pandemic.

Steve Lumb also established Terrace Cult in lockdown to which he says:

'Who'd start a clothing brand in a Covid pandemic where they've banned football?' Who? Terrace Cult that's who. Bosh.

'We set up just before Covid. It was a good vibe, everyone sticking together and trying to keep the morale up. It was a scary time as nobody was going out or going to the football, so they weren't buying at first. But, as the end of Covid started to come nearer, people started to use the money they'd saved to buy new clobber and our sales started to improve a lot.'

Neil Primett agrees and has seen the recovering, Covid-fucked consumer really kick back into life, both online and surprisingly on the high street, believing that people want this physical experience once more after being cooped up so long. To have a mooch, a bite to eat, to make a day of it:

'Post Covid my own two stores have bounced back to trade 20% higher. If the destination satisfies the consumer, then he can spend all his clothing money with you, his missus can pop to her neighbouring favourite shops, or a group of lads get to bars and restaurants after a shop.'

It will take a long time for normal service to be resumed. Yes, high-end brands have had the time and resources to adapt accordingly to the market and come out stronger the other side, but the high street and independent brands haven't had the luxury. Shopping, and other perceived trivial pursuits, such as sport and leisure, have took the biggest kick in the bollox, the sacrificial lambs in what is deemed essential spends in our most frugal and paranoid of times. They were the first things to be closed and last to be opened (and arguably rightly so), but now we need sport and shopping and spending back, and they need us just as bad.

The mutual impact of sports without spectators, and spectators without sports, is only just being researched. Grix, Brannagan, Grimes and Neville are investigating the impact of Covid-19 on sport, the knock-on effect from the loss of the feelgood factor of the large groups of spectators, who typically bring passion, energy and noise to stadia, when they are no longer there.

We know better than anyone this crackling atmosphere that can be experienced at matches; that when the audience is flat this can influence the game itself. It is this 'collective effervescence'. It is the 'rush of energy stimulated by assembled social groups', as highlighted by Durkheim in his research, that heightens the feelings of belongings at football matches. Replace the stadiums for the pubs leading up to the match and you will have the fizz of anticipation, anxiety and excitement brimming over. With no spectators, that fizz is flat as fuck with both parties missing from this Covid-induced ceasefire. The hustle and the bustle, the new clobber, the pride in what you are wearing, your mates, your club, your town, gives football this magnificent and unmistakeable 'feelgood factor', and with weekly games, the cycle of footie life continues. As Grix et al investigate further:

'It is this 'collective effervescence' of the sporting event that is understood as working a communal remedy, refreshing and re-setting individuals psychologically, allowing them to face their everyday lives.'

Without this routine however, without this stage on which to strut, did this have an effect on the football Casuals and their clobber? With football matches redundant through lockdown, what was the point of peacocking if there was no audience? Did they still parade their new garms without a theatre of dreams in which to show off?

The Italians use the phrase 'sprezzatura' to describe an effortless style, to be able to wear something over anyone with a nonchalant coolness that cannot be faked or replicated. And to show off their style, they would take a stylish sartorial walk in the ultimate game of one upmanship.

Neil Summers told me more: 'It's like in Italy, you've got the Passeggiata. In Italy it's hard to get a house, and it's not a lot of money there, but they have this thing called the Passeggiata, and it's like this road we're on now, in the evening, everyone puts on their best gear and goes for a walk. It's a fucking pose.'

I fully believe that matchdays are the UK's Passeggiata, the Casuals' opportunity to display their shiny new purchases and bask in the jealous glow from their peers. But through Covid, and through the absolute dilution of terrace culture and the Casual subculture scene, where do they strut next?! This is the $64,000 dollar question!! Why still wear Casual brands, or labels associated with Casual style and football culture, if it no longer exists and nowhere to wear it?!

But it must exist. This confined yet highly anticipated communal letting off steam, has arguably exploded and gone all over the show. It appears to me that being caged up like tigers has created a surge in testosterone fuelled footy violence. Once the matches started again, there has been much in the media about football hooliganism. A cultural renaissance or just a familiar media-fuelled principled panic. Middle-of-the-road, beige programme *Good Morning Britain* covered pitch invasions and football violence (scuffles) at the end of May 2022 and accused social media of driving this. The faux outrage made me almost choke on my brew. Some middle-class benign reporter continuing the moral high ground by citing football fans as rowdy and boisterous and damaging our bid for hosting the World Cup. Who says we even want to host the World Cup? It is past being against modern football, more about being against corrupt football officials siphoning off loads off brass but having the audacity to blame football hooligans and violence as the root of all global football problems.

'But we're never gonna survive, unless

We get a little crazy.' Seal (1991).

We have finally been let out of our padded lockdown cells, so we were always going to go a bit mental surely. Has this increased the violence or just the attention to any little bit of violence? Has football hooliganism come full circle?

Casual Ultra: 'I think Covid had a strong impact on the football scene overall. After almost two years without entering the stadium, people became more fanatic in supporting their club in and outside the stadium. Because of this, football violence and hooliganism gained a boost as well.'

Oliver Beer: 'It's a tough 'un. People now, after Covid, people were scared to go out. A lot of people are shitting themselves about catching a cold!

'It's like, so you go to the match and there's numbers of people… no, I can't see it kicking off again. I can see little pockets of fighting and stuff like that, but I can't honestly see that we'll ever have a time like the eighties.'

David Elders: 'Possibly among the young (there's a resurgence in hooliganism), but I think it's less to do with Covid and more to do with the fact that since the heyday of the Casual scene there hasn't been a new youth culture come along to replace it and do its own thing. You had razor gangs in the '30s and 40s, Rockers in the '50s, Mods in the '60s, Skins and Punks in the '70s, Casuals in the '80s and '90s but since then there's been a vacuum. I think the young lot are looking nostalgically at the old heads and trying to fill that vacuum they once occupied. Society has changed since those days though, sentencing and policing certainly has, few stretches for bouncing around in the middle of a road with no actual row will soon put an end to that.'

Riaz Kahn believes it's a combination of underlying factors that is bringing it back to the forefront:

'Online shopping is big at the moment due to lockdowns and with the access of Netflix and other channels, films regarding, football culture are readily available. Covid has affected cultures but due to lockdown people have more time on their hands and this means they access more stuff on the Net. Also being couped up can be frustrating, so when the matches are back open to the public you will see the odd skirmishes here and there but that will never compare to how it was in the golden age of the Casual culture. The media will pick up on this and as usual will exaggerate the violence.'

50|

Stop Press; the Media's Role in Vilifying the Casuals

Slow News Day, Yeah??

Whilst researching this book, throughout 2021/22, I started to record reports of football violence, not only from the mainstream media or 'heavyweight' politicos such Garraway and Shepherd – lol – but also from fan sites on social media. Stoke City appears to have been at the forefront of all this action with trouble at Huddersfield and Birmingham games in early 2022. Shocker.

When discussing the Huddersfield v Stoke match, wizened Stoke lads mused about the trouble there, as there is apparently a friendship/allegiance between the two.

Football Awaydays (Twitter):

Anonymous: 'What's happened to the love in?'

Peter Mcloughlin: 'Thought the young 'uns were all mates?'

The same young 'uns attempts at some forms of hooliganism were totally dismissed by elders on similar fan pages:

'These youngsters that dress the Casual way and pretend to be football hooligans nowadays are so funny. They missed the boat by about 20 years... bless 'em. Stoke City were a very formidable firm in the '80s. The Naughty Forty had a couple of memorable encounters with towns (in this instance), the Dirty Thirty, and it resulted in quite a rivalry building up over the years. But these young 'uns now. Turn it in boys. It's done.'

A Dadual puts these Casual idolisers/wannabes firmly in their place. The roasting continued with more joining in on Nouveaux bashing:

'I thought the same thing. All you need now is a baseball cap and a Stone Island jumper and you're part of the firm. Every club has them, usually standing in huddles of 5 or more haha.'

'That's what caused it. One 14-year-old told another his Stone Island was fake lol.'

A Dadual joke if ever we heard. But while they all chuntered online then ultimately leaving the chat, the tabloids started screaming headlines like:

'Fan violence mars Stoke's fightback!' and 'Four arrests after trouble flares as Stoke City take on Birmingham!'

Whit whoo. But as an anonymous reader quite rightly tells the shithanger local North Staffs rag, *The Sentinel*:

'There's been trouble at football for nearly 200 years. Football is tribal. Village versus village when it first started, and 90% of the time the ball would be forgotten about during the game and it would be one big brawl. It's come a long way since the days of the 70s, 80s and 90s, but there will always be that tribal element involved and there will always be minor skirmishes.' Was this Steve Redhead in disguise?! If I could have 'liked' his comment a million times, I would have. Spot on!

Social media may not be the most real of realms with fake insta-worthy lifestyles and sarcastic troll comments punched from the safety of a laptop rather than a toe-to-toe fight. And yeah, the keyboard warriors maybe full of shit, but then, isn't the mainstream media?

Sensationalist, salacious, frenzied reporting of football hooliganism is nothing new. There has regularly been a vitriolic bias towards the young, white working-class male, with many frothing journalists misunderstanding the whole concept of hooliganism.

'Conservative politics, with its emphasis on possession – car, house, wife etc. – is directly linked to male violence. To be a "real" man, the male must have affluence and therefore power. Witness the rise of the yuppie or the self-made millionaire held aloft as an ideal image: well-dressed, married, refined accent. If a man does not have these qualities, he must turn to that "essential" characteristic: strength. Strength combined with deprivation means violence. This becomes the poor man's only viable means of protecting his maleness. It is at football grounds that this problem may be seen, bound up in clannishness, uniforms, notions of territories, class and racial divides. The football then becomes a breeding ground for frustrated maleness,' writes Michallat.

This frustration which spilled out onto the terraces was picked up by the media and turned into a commercial advantage, exploiting their fellow countrymen's misery for profitable gain in newspaper sales. The hooligans' misfortune was also their Achilles heel; an easy target to blame, which they wickedly did so, most infamously at the tragic events at Hillsborough.

'The Hillsborough Disaster occurred in an historical media framework that already labelled Liverpool as rebellious and anarchistic. The 1980's were the heady days of the Militant dominated council in the city. Not only the Thatcher government but also the Labour party under Neil Kinnock waged war on the leaders of the City Council (Derek Hatton and co). In reality, they were waging war on the people of Liverpool – they became the real victims as they suffered the direct consequences of harsh measures imposed but also as they gained an undeserved negative reputation not only nationwide but internationally as well. It was this context which enabled the media to act so appallingly in relation to the Hillsborough Disaster.' This expert analysis comes from Contrast.org.

The immediate reaction of the press following Hillsborough was to blame the fans; *The Sun* (from hence forth known as The S*n) infamous headline:

'*The Truth; some fans picked pockets of victims; some fans urinated on the brave cops; some fans beat up PC giving kiss of life.*'

Steen believes, 'it would be wrong to suggest that the English press did not sensationalize hooliganism at all. "Shock! Horror!" headlines sell papers, and there can certainly be no defence for Kelvin Mackenzie's decision to emblazon "The Truth" across the front page of *The Sun* with such callous abandon.'

The Scousers were at the bottom of the hooligan hierarchy from the media's perspective, helped by manipulative whispers from football officials, politicians and the police.

'Hughson and Spaaij contend that anti-Liverpool sentiment widespread in the establishment, and the media, had driven a media mob kicking of the city. Such press hostility is now being conveniently forgotten, as the truth finally emerges,' writes Dr Raj Persaud in the Huff Post.

Now I'm not saying that all media are guilty of this. In former football journalist, Rob Steen's 2016 study, he also felt:

'Defensiveness, not unnaturally, arises when reading criticism that the media were not only guilty of sensationalizing hooliganism in the eighties, but actively encouraging violence by reporting it. To allow such views to pass unchallenged would be an abrogation of responsibility. Just as it is wrong to even hint that all football fans of the era were hooligans, it is equally wrong to cast all football reporters as muckrakers.'

But some did shit-stir and have done a pretty good job in creating and maintaining an exaggerated and cartoonish image of football hooligans. No, hoolies and Casuals did not always display angelic behaviour to say the least, but to blamed for some of the atrocities that were due to the authorities is an absolute piss take. The Hillsborough/Heysel hangover continues to do this day with The S*n reporting of lots of Scousers climbing over or rushing the gates for the Champions League final between Liverpool and Real Madrid in May 2022. The whole organisation of the match appeared to be an absolute shambles with police pepper-spraying fans indiscriminately. UEFA also blamed Liverpool fans for having fake or no tickets causing a pulsating and claustrophobic bottle neck.

Is this a sign of the times? Is this the full circle of football Casual culture returning full scale with the same prejudiced media and police lurking in the shadows?

51|

Ultras; the International Scene & Football Fandom

When Neil Summers and I discussed whether we thought violence was having a comeback, it brought a very valid political perspective into the equation:

Me: 'I don't know whether it's me, but after Covid, does there seems to be loads more rows and stuff at football now or is the media just really focussing on it again?'

Neil: 'That's what I think there should be more of. That's what kind of annoyed me about football hooliganism, I totally understood where it came from in the '70s and '80s. People are really angry because of political situations, but it's like anything. It's like, don't kick the fuck out of each other. Go to Downing Street and kick the fuck out of them. Do you know what I mean?

'It's like television and religion, it's that opium, the masses thing where it's like, "Just give them something to do – let's get pissed and batter each other." I'm not a conspiracy theorist, but it's like in Liverpool and Manchester. In the '80s they definitely turned a blind eye to heroin going into those places, because there were riots, the early '80s was loads of riots. You didn't get any riots after all the heroin came in, because everyone was just like, "I haven't got time for a riot. I've got to go and buy some drugs, or I'm going to be really ill." It's that thing isn't it. "Shut up dickheads, just go and watch football, or go and watch *Coronation Street*."'

Me: 'It's divide and conquer, isn't it?'

Neil: 'Exactly. That's what I love about places like France, Spain and Italy, they're a bit more, they get off their arse a bit and go, "We're not having this."'

Not only politically, but at the football, it seems our European counterparts are game as fuck, both on and off the pitch.

Riaz Kahn: 'I attended a Europa match recently where Leicester City played Legia Warsaw. The Polish lads brought a firm and they wanted it. They walked through the city centre chanting, one hundred strong but not well dressed. Once in the ground, the Polish fans let off flares (which was amazing to watch and a signal for them to get ready) and tried to get at the Leicester fans in the stadium but the police formed a line. The Poles then started attacking the police! The Eastern Europeans are still at it! Imagine if we attacked the police in Poland!!'

Before we go into the type of clobber and other tribalistic rituals appropriated by the Ultras, we must first understand a bit more about this faction of football fandom who are typified by their violent tendencies, chanting, assumed political interests and love of pyros and 'snide' designer clobber. You know if you ever went on holiday abroad and the music at the hotel discotheque was about ten years behind ours, then the same has often (unfairly?) been thought about the Ultras' outdated style. But that is clothing, the Ultras are more renowned for their love of (often politicised) conflict.

Spectator violence aka football violence, was originally labelled the 'English disease' which was just another term aiming to further demonise football hooligans, grouping them all together under the collective umbrella term of football hooliganism. In Spaaij's study, he aims to analyse football hooliganism as a 'transnational phenomenon' and he looks at the differences within this subculture, concluding that they cannot all be lazily dumped then lumped under one pigeonholed label.

Spaaij theorised even back in 2007 that:

'Despite the ongoing globalization of football culture and societies at large, there remain important cross-national and cross-local variations in the level and forms of football hooliganism. These dissimilarities thwart efforts to conceptualize and explain football hooliganism as a homogeneous phenomenon.'

There are many layers and gradients of fans, the pecking order often defined by levels of violence, loyalty and self-expression.

'The violence is predominantly done by the first line of good guys. Not only are these the most skilled fighters, but they also embody a specific masculinity exhibited in their clothing, comportment and demeanour,' Doidge and Lieser discovered in their research.

This proclivity to violence is what the Ultras are notorious for, but there is more to this than just neanderthal chest pummelling and giving it the big 'un at matches. The Ultras originated in Italy and mutated across Europe, then further afield such as the USA and Indonesia. They are loud, proud, choreographed, militia-esque and carnivalesque.

'The Ultras have become the most spectacular form of football fandom in the early twenty-first century. Thanks to global media, social media and increased travel, engage and interact with a range of other fans from across the globe...Not only does this demonstrate the prevalence of the ultras style of fandom across the globe, but it also shows how football becomes an important cultural arena to see the intersections of globalism and localism,' continue Doidge and Liesre.

Reading academic papers on the (limited) research of the Ultras, it becomes apparent that there is more depth to them than their image portrays; that although violence, rivalry, politics and powerful displays of fandom unify and describe the Ultras' form of fandom, what really binds and bonds them is their staunch, unfaltering commitment and support of their club.

Understanding this concept well myself. 'Vis Unita Fortior' is Stoke City's motto, which translates as 'United Strength is Stronger'. This encapsulates the whole Ultra and Hoolie/Casual psyche. The united strength is displayed by the Ultras through their consumption, not just of brands, but of football hooligan culture in its entirety, including banners, songs and violence. This 'communal effervescence', this energy generated that you can physically feel reverberating throughout the stadium, is not just directed at the rival clubs, but against football politics altogether.

52|

Against Modern Football Part 2; All Cops Are Bastards (Acab!)

The question of whether terrace and football Casual culture is dead, dying or weakened, is what underpins this entire book and is what inspired to me ask the original Casuals, the Nouveaux, the Ultras, the brand owners, the social commentators, the artists and the authors about the status quo of this subculture today, to ascertain its fragility or strength through the followers' keen and continued collective and conspicuous consumption of typical Casual brands.

Without exception there is a universal agreement that the golden era of the Casual age will never be recreated. Whether or not it can be reimagined for the Millennials and the Gen-Zs in this post-pandemic, pre-apocalyptic, totes fucked up world, remains to be seen. The gluttonous commercialisation of modern football is one of the main factors in the decline of this subculture, and the Ultras are just as set against this cannibalisation of the beautiful game, with their protests often aimed at club owners and the government at both local and national level.

'Various football supporter actors have been expressing their discontent with the intense commodification of football ever since the process began roughly two decades ago.

'Against Modern Football is the common denominator of a worldwide, heterogeneous social movement comprised of various actors and the methods of conflict: simple, symbolic actions like slogans written on flags, banners or walls; boycotts, petitions, demonstrations. The movement is primarily focused on the fight against the rigid commercialization of football and against turning supporters into consumers of football merchandise,' write Perasović and Mustapić.

The choice to consume or not is a form of the Ultras rebellion; refusing to line the already heavy pockets of the greedy club owners, the evil diablos who have changed our grassroots game into just another corporation, with shareholders, stakeholders and piss-takers galore. This is something the Casuals arguably do, but with less organised political fight, and more general disdain of the Shirter brigade. The fact that, as Didge and Lieser theorise, Ultras use consumption as a form of resistance to global corporate football is evidence of how any form of consumption, conspicuous, collective or ceased, can be symbolic of a subculture and how they are expressing their identity and values.

The efficiency and political dissent are what differentiates the Ultras from the hooligans and Casuals who debatably are more easily misled on match day (bungle and beers) and have a general political malaise. This political unrest, combined with a rage against the machine, the authorities that are hellbent on taking out the bleeding heart of local communities, unites all Ultras. While studying old-school Ultras Torcida, from Croatian team Hadjuk Split (incidentally, I watched Stoke beat them at the Brit in the third qualifying round, first leg in the UEFA cup back in the golden Pulis era of 2011/12. We beat them again away in the second round. We have not been in the UEFA cup since. Shocking I know). Perasović and Mustapić found that Torcida were more than proactive in voicing their opinion and vocalising their fight: 'against the football establishment, surveillance, control and commercialization. There is also a strong wish for Hajduk, as a public company, to remain a "people's club" without a private majority owner...

'We have noted that Torcida uses numerous flags and banners with the slogan "Against Modern Football" written on them, one-off messages in stadiums (also connected to the movement or expressing solidarity with other actors in the Ultras movement), graffiti on walls, messages on t-shirts and stickers, etc. Slogans and motifs inspired by AMF can also be found on the internet, ranging from individual activities (icons, symbols, photos, nicknames or other representations) to group internet activities. All the Torcida members interviewed believe that they, as an Ultras group, are a large supporters' movement that shares a common set of ideals and fights for a common goal.'

When I set out to write this book, specifically this section, I had assumed that the Ultras were much more political, with Far-Right inclinations. They are indeed political in terms of their proactive protesting against authoritarian establishments, not necessarily due to socio-political beliefs, but more steadfast loyalty to their club, their town, their territory. Gutu discovered that:

'Today, we notice the Ultras becoming ideologically moderate, some of them getting involved in democratic causes of civil society.'

Doidge and Lieser add:

'Ultras have become synonymous with violence, particularly as they became influenced by British hooliganism. The antisocial elements of Ultras culture have provoked the ire of those in authority – clubs, football federations and police. Although many ultra groups consider themselves to be ideologically apolitical, they frequently engage in football politics. This means that groups will protest and campaign against laws and regulations that are affecting their enjoyment of the game.'

Whereas the British scene is typically working-class, many Ultra groups in various European countries are middle class. The class structure of the Ultras is complex, particularly if coinciding with any aggressive socio-economic issues from serious political episodes such as war and far-right/far-left uprisings. In the ethnographic study of Holland's Sparta Youth Crew, Spaaij researched the development of the Dutch Ultra subculture:

'The emergence of football hooliganism in the Netherlands, in the early 1970s, should be within the context of post-war social changes. Youth began to emerge as a distinct social category with their own cultural practices and styles and were increasingly inspired by British youth subculture.'

Spaaij also discovers that while most British youth subculture has an undeniable working-class background, there was a noticeable class diversity amongst the Dutch Ultras. Rotterdam's 'Sparta Youth Crew' differentiate themselves from Feyenoord hooligans.

Whereas Feyenoord are portrayed as rough, hard-core criminals, the Sparta hooligans view themselves as a more sophisticated, fashionable fighting crew. One Sparta Youth Crew (SYC) member when interviewed in the study, explained:

'Feyenoord hooligans have very different backgrounds. Many of them have no education, both parents on drugs, brought up in a culture of violence. Our group is completely different. We come from stable families, quite well-off, have certain values in life, an education. They will still be doing their business when they're 35. I certainly won't.'

Roughing it with Daddy's money lads? Temporary Ultras?! It's meant to be a lifestyle not a phase! This kind of blasé, pick and choose mentality really boils my piss. Apparently, and worryingly, this is not uncommon, and that more (bored) rich kids are jumping on the bandwagon.

Wishing to remain anonymous, 'My friend in Norway' has a colourful, transnational Ultra background and reinforces this notion by discussing the increase in Norwegian posh kids boy-crushing on the subculture; upper middle-class boys swanning around pretending they're lads because they've got Stone Island on just like their 'heroes'.

'Here in Norway, it's the same as the UK. Stone Island was the main Casual brand, but it has become a rich boys' brand. Fana boys (kids from a rich part of Bergen) are wearing it to show how much money they have. The problem now is people don't appreciate the brand. The schooligans wear it to look tough and then the celebrities like Drake and Ed Shearon have no clue as to its origins. The fact the Scousers robbed the shops in Italy in the 90s to bring it back to the UK is lost on them.

'It's weird here. The closest rivals are usually two to three hours drive or a plane ride away. It does happen though. Only last night between Brann Bergen and Start there was an organised fight outside a pub in the city. None have a real idea of what true football fighting is about.'

There does exist commonalities between the harder factions of this subculture with the Ultras becoming synonymous with conflict as they became influenced by the British Hoolie. The level of violence however ironically differentiates them within their own group, how the violence is expressed differs greatly to create a hierarchy of machismo conflict. As exhibited by the handbags at dawn, skirmish-lite Fana/Fanny boys of Bergen, some wannabes will talk the talk but simply cannot walk the walk, even if they have Klarna'ed a new Stone Piece. In some studies, they use a certain term, 'carnivalesque' to differentiate these aspirants from the more 'street' of the Ultras. The more carnivalesque will join in with the shared rituals, the drinking, the chanting, the pyrotechnic displays, whereas the 'real' Ultras add violence, political agitation or local rivalry to enhance the pleasure and the adrenaline of the day. Colloquially speaking, these carnivalesque lot are the jokers of the pack, or as we like to call them, Shirters. Game for a laugh, have a couple of beers, wear some of the clobber, might go on a few away days or derbies (never make it on a cold Tuesday night up Stoke), but when the shit hits the fan, they are nowhere to be seen. Like a microcosm of society, the pecking order of violence and clobber is a telling display of the one-upmanship games intrinsically linked to football subcultures.

53|

Casual Ultras

The Casuals phenomenon has become romanticised, internationalised and politicised. Picked up on, adopted and gaining momentum across Europe, it was through conspicuous consumption of certain brands that would allow these new fanatical supporters to identify themselves. I interviewed several lads from varying Casual fandoms: Ultras/ex-Ultras/social media commentators, to get an insight of how and why they appropriate and consume the brands that they do.

First up was The Casual Ultra, a page on Instagram I have coincidentally followed the longest. An SC Cambuur supporter, the founder of the page explains the background to his Casual addiction:

'I got involved in the fanatic football scene when I moved from the main stand (where I had a season ticket together with my dad for a couple of years) to the stand where all the fanatics/Ultras/hooligans are standing together. I was 17 years old by then.

'During that time the Casual culture was already a big part of the football scene (almost everyone, from Ultras to hooligans are mostly dressed as Casuals) over here in The Netherlands. So, during that time I slowly started to wear Adidas shoes and jackets like Stone Island, CP Company, MA. Strum etc. Not only because of the move to the fanatic stand, but during that time I really started to follow the Casual, Ultras and hooligans scene. That was also the start of Casual Ultra, because I liked to keep people updated about the scene since I really liked it myself as well.'

Fellow Dutchman, rival supporter and friend of Stoke City, Robert Van der Weijden (Ajax), tells me:

'When I was around 15 years old, I began to learn about some lads of Ajax. I was always interested in hooliganism; that was also the time when I saw the Casual clothing all the lads were wearing. So, I started wearing it when I was 16/17. Stone island, Aquascutum, CP Company. But Aquascutum was not for sale in Holland so I got it from websites in England.'

The big hitters and obvious favourites of Stone Island and CP Company are undeniably popular everywhere, but interesting that they turn to English retailers. The Casual Ultra agrees:

'I had to order my clothing via the internet, because we only had one shop over here selling Casual clothing. So mainly all my clothing came from Terraces Menswear (and still do). Because they did/do some great discounts, it was really affordable for me during that time.'

An anonymous associate in Montenegro tells me:

'Right now, Casual culture is mixed here since there is only one well organised group called "Varvari" (Barbarians) fans of Buducnost. Mainly on the stand you see North Face, Adidas, Nike etc. Away days are a must and since there are only two rival groups in the country, we mainly fight with the police. Mostly we are just having fun and if the police get frustrated by it then we get into a fight with them.'

The similarities in 'this thing of ours' all starting with male influences does not end there. Much like Bowie and other music artists inspiring early Casuals, European Ultras started their British Casual brand obsession through films such as *Green Street* and *Football Factory*. In Dinu Gutu's case study on Dinamo Bucharest, he researches into the differing European styles of Ultras, where they drew their influences from, and how this sometimes created an inner disparity between the older Ultras and nouveaux Ultras:

'For the Romanian Ultras, the adoption of the British hooligan dress elements emerges with the release of films which romanticise the stadium culture: *Green Street Hooligans* and *Football Factory*, as well as the usage of internet forums. From this point of view, we can say that there exists a strong postmodern element in the emergence of this type of symbolic consumption in Romania: the globalisation of consumption, the manipulation of tastes through media...'

Who would have thought Frodo Baggins (Elijah Wood), was such a cross-continental, cultural poster boy for hyper consumerism?!! These football hoolie films had a reach across Europe: even our friend in Norway has seen the tentacle reach of *Green Street* et al:

'The Casuals here though tend to be around 20- 25 years old and influenced by the hooligan films.'

These films, along with the football, the fandom and social media fan pages, have had a huge impact on the dissemination of British football culture and is where many gain their Casual clobber references. Matt Snell of Casual Client Clothing explained:

'My followers are from all over the world. As the page has grown, the net gets wider. 50% of my following are from the UK. But they go as far as Indonesia, Malaysia, Russia, Italy, Argentina. The list is endless.'

Even Matt says that his entry into Casual culture was film-based:

'Shortly after I started to notice the (Casual) dress code, *Football Factory* came out in 2004. And that just intensified the interest.'

This film really has a load to answer for, a load of wannabe Danny Dyer cockneys bowling round in some Stone Island which automatically makes them a hooligan. Indeed, it can be said that the other countries' perspective of Casual culture is skewed by these caricatures and exaggerated versions as represented in the media and helped the resurgence of hooligan culture which had pretty much died out when these films came out.

In certain cases, the Casuals were revered to almost God like status, well they do say imitation is the sincerest form of flattery. Leo Gregory who plays the infamous Bovver in *Green Street* and is a Weekend Offender brand ambassador, is held up as the epitome of a football Casual to international Ultras.

Perasović and Marko Mustapić write:

'The Ultras scene and the phenomenon of football hooliganism are far more alike than was initially suspected. The revival of Casual style is strong in the contemporary Ultras scene, both in fashion and behaviour. In fact, the contemporary Ultras movement nurtures both traditions equally – both the loud and fanatical cheering and rituals in and around the stadium, and the English tradition of Casuals.

'The impact of mimicry on consumer choices and preferences has been discussed in prior literature. Studies have shown that individuals mimic aspects of others to create rapport and empathy in social interactions. Although previous research has focused on the pro-social emotions and behaviour of mimicking, what has not been properly addressed is how acts of mimicry can have negative effects on the groups they target. It is thus important to explore the extent to which imitated consumption-oriented behaviours affect subcultural communities.'

These Ultra-Nouveaux are wanting to be accepted by the original Casuals, 'to maintain a relation of homology and to be recognised as a part of the group by the other members, by maintaining the same symbolical consumption,' explains Gutu. By adopting brands favoured by Casuals, it signifies an affiliation with this tribe, or at least attempts to.

By mutual agreement from Ultras across the globe, their inspiration has always been British Casuals albeit with localistic differences or shall we say, 'Ultralisitic' tendencies.

Terrace Cult owner in Holland, Davy Pennings (PSV Eindhoven) explains:

'I notice in England the colourful range is more popular than in the Netherlands where people wear darker tones. But the style is copied from the English.'

Our mutual friend in Norway:

'There is a tendency to wear all black here. This also has a lot to do with how dark it is in some cities due to the Northern lights.'

Kevin Feliz (Man Utd) who is involved in Terrace Cult USA agrees:

'We Yanks love the UK Casual scene and have always admired what comes out of Europe.'

Kevin understands that the British Casual heritage is of one that cannot be forgotten nor recreated:

'My favourite brand besides Terrace Cult has to be Stone Island. The history behind it is something that most of us here in the US wished we could have experienced growing up.'

We know we're the dogs bollox, our legacy lives on. Clobber magazine blogger and creator, Paul Smith, totally gets our bragging rights in terms of our superiority in style and originality in Casual culture, quite rightly naming us 'custodians' of the subculture itself.

'(Ultras); granted they wear a lot of snide copies but they've fully taken on the whole Casual lifestyle, right down to their own little footy firms (big shout out to the Bandung Casuals!). It also makes me really proud to be British, I mean, any decent subculture worth its salt has come from the UK and I love the fact that others around the world are now wrapped around it.'

The Ultras' self-confessed love in for British hooligans/Casual style underlines their style foundation, but it does vary from region to region, often depending on political factors and geographical variables, all with deep undertones of an Against Modern football/military-esque vibe.

'The Polish always had more shaved heads, more hoodies, more tattoos; the Serbs always went to fights in tracksuits and with those fanny packs around their hips.'

Gutu interviews a Romanian Ultra who told him:

'I think that we are still dressing Romanian. We have from the Italians and from the others. But it is still our style. What I like about Casual? A lot of people in Europe, who are somewhere between Ultras and Casuals, are still closer to Casual. At a certain time, clothes give you that reputation.'

The Casual Ultra muses when I ask him about whether there is an obvious heterogenous choice of brands between the Casuals and the Ultras:

'Overall, I don't really think there is a big difference between the Casual brands over in the UK and the rest of Europe (besides people in the UK wear running shoes when going to matches haha). The brands that are popular in the UK, are also popular in the rest of Europe. I don't think there is a delay or something. The UK is still very much attached to the Casual scene, while in the rest of Europe the Ultras scene is the most important. In that Ultras scene, the Casual brands are not important at all, and supporters often wear clothes from their own supporters' group.

'There are some countries however where some of the Ultras are also linked to the Casual scene, such as the Netherlands, Belgium, Denmark and Italy. I can't really choose which culture appeals to me the most, the Ultras or Casual culture. I think it's a mix of both. I still find Casual clothing fascinating and the most beautiful clothing style, while the way of supporting your club, like in Eastern Europe appeals to me very much. The use of big tifos, pyro and massive singing is one of the most beautiful and best things there is!'

Robert Van der Weijden from his Dutch viewpoint:

'Here we wear more like the Casual style like in England. My favourites are still Stone Island, CP Company and Aquascutum. Also, because every year Stone Island and CP Company have different designs. But it's a shame Aquascutum is out of making new clothing. I know that in most of Europe and the South of Europe there are more groups calling themselves Ultras. They aren't as into Casual clothing as in England and Holland, Belgium etc. They wear more brands like Fred Perry, New Balance, North Face.'

The 'roadman' aesthetic continues across Europe with our friend in Montenegro noticing close regional trends:

'Around Belgrade there is mainly so called 'Dizel' style which comes with Nike AirMax, nylon trousers, some Nike, North Face and Napapijri T-shirts and jackets etc. Also, a bag around the waist is a must.'

These JD labels are so omnipresent, a sportswear style that is adopted by youths all over the continent, with many assuming they are representative of Casual clobber:

'Over here people think that they're Casual when they wear Lyle & Scott, The North Face or Ralph Lauren they're Casual, while in my opinion they're not. The North Face is linked to the Ultras scene, Lyle & Scott is just a cheap and popular brand among younger people over here, it got a bit of the same look as Fred Perry. And for Ralph Lauren, I think the brand's time has slowly come to an end and not really a link to the Casual scene anymore,' according to The Casual Ultra.

When asked where they purchase brands, whether there is a pan-European alternative to JD, the answer was mixed:

'We have a couple of multibrand stores but nice piece clothing we usually get from guys who have private stores in apartments because they bring clothing from abroad. They do a couple of months sniffing shops around Europe and they bring what they get back with pretty good discount prices,' as per the opinion of our source in Montenegro.

'More from online stores, but my trainers I buy in sports shops, like JD indeed,' adds Robert VDW.

'I only buy Casual brands like MA. Strum, Marshall Artist, Pretty Green, Weekend Offender, Henri Lloyd, CP Company, Stone Island. But do you count Ellesse, Fred Perry etc. under sports brands?' This questioned being asked by The Casual Ultra.

This is a good point. With the convenience of these brands, their ever-present availability and undefined role in Casual culture, some believe labels are more Casual than others, that brands such as Ellesse and Fred Perry are sports brands and un-Casual/more Ultralisitic/roadman attire, whereas as we know in the UK, these brands are having a huge eighties Casual revival.

Could it be an economic factor which sways European fans to choose certain brands over others? Our friend in Norway says:

'The real lads here now are going more to CP Company but again in the UK that's becoming like Stone Island. A lot of Lacoste and Fred perry here too. The price of clothing, and pretty much everything here, is crazy expensive. It is around £11 a pint of Guinness so you can imagine the cost of designer gear. It is also hard to get. If you buy from abroad, it gets held up and tax is added at 25% so there's no point ordering from UK. Adidas is huge here, most lads wearing the trainers. Jeans are usually Gstar or Levi's. Ralph Lauren is very popular with the football lads as it's easy to get and not too overpriced.'

The saturation of the Casual brands, the ease of consumption and lower than Stone Island/CP Company price of the products has most definitely helped create the Casual Ultra European look, but it begs the question of who defines these brands as Casual or not, who sets the clobber agenda within the subcultures of the football fandom of each country. Every region has their look, whether they be the purists wearing only Stone Island and CP Company or wearing watered down Casual brands just to have that smidge of an affiliation to Casual culture.

Some of the lads I spoke to are on the periphery of the Ultra-subculture, balancing and wobbling on that very thin line that does differentiate the Casuals and the Ultras. There are aspects of both subcultures, combined to create a hybrid of the Casuals and the Ultras, lads that dress better than Ultras but are arguably more violent than the Casuals. Et voila! There you have this Ultra-lite, Casual-lite combo. Best of both worlds?

Blissfully ignorant of the regional nuances of Ultra couture, Casuals have a preconception of the more Eastern of Ultras to be rough, (snide) badged up, cloaked in black with the ubiquitous goggles, going for prearranged rows in forests. They are at least up for it and seeing as the 'Modern Football' disease is creeping everywhere, even this lot are staying away from the Big Brothered up CCTV at the grounds and meeting up with rival firms in organised fights.

Tragically, or conveniently, some of this fighting and training in the woods may have come in handy for certain Ultras. As of February 2022, when Russia invaded Ukraine, hooligans from Dynamo Kiev and several other Ukrainian Ultras volunteered to defend their country. Literally, two tribes going to war. Wonder if you'd get our Stone Island overshirt army #gettingthebadgein whilst dodging the shelling of their towns? I'd hazard a guess and say doubtful.

The documentary *Frontline Hooligans* looks at how members of rival Ultras are joining forces to defend against the common enemy of Russia and also in the earlier internal conflicts against the pro-Russian government.

'Football hooligans are playing an outsized role in the Ukrainian war effort, with many firms having formed into militias. The Azov Battalion emerged from the fight clubs of FC Metalist Kharkiv, with an estimated 60 per cent of Azov fighters at the first battle for Mariupol drawn from the terraces. When Ukrainian soldiers die in battle it has become common to see them commemorated with their team colours.'

'We don't have arguments now because we have war on our land,' says founding member of HHK (Hoods Hoods Klan hooligan firm of Arsenal Kyiv) Anton. 'Let us resolve this first and everything else will be handled later.' Poignantly, he adds: 'Do I look forward to a return to the terraces after the war? Maybe after this I won't be interested in hooligan stuff.'

Is it any wonder they are all cameoed up to fuck in black paramilitary gear, defending their country and dodging bear-wrestling Putin wannabees?

54|

Auld Enemies; By Order of the Peaky Fucking Blinders

In recent years, one group of Ultras has been pictured on mass dressed like the Peaky fucking Blinders. A cultural phenomenon, *Peaky Blinders* was a mint TV programme based on a factual Birmingham gang. The programme with its sex, drugs and violent storylines set against a backdrop of huge historical occasions and a cool, deep soundtrack, the characters soon became idolised with many a young lad dressing up in a suit and flat cap to emulate the anti-hero (and fit as fuck!) Tommy Shelby.

I find this connection and influence extremely relevant in terms of clobber; in the programme *The Real Peaky Blinders*, creator Steve Knight describes them as the first modern youth cult:

'Their clothing, their sense of style, even their own language, it makes me think that in an environment where you have no control, you have no authority, everything's pretty grim, the only thing you can do is make yourself the thing.'

This describes the emotion behind the early Casuals perfectly. When describing the Peaky Blinders women, all dolled up in their best clobber including big collars, furs, extravagant hats, trying to blend in and look like a more affluent person, often apprehended for stealing boots, watches, shirts and clothing, they sound more than familiar.

This working-class blueprint has been engraved in the psyche of generations down the line, the subversion of style, the sense of self elevation by clobber. And it's easy to see why men dress for the Tommy Shelby affect. I love a man in a sharp suit; a man in a sharp suit with a flat cap, piercing blue eyes and fag dangling nonchalantly out his mouth, is a no brainer.

Djurgardens Ultras dressing up like Peaky Blinders, chanting loud, proud Ultra songs on their annual dress up away day albeit looking more like Arthur than Tommy, is something I love to see. It's different, it's smart(er), they're wearing hats (I miss hats). Sometimes I would prefer to see a group of lads daring to be different at the match but with the same sensibilities as the Casual aesthetic. Skinny mod suits for example, or a uniform of Sicilian-mob style looks, regalia of a considered style. I would rather see that than the same sea of uninspired, insipid, uncreative, yawnsome basic Stone Island crewneck jumpers or worse, the dreaded overshirt.

But the *Peaky Blinders* connection with football doesn't end there. The *Scottish Sun* reports:

'Rangers fans were sent into meltdown after Peaky Blinders leader Tommy Shelby exclaimed "We are the people." The head of the fictional Birmingham crime gang made the declaration in a speech to Parliament on the BBC hit show.

'In series five the Shelbys battle a Glasgow gang boss based on the head of the feared Billy Boys. Notorious Glasgow razor gang boss Billy Fullerton – the inspiration for the 'Billy Boys' chant sung by Rangers fans – was the inspiration for the next villain in the BBC hit.'

Once again politics and paramilitary undertones are still embedded within neo-tribes in football fandom today. When asked if there was a correlation between British Ultras and paramilitary affiliations, an anonymous football source in Scotland explains:

'Celtic have the Green Brigade and they like to highlight the atrocities in Northern Ireland. I have no doubt that some have links to the IRA. Rangers have a newer group who call themselves the Union Bears, most are kids. However, given the numbers that travel to Rangers from Northern Ireland, they are growing. Things like UDA and UVF are topics on match day.'

Coincidentally and just as controversially, the Rangers Union Bears Ultras displayed a grand show of respect at their game versus Napoli at the time of writing this chapter, when Queen Elizabeth II passed away, commencing a period of national mourning and outpourings of grief. In a game after her passing, the Union Bears were behind the Rangers fans decision to defy a UEFA ban by roaring a powerhouse rendition of the National Anthem and decorating the Ibrox with a huge tifo of the Queen's image on the Union Jack. Despite warnings, they quite clearly didn't give a fuck:

'Chelsea and Manchester City, as well as the 'Gers, saw special requests denied by UEFA in their first matches since the Queen's death. Rangers stood defiant regardless, alerting their fans via social media that they planned to go ahead with the show of respect.'

The patriotic display was not unnoticed by the football fraternity, many applauding them for their two fingers up to UEFA/modern football and being loyal to the crown.

'Spine-tingling.'

'Absolute goosebumps, can't stop watching it.'

'Class act. Who is UEFA to say the National Anthem can't be played. No respect.'

It went down particularly well with the Stoke lot, no doubt due to our connection with Rangers which apparently is:

'A British thing as Rangers see themselves more as an English club rather than Scottish and are also anti-Catholic/IRA...and Stoke share these values,' explains Fine Casual Element (Stoke City). He adds about the display:

'They were better than any English club. They got told by UEFA not to play the National Anthem, but they did so instead of the UEFA anthem, they'll probably get fined.'

When it comes this kind of politics and club allegiances, I try to stay apathetic and apolitical due to my mongrel mix of Russian/Scouse/Jew on my mother's side, North East with Irish connections on my father's. I'm sure that helps explain a lot about my character (lol).

Not everyone was loving the Rangers actions, however, but they favoured it over the Scousers and Celtic's own personal tribute to the Queen.

"It was better than the Scousers booing in the minute's silence and Celtic flags saying, "Fuck the Queen." Horrible twats.' Anonymous.

Not really a shocker that the Irish-immigrant, anti-royalist, pro-Scouse republic fans booed the Queen. All this contention makes me wonder if there is a correlation between the newer Ultra converts and sectarianism within the UK. In other words, are the areas where there has been religious and political upset and/or have paramilitary sympathisers more prone to adopt the more militia inspired Ultralisitic uniform? But then how do you explain Crystal Palace's Ultra faction, the Holmesdale Fanatics?!

@huyvfhj: 'The Ultra scene has been big in Glasgow for about a decade. Came from European away days and friendships with German/Italian clubs. Clobber is still big in the scene though.'

This scene has travelled across the Irish Sea with a small tribe growing there, despite being in the shadow of Gaelic games and rugby. Self-confessed Irish Ultra, Darren Broomfield, is deeply entrenched in these infant days of the Ultra scene there, even being part of one of Ireland's longest running fanzine's, Red Inc. He talks to me at length:

'My team in Ireland is Shelbourne and my English team is Leeds. I go home and away to Shels games and usually get over for three to four Leeds games per season. I have always loved the rhythms and rituals around football. I've a huge interest in design and fashion too so I suppose all of that has contributed to my interest in Ultra culture. Ultra culture in Ireland probably maintains a resistance to everything else; our league is small and poorly covered in the mainstream.

'Like most Irish football fans, whether they like to admit it or not, British football is hugely influential. I think the classic Ultra look is quite ubiquitous; you see boys and girls in Ireland, the UK, Italy etc., all wearing Adidas and Stone Island. I don't think there's anything wrong with this necessarily but it's a consistent look.'

The sense of belonging to such a cool collective such as the Casuals or the Ultras translates exceptionally well, feelings felt strongly by young lads (and ladettes), across the globe. Clobber may vary, brands may differ, but that unfaltering passion burns bright and never dies. Darren agrees:

'The line from *The Sopranos*, "this thing of ours", is one you see on stickers here. It's a release for young lads who may have little else, particularly from the more marginalised community. Travelling to games, messing around, it's a bit of fun.'

A universal language we all understand, reimagined with our own colloquial tweaks, twangs and slang.

Clobber as a language has always had a strong dialect, no more so then in Scotland. The ASC (Aberdeen Soccer Casuals) are held in the highest of regards in terms of the original Casuals, long renowned for their steadfast love of Casual culture. Speaking to Aberdeen's version of a James Bond villain, Mr M 😊 , he recalls his own experience:

'Back in Aberdeen in the early eighties, the Casual (dresser) scene was huge. Many like myself then started going to the games at home and then travelling to away games and going along with the more established lads in the ASC. Back then you would beg, borrow and steal to try and keep up with the trends, always looking closely at what other mobs were wearing when you played them and seen their lads.

'There was a subculture surrounding the scene and it wasn't all football; many music and bands played a huge part and lads would swap record, tapes, go to gigs together. The whole clothing, music and fashion all came together to form the biggest youth subculture seen in the UK since the Mods in the early sixties.'

That, my friend Mr M, is the perfect storm, the zeitgeist that brought it all together. As we learned from earlier chapters, we know that this storm no longer exists, so what's the crack with Daduals and Nouveaux across the border right now?

'The older lads know no different from the styles and labels we wore when younger and still wear today, it's just toned down a lot more. The younger lads see the labels as a way of identifying themselves as Casuals or Ultras and are basically just carrying on; clever online marketing and targeted advertising allows certain labels to keep a prominent place in the fashion stakes. TV celebs wearing certain brands and certain bands wearing labels all help the younger generation wear the same labels year in year out. There's no real change of style coming in at all for the last decade at least and it's all become very stale in my opinion.'

55|
"SCRUFFY FUCKS"

Ultras and football hooliganism, like most things, has become globalised. It is becoming increasingly apparent however, that throughout the whole of Europe, there are patterns of differentiation. Different countries have their own cultural practises, and they are also engaged in mimicking others. Cross-cultural examples include, 'the introduction into British fan culture of Continental designer-clothing (Casual) styles in the early 1980s. Additionally, the Ultras subcultures dominant in countries such as Italy, Spain and parts of France have come to influence supporter groups in Northern Europe, with similar fan groups being formed in countries such as Germany, Austria, the Netherlands and parts of Scandinavia...In the 1990s British fan subcultures also started to experiment with aspects of the Southern European model, through the use of Latin chant patterns and musical bands,' Spaaij explains.

So, we've all appropriated little bits and bobs from each other, even, and especially, us Brits! Yet there is a sweeping disparaging and snobbish opinion towards the Ultras.

An anonymous scathe:

'Scruffy fucks. Crazy. Dynamo Kiev were mental. Not aware or arsed about their clothing consumption. They've got nothing to lose. See how they'd be twenty years ago.'

Riaz Kahn says:

'Snides! As for Eastern Europeans they are slow on the uptake when it comes to terrace fashions, they seem to be wearing all black and they also seem to be more interested in the violence of football culture. They really go to town when they meet up whether it's in the woods or outside a stadium. The use of iron bars and other types of weapons is evident, and they really want to damage the opponent. We Brits are refined, it's not just about the violence and we have rules of engagement. Take for example the Russians in the Euros 2016, they attacked normal fans, they could not distinguish between the hooligan and the supporter. They are some European nations that are interested in the clobber (Swedes and Danes), but the rest need to catch up!!'

David Elders (Original Casuals):

'Very few of the international football lot ever really got into the Casual scene. Lots of European teams had big hooligan firms but to be honest, barring a few notable exceptions, it was few and far between as to the ones that were worth their salt. Likewise with their dress sense LOL! As for the Eastern European lot and these forest meets with tops off, that's hilarious!'

Why has everyone lost it on Ultras and forests?! And where the fuck is this mythical forest?!

Online football fan pages are the perfect platform to proudly boast about match day escapades, whether it's because I follow said pages or keep a beady eye out for all things football 'hooligan' related in the media, there seems to have been more than a few rows of late, and even more sartorial territorial pissing with British Casuals looking down on the clobber, clothes and culture of the Ultras.

The clear need to differentiate and stamp authority over the Ultras was evident when I went to the dark side and asked on my Instagram story for any Ultras to get in touch with me to discuss all things clobber. A Pandora's Box of fiendishness was most definitely opened. My research is ethnographic in theory, through structured and unstructured interviews, polls and an online call to arms. Asking any Ultras to DM me through my Insta account certainly resulted in a mental mix of the send nudes brigade, real Ultras, Casuals and 12-year-old English kids desperate to #gettheirbadgein. Not the required demographic but alas too late, the social media floodgates were wide open, and the outpouring was a mixture of wannabe fandom and unimpressed Casuals that I had used the words 'Ultras' and 'Clobber' in the same sentence. The term scruffy appears to be used indiscriminately.

'Ultras' clobber side...?! They're all scruffy cunts! I'm Palace and 98% of our fan base hate the muggy ultras. We have, in house fighting with them week in week out. They're embarrassing. To be fair there's about 200 of the cunts at ours now, one of my old pals who used to come with us in the eighties actually goes with them now.'

'Anyone from England who thinks they're an Ultra is a knobhead don't waste your time.'

Anonymous in Dundee:

'I first encountered Ultras in Milan about 15 years ago. Been an AC Milan season ticket holder for the past ten years. Seat is in the heart of Curva Sud. The Ultras are a very well organised group. You have your leaders who oversee everything, then soldiers who have their own squads to look after. Kids are groomed to be Ultras. They sell merchandise at games. All displays and chants are choreographed by guys on railings in front of each section. The organised marches to San Siro are amazing. It is only now that British clubs are trying to emulate this. Mainly wee boys being copycats. They don't go as far as having fight training. Back in my skinhead days, we would wait at the station for any mobs. Get off train. Takeover first pub we saw and wait for word to go round that Dundee were in town. Then Casuals came along, now they wanna be Ultras. It's funny when you see the Rangers

Union Bear Ultras at a match wearing balaclavas. Son, it's 28 fucking degrees dafty!'

This so called 'call to arms' of mine surprised me in terms of how many Casuals were identifying themselves as Ultras and that there was a potentially significant British Ultra scene after many had merged or transitioned from being a Casual. The number of circles this appropriating is going in, the never-ending cycle of clothing influences and cultural copying, is dizzying.

Scotts Menswear's blog discussed this in *Ultrafication of British Football*:

'The reasons behind this shift in culture are numerous. With the repeated expansion of the Champions League, and the rebranding of the UEFA Cup as the Europa League, more fans are coming into direct contact with the Ultra-style of support. On top of that, beginning with Football Italia in the 90s the increased access to European football on the television has brought ultras into the living rooms of fans from Burnley to Bournemouth.

'Ironically, when the Ultras in their modern form emerged in continental Europe in the sixties, seventies and eighties, they took inspiration from the atmosphere created on British terraces. However, that this has gone full circle is not altogether surprising.

'Fundamentally, this adaption of Ultras culture taps into the longstanding sense of one-upmanship amongst British football supporters, particularly within organised groups such as the Holmesdale Fanatics or Red Faction; recent lower and non-league groups such as the Jorvik Reds at York or the Ultras Barovia at Barrow; as well as groups north of the border at Rangers, Celtic and Aberdeen amongst others.'

Is the Ultra scene that prevalent in the UK, however? Being the intrepid reporter/nosey bastard that I am, I delved back into Insta's dark side.

'People still want to belong to something, so as the Casual scene has died due to police/court activity, the ultra scene has flourished as you're less likely to get jail for it. It's still a way of marking themselves out as more than an ordinary fan; I mean the fashion is there but it's not what Casual was about for me.'

'Ultras ain't really a big thing. Closest thing would be Palace.'

'I think the Ultra scene is a bit embarrassing. I get Casuals have always been a thing, but the likes of the Palace lot with huge flags and claiming to be Ultras is pathetic.'

'The Ultra scene is embarrassing!! I hate it. Casual all day.'

'The Ultra scene seems to be just kids bouncing about waving banners. Walking in mass to their home grounds; to an outsider it seems pretty tinpot and embarrassing. Hope I never see it at Elland Road.'

'It isn't (a scene). It's spotty 18-year-olds with snide CP and Stone Island.'

'They just can't afford the clobber and H & M Black hoodies and boot cut jeans are more affordable.'

A subculture hijacked by Gen-Zs once more then? Or a general blurring of the lines between Casual and Ultra in which the young lot believe that wearing the badge or the lens automatically makes you belong to a group.

An anonymous Insta follower theorises: 'Seriously, I think the ex-Casuals of a certain age are trying to stay relevant. I think in this country, Ultras are the kids coming through not happy being the under 5s, yooth etc. So the young 'uns have taken on the ultras tag to perhaps reinvent themselves and move away from the old skool football Casual? Football Casuals are a staple point in the British football hooligan scene, but modern-day Casuals don't necessarily like a scrap. Literally can't move at West Ham these days without seeing Stone Island, these lads don't want a scrap, they just wanna look the part around the East End!'

Kids! CP Company and Stone Island do not a Casual make! And I'm pretty sure there's more to being an Ultra then pulling down the goggles!

56|

A Whole New World

Stoke-on-Trent is Casual as fuck but it's also small as fuck. What about our Casual brothers on the other side of the pond, and on the other side of the world? 'Sappening in terms of terrace culture overseas?

Social media and these fucking hooligan films really have opened up new audiences to the 'past-it' Casual scene, but the new devotees' clear passion and dedication to the cause seems to be helping the renaissance of the scene, the revival and the reignition of the flame. Does this mean terrace culture is genuinely back up and running, or like actual Casual brands, just become an existing watered-down version always chasing rainbows?

The rise in Ultras directly correlates to the rise in global followers of Casual fan pages. This is probably due to the lost-in-translation perception that Ultras are Casuals and vice versa with a love of shared labels. This misconstrued concept also caters to the belief that you are Casual just by wearing Stone Island, CP and Weekend Offender. The page founders I spoke to say that the majority of followers are from the UK, but go as far as Indonesia, Malaysia, Russia, China, Japan and Korea.

Lorenzo Osti and I spoke about these new territories and how they are adopting CP Company for their own twist on Casual culture; not even necessarily purchasing the brand but appropriating its very identity to further their terrace culture cause.

'The biggest countries for us for CP are the UK and France now, France has never been like this, it's a new phenomenon, and Korea, historically, has always been very popular. What is interesting, the third country origin of tracking of our Instagram account, is Indonesia.

'We have no clients, we don't sell anything (there). They fell in love with UK football, so they adopted the same brands that you were using. The connection is, there is a Casual scene in Indonesia. For me, it was a super weird surprise, but nice. Also, these guys are really young, kids, but yeah, it's weird how subcultures can connect.'

It is a bit mental how the scene and the typical brands are really taking off in Asia and it's not the first time I've encountered the almost fanatism from Indonesians towards Casuals; there are many huge social media pages documenting their love of all things Casual – despite no football and no actual (direct) consuming. The emperor's new clothes or hero-worshipping on a massive scale?

Paul Smith says:

'I think it's great! Clobber Magazine has a huge following in Indonesia! They are bang into their retro tennis gear, Stone Island, CP the lot, although granted most of it is snide.'

Agreeing, Matt Snell tells me:

'When I started the page (Casual Client Clothing), I didn't know how big the Casual scene is in Asia. It's huge! Malaysia has a massive love for it. However, coming from that area, you notice a few fakes knocking about. But still, the want for it is there.'

Matt Banks discusses Terraces' international customer base and the (literal) lengths some fans will turn to in order to get their fabled Casual clobber:

'Over the years we've seen our customer base massively grow globally, not just around Europe but as far as Malaysia, America, Brazil, Jamaica and Mexico. Our main Terraces HQ in Hanley in Stoke, has seen visitors from Malaysia, Holland and Scotland.'

From Paninaro to Pan-AM Pacific via sunny Stoke-on-Trent, football culture is going increasingly berserk abroad, including flashbacks to the very darkest of troubles relating to over-zealous police and hooligans.

'More than 130 people were killed as they rushed to exit a stadium in East Java in one of the world's worst sports disasters. A football stampede in Indonesia that killed more than 130 people was caused by tear gas,' reported *Al Jazeera* in 2022.

Let's hope this horrific event signals the end of massive-scale football atrocities and the fans continue their love affair with the terrace fashion element only.

Oliver Beer:

'I know CP did an Asian market years ago, so there must have been something there. You'll always find Japanese and your Chinese market different – and they would see our stuff as different. Perhaps that's their way – they're all one culture, their way of being different is wearing something different. So instead of being part of the biggest communist group you wear something a little bit different to stand out.'

Agreeing with this desire to stand out yet paradoxically looking the same by choosing to wear the generic brands that scream 'Wannabe Casual' as opposed to 'Casual', I explored the theory further with Jared Latimer:

Me: 'You mentioned Weekend Offender. Now, they have a real big following, in places like Indonesia and Korea and that. And they are places that seem to have a rising Casual scene. I don't mean like a real one, but to dress like one. Do you think that's where markets are going that way, and do you think that's why brands are catering for that?'

Jared: 'Possibly, yes. I think what is normal to us is obviously exotic to others. Obviously, a Stone Island originally was something from Italy that was super cool. And the same as some of the Japanese brands – Evisu – appear so much cooler to us, because we're not used to seeing them. So, I just think some of the other countries have seen that on the opposite side of things. Things we are used to, also making it super cool. Brands like Fred Perry, which still sells strongly in the UK, but abroad, it's seen as that strong, English thing, like Burberry as well.

'I know, when I was living abroad, a lot of the lads I was with, the Scandinavians and Swedish lads, they were just absolutely crazy about this Stone Island thing. But instead of them getting it from Italy, they sort of got their ideas from us, and obviously we got it from Italy.

"Scandinavia is known for its quality, and a lot of their clothing brands are really good quality. But again, I think, no matter what country it is, if everybody looks the same, it then dilutes it, it's not interesting anymore.'

57|
Admit Nothing

Weekend Offender is a brand that has been adopted by almost every (Casually motivated) country, and their personalised city or country of choice t-shirts solidifies their position as a world renowned, global Casual brand. Does this mean the brand is diluted or just extremely successful?

I spoke with Weekend Offender co-founder Adam Keyte about the international phenomenon of their City Series collection, being relatable to football lads in a wink wink, nudge nudge capacity, and how his background in Ibiza and acid house has ultimately helped him achieve this.

Adam (Villa) is a veteran of the perfect storm of eighties and nineties music and fashion culture; with his knowledge of the party and football scene, he and his partners started out creating cheeky and provocative t-shirts (trips and garys anyone?). This gradually evolved into designing coats, jackets and smocks which had either hangover cures provided in the labels, an actual toothbrush and paste for the dirty stop-outs amongst us, and even real embassy contact details for prime party hotspots such as Ibiza and Bangkok just in case you end up *Banged up Abroad*.

Knowing he was onto a winner with these comical, relatable – and possibly lifesaving – touches, Adam explains:

'Between the three of us we came up with ideas that harked back to our heritage also. Cult films, the 'Admit Nothing' label designed as an old cinema ticket stub...we are creative with the labels which we know connects with the perceived end consumer.'

Weekend Offender customers can relate to the brand because of its nonchalant, non-contrived identity. The founders are genuine, their jargon speaks to those in the know, the designs are a pisser. We don't give a fuck if we are wearing drug related designs, Weekend Offender knows this, and caters for these little bad habits ☺.

I ask him about their City Series collection, t-shirts which emblazons your country or city in a way that is unmistakably Weekend Offender yet allows folk not from typical large or capital cities to have a piece of their own personalised locality on show; not many labels cater for cities such as Stoke, Rotterdam and Jakarta.

The success in Indonesia and Russia is 'organic' says Adam, and is evident once again of these territories adopting the Casual culture. Weekend Offender is totally ingrained into the Hall of Fame of Casual brands, and whether or not the Nouveaux continue to consume the brand, it is without question that the international Ultras will most definitely, and willingly, take up this mantle.

Aspiring to our undefinable, inimitable football subculture will never be realistically achievable. The Casuals existed through an organic evolution of styles formed geographically across the UK through FASHION, FRIENDSHIP, FOOTBALL (Original Casuals). This does not stop the world in trying to emulate us, however.

Kyle Dixon, Archivio Clothing:

'Terrace culture will always be here as places like Asia try and replicate the English terrace culture, it is seen as something to look up to. The fashion, music, drugs, lifestyle, the character and family you make along the way; there's so much to be said about it but while football is always the number one sport in English eyes, the terrace culture will always be there. Compare the hostility surrounded with it compared to rugby or basketball or even the way other countries see their top sports. The Americans are a good comparison, not known for their brilliant chants or even having an away end.'

Speaking of the Americans...

58|
Gold Rush

Historically, the United States has been an untapped source, a country so vast with deep resources, that the Europeans flocked there to stake their claim. If Casual culture wanted to expand and get more recruits, then America certainly seems ripe for the picking.

The New World does indeed appear to be experiencing a surge in 'Casuals', primarily in LA and Miami where the Major Soccer League (MSL) has its stronghold. And with Stone Island becoming a Rapper's Delight, the brand du jour of 'you know who', it appears the Stateside reception to heritage Italo brands is warm. As many of the lads I spoke to, America is one of the countries that is becoming host to noisily growing fans of Casual brands and culture.

Matt Snell (Casual Client Clothing):

'America's football is years behind everyone else but the fans really are trying to make their mark and there is plenty of money washing around. Tifos, flares and banners show they are trying to recreate Europe and South America so the clothes won't be far behind. Also, with America being exposed to Stone Island more through Drake (noooooooo!) and other outlets, I can see them becoming big buyers.'

Steve Lumb, owner of Terrace Cult, has realised the potential for business with the Nouveaux-Yank Casual scene:

'We saw the Casual scene growing in America and we thought we need to get a head start over the pond. We knew Kevin (Veliz, Terrace

Cult USA), was a massive fan so we offered him the chance to use our branding in the states sort of like a franchise; no pressure from us and no targets for him to hit, just a relationship based on trust and love for Casual culture. So far, it's moving ok. Lots of American fans, especially in LA and New York, love Terrace Cult and love everything the brand stands for.'

Steve may be right in pre-empting the Casual gold rush as clearly there is a developing attraction to the football Casual culture in the US. I spoke with Kevin Veliz:

'The Casual culture here has definitely grown and it's getting even more popular because of the MLS Casual groups travelling to away games. Here in Los Angeles, we have a huge Casual scene. Everyone is wearing the trainers, Terrace Cult, Weekend Offender and Stone Island.

'We Yanks love the Casual scene and have always admired what comes out of Europe. We buy the clothing brands because it separates you from the normal fans and it's a badge you wear here with pride. Los Angeles is leading the Casual scene in America.'

Interestingly, American Casuals have created their own rituals. Kevin continues:

'A few years back we started a tradition where we raise our left trainer for when our Captain, Carlos Vela, scores with his left foot. That started a whole Casual movement and that is one reason why many started wearing the Adidas trainer.'

So how do they consume their brands and satisfy their Anglophile desires?

'We sell trainers between the Casual community online. I personally don't buy through fan pages; I'd rather buy straight from the source. Before I started selling Terrace Cult, I used to buy directly from Terrace Cult. 80s Casual Classics is another website we use a lot here in the US. That's where we buy most of our trainers and other Casual brands.'

They are clearly taking this shit seriously; Steve backs up their commitment:

'They're getting into it big time, and I mean big time. Getting Adidas trainers, getting Stone Island- they're even coming into Europe to buy Stoney bits. They're getting stuff now; the Americans are getting it. They're watching movies, watching ID, watching *Green Street*, they're contacting us all the time.'

Like the European Ultras, there is an element of violence to the Yankee Casuals, although more South American and/or gang related as opposed to paramilitary backgrounds. Steve explains:

'The MLS is twenty years behind. The fans in the MLS used to be popcorn and candyfloss, and I think a lot of the Hispanic teams, they've got a bit of that football culture about them already, the South American twist. And I think they wanted to bring it to the terraces in North America and LAFC, not LA Galaxy. LAFC have a group called District 9 and they're very, very close to a European style Ultra group.'

Fittingly for Terrace Cult, the culture is indeed slowly spreading, appearing cultish for sure especially when we consider Derek Diablo – a notorious Casual evangelist, spreading the word, a self-confessed 'Del Boy' devotee to the movement, on a seriously 'naughty' mission:

'My goal is and has been since I began with my online hooligan exploits in 2018, to spread awareness of football hooliganism in America with the intention of propagating Casuals as a significant subculture here.'

A fine manifesto if ever I heard!

Derek Diablo has come into the Casual consciousness with a video called *Millwall vs Miami: Who's the Hardest?* At first the viral video seems a parody, a proper piss-take sketch you'd see on *The Fast Show*. Yet the pastiche is real and Diablo, he of many teams (Inter Miami,

Man Utd, Plymouth Argyle) is serious about Casual culture. The snobby UK and European Casuals may sneer but reading through some American hippy dippy new age terminology, certain valid points are made.

At first Diablo began dressing like the fine British subcultures of Punks and Skinheads which then naturally evolved into the Casuals, astutely understanding the symbolism and rituals of these subcultures:

'There is much familiarity in the way of shared culture, street ethics, adherence to underworld codes, and then the livery or trappings of a particular shared culture/subculture which may or may not include shared dress codes or a shared fashion. Casuals have a defined fashion sensibility, if difficult to pinpoint. From Mod, to Skinhead, to Casual, there is a thread; a tough, clean, mean sort of look which reflects the mindset and character of its proponents.'

So far, so good, so Casual. And Diablo gets the fundamentals, continuing:

'At the end of the day, apart from the one upmanship element, we are talking about high quality stylish clothing, and with this as the foundation, it's easy to see how the brands have such staying power. In contrast to the Chav style, Casuals are not into tacky or garish sorts of presentations, the brands aren't put so front and centre that you become a walking billboard, everything must be done with a bit of class.

'For me, I will continue to support and collect the established brands as well as the newer ones and those still to come. Another attractive feature for me with the Casuals' style is the freedom and constant evolution of the fashion in contrast with the Skinheads who had an established uniform.'

Diablo and other American Casuals get it, but will they ever really 'get' it? They're saying the correct sweeping statements, they have profound knowledge of the chronological order of Casual brands, but will they really understand the golden Casual era of the late eighties/early nineties? Will they ever longingly aspire to the clobber they've seen in The Face or L'Uomo Vogue?

Derek does, apparently.

'It's art really, the collection of one's clobber, deciding when to wear it and how, it's walking art and the assembling of a collection can be viewed identically to that of any other sort of art collection. Football hooliganism is a violent, outlaw culture, but the Casuals' style is a thing of beauty.'

Choosing the obvious favourite brands; Lacoste, CP, Stone Island, Weekend Offender et al, Diablo does accept that his style is growing and evolving, much like the American scene itself:

'I foresee North America becoming a mecca for the Casuals scene in time, just as it has been for the Skinheads... America and Americans are always after the next trend, the next fad and this is on a cultural as well as commercial level. I want to see Casuals become the dominant subculture in America.'

The fanaticism concludes:

'Anyone who is interested in the furtherance of the Casuals scene and is willing and able should think how you can contribute. Everyone can make a difference whether by writing blogs, books, magazines, videos, documenting the history of their firm, reviewing clobber, creating online communities, and simply be willing to bring the youth up according to the traditions of this cult.'

Are you converted yet?! The guy is a Casual zealot for sure but is his spearheading perception of Casuals in the States damaging or furthering Casual culture? Does the culture even want to expand and recruit American Casuals in order to survive as a 'species'? I'm confident most of the originals would rather die out then this satirised version. The Americans don't get our dry loftiness, the very slight British/European subversions that make Casuals 'Casual' – it's all in the detail.

The playful references, the subtle threat, the knowing wink, the flick of the hair, the silky hankie, the purposeful sock, all these nuances are low key and potentially be missed by not being loud and in your face.

The brash smash 'n' grab approach to appropriation even lent itself to football chants. In what can only be described as a fucking pisser, Millwall's *No one likes us, we don't care* song was adopted by American MLS team Philadelphia Union's independent group of supporters, the Sons of Ben. Sounding like a Netflix series, this lot sing throughout the game, bizarrely using Millwall's infamous song. When asked why in an interview online with the Brotherly Game, they responded:

'I think it's because when it comes to the City of Brotherly Love, and especially our sports, there's no middle ground ... You either love it with every bit of your existence, or you hate everything about it. And we can go to any bar and sit next to a complete stranger, but as long as they're cheering on our team, you're instantly connected.'

Interviewer: 'How do you feel about some Millwall fans having a negative reaction to another fan base singing the song?'

'I don't care.'

Millwall don't care that you don't care that they don't like that you don't care...

This Coors-Lite American football fandom comes across as fiendish, no more so when they are describing 'firms'. It gives Casuals about as much gravitas as Get the Badge In. According to Diablo in one of his You Tube rants, he mentions the rivalry between Stoke and Port Vale. Unquestionably, we all hate the Vale, but to describe it as a tête-à-tête, Ton sur Ton, heavyweight hooligan battle is a tad farfetched.

But are our American cousins not loud and exaggerative in their natures? At least Derek Diablo is being passionate about the Casuals, and I'd bet his bottom dollar that he'd be there at the match smashing up the Vale toilets ☺ .

59|

Just Say No; Clobber Addicts & Fanatics

Casuals, Hoolies, Ultra. Whatever the tribes may call themselves, they all sit under the umbrella of football fandom, and are getting a serious arse kicking for their collective consumption; that is, their image has become so mocked due to the piss-poor watering down of the culture and the brands that are used to symbolize and represent them. Being ridiculed by their own 'kin' is one thing, but what do normal folk think of it all? Do regular people buy brands like CP Company and Stone Island knowing full well the connotations, and despite having no personal footie connections, still wear regardless due to the pull and the attraction of the brands? Perhaps they have heard only of the media-engorged Hoolies rather than the neat and precise dressers of the Casuals and thus stay away from the more stereotypical Casual brands? Or maybe they just like the brands?!

Soccer Am Presenter Fenners is well known for his sharp attire and immaculate collection; and although a self-pronounced non-hoolie, more a clobber connoisseur, he still knows his shit and can be perceived as being influential to both old and new Casuals, often being mistaken for one himself.

Fenners: 'Because people see me on the telly, you'll get people going, "oh he's this, he's a fake Casual. Oh, you're a fake hooligan." And I just laugh and say, "well I've never been a hooligan. Never wanted to be a hooligan."'

He continues: 'I'm just an enthusiast. I'm a football enthusiast, I'm a music enthusiast, I'm a clothes enthusiast. I'm not an aficionado of any sort. I wouldn't class myself as a collector.' He does, however, have a remarkable gift for squirreling out some unreal pieces, the way he facilitates his brand consumption allows him to uncover some hidden gems, the pleasure heightened even more if no one else has these coveted items.

'If you can find it, you can get it. If you get the enjoyment from looking and searching and finding, and getting something that you like, a lot of lads don't want stuff that no one else has got. They want to be like the other lads. They want the same stuff.'

Ingeniously, Fenners goes on to explain how he deploys his strategy in unearthing some serious clobber through largely the vintage sites:

'Most of the stuff I wear is second-hand, you know, pretty much everything. If you said to me, "Here you go, Fenners, there's £500, go and buy something," the first place I'd go to is Depop. I'd go to Depop, I'd go to eBay, I'd go to Grailed, I'd go to Etsy, I'd go to Vinted, and I'd scour them and scour them.

'It's like stock markets. Get up in the morning, see what's there. And you think, oh, you know, if you go on a Sunday afternoon, then you'll have a lot of lads who've been out and they've probably spent up on a Saturday night, and they've probably got a few quid in, so they're probably popping something up.'

Also recognizing there is bound to be more clobber bouncing round towards the end of the month is just as brilliant. A masterpiece in brand consumption in the reseller market, when timing is everything from both buyer and seller, to be in the right place at the right time when the right clobber drops, is poetry in motion.

Fellow non-hooligan but just as respected 'in this thing of ours' scene, Neil Summers has always been bang into the clobber scene, mirroring Fenners in being obsessed with the music and clothes first and foremost.

Neil: 'I'm not remotely interested in football. The people I grew up with weren't into football, it was all about music. So, I came into Casual culture via the music scene, really. My first thing into it was seeing kids with flicks. In Manchester they were called Perry Boys.'

Neil is much more original than the typical clobber whore and stays true to the rugged outdoors aesthetic adopted by the Casuals early on, citing Patagonia, North Face and Berghaus as favoured brands. Hiking chic is mos def Neil's vibe, and sensibility has always formed part of a Casual brand's identity due to the dual functions of being practical in any situation and just looking cool as fuck:

'I'm massively into the outdoor wear scene…If you go out to a football match or go out in the rain, you need a fleece or waterproof jacket, do you know what I mean? I used to go clubbing at Shelley's. I used to have a little pack to take with me, a little pack, and it would have a carton of Ribena in it. I'd have a clean sweatshirt, I'd have 40 B & H and a load of skins. I'd have a Berghaus fleece as well, because it's like, you go raving in Shelley's for four or five hours, and you'd come out to a cold transit van in January. That fleece is going on and you're off to the service station. We were going on expedition. They weren't up mountains. They were in nightclubs.'

Shelley's was a legendary club in Stoke-on-Trent. Somewhere not even Bear Grylls could endure without that essential survival kit. Ebeneezer Goode indeed 😊.

Similarly to Fenners' all hours trawling for the best vintage pieces, Neil too cannot resist the lure of a new bit of clobber:

'I'm one of these people who's trying to stop buying stuff, and you know, I'm 50. I've got loads of fucking shit I don't need anymore; I don't need anything. It's like a drug dealer, isn't it? It's like, "Oh, someone's waving a bag in front of me." I've got people who just send me links to stuff. The internet is good at that. Something will just pop up that you like.'

This addiction, this need for old and new clobber, is no joke, folks. Happens to the best of us, we become obsessed with the next fix, taking over our lives, even our homes 😌 .

Oliver Beer:

'I had a stupid idea one day. I thought, I like my clothes. I'm not a collector, I wear everything that I buy…I might wear it once a year, or once every two years but I'll, I tend to hoard them almost. But I thought, right, I want a jacket every day of the year. I got to three hundred-ish. I couldn't fit them in the house. I had to, I had a business unit and put them in just because I couldn't fit them in the house!'

When the fun stops, stop. Or just say no. Ask Zammo.

Casuals are afflicted with brand addiction, those on the periphery of the scene could be described as having deep brand attachment. Seung-Hee Lee and Jane E. Workman write from their research:

'Brand attachment is explained as a strong association or connectedness between the brand and the consumer's self. The stronger the consumer's self-brand relationship, the stronger the consumer's attachment to the brand.'

According to Ball and Tasaki, 'objects that are socially visible; expensive; reflective of an individual's roles, relationships, accomplishments, and experiences; and usually "personalized" by the efforts of their owners are clearly more likely to reflect self.'

There are unquestionably superfans of Stone Island out there that will champion and have a deep affinity with the brand. One such fan is Lenny Urban, car specialist and well known, lifelong Stone Island consumer. Lenny gives me some background into his story, of how a non-footie lad became just as respected for his clobber collections than any Casual.

Lenny: 'I watch football, but I wouldn't say I'm an avid fan of anyone in particular. I used to be a big Arsenal fan back when I was a kid because they were my closest Prem team but as I got into my late teens I just fell out of love with the game and became more interested in cars and clothes.

'My favourite brand is Stone Island all day long. I bought my first jumper 20 years ago when I was 19 after seeing a couple of the older lads wearing it in the pub. One of them had an awesome cream trench style jacket and I asked what the make was – that was the start of the love affair for the brand! I rarely wear anything else now.'

When asked why though, why this love of the brand, Lenny responds:

'I've never been into current fashion trends. I like clothes that are dateless, which is what Stone Island is. I can wear one of my ten-to-fifteen-year-old jackets with a nice fitting pair of jeans and trainers and it's just a classic look. That's why I don't mind spending the money on the jackets and coats – the pieces I buy are never going to really go in or out of fashion.'

He fully understands the problematic and currently incessant weakening of his beloved brand:

'I'd like to think I'll always wear Stone Island and won't be put off by it. I have a fairly strong online presence due to my work in the luxury car sector, but a lot of my followers know my love for the brand too. It makes my teeth itch watching TikTokers talking about getting the badge in and acting all Football Factory – that ain't what it's about for me. The history is greater than that and I'm sure Massimo Osti would be rolling in his grave seeing how some of his brand is being worn.'

Lenny's brand attachment, like thousands of others, means he will continue to have this brand loyalty even when its image starts to go tits up. To save the credibility of Stone Island, these superfans will continue to source out the more independent sellers, looking for those rarer pieces, and to not lose hope that this once mighty brand will eventually shake the more CHAV/Nouveaux Casuals and go back to its roots.

'I'd like to hope that Stone Island just carry on doing what they're doing. Creating classic pieces and pushing the boundaries of design and innovative materials. I can't see myself changing into anything else!'

Reseller Kyle Dixon of Archivio Clothing supports this theory that the garments' ingenuity creates a longevity, and along with smart brand positioning and equity, Stone Island manages to stand the test of time with Casuals and collectors alike:

'Brands that have high price tags and are seen to be popular will always have people wanting them. But the creativity of Massimo Ost and all that still carries through to what we have today. The imagination, creativity and rarity are some key reasons, along with great investments and a brand that has always renovated with the times. Look at the 1982 teal capes and now look at the nylon metals, smocks, overshirts etc. They are always at the forefront smashing out fashion pieces. The amount of badges bouncing around everywhere you go now is crazy!'

At its inception Stone Island has always been a trailblazer; I think it's time to rekindle our love and affection for the brand and take back ownership. The future's bright, the future's Casual?

60|

"Fashion Fades, Only Style Remains the Same."

The past decade has seen some instrumental changes in the world and our Casuals have had to negotiate seismic changes including social media, #Getthebadgein cranks, Drake etc. Frankly, the list is endless. Terrace culture has been limping and licking its wounds, wondering which direction to turn next.

Paul Smith, Clobber Magazine:

'It's been plodding along I guess, but with the older lot (like me) finding the internet and social media, it's really developed a whole new edge (not all of it good either)! It's a peculiar mixture these days, made up of the old guard, that is, proper terrace legends, top boys and dressers.

'Then there's the younger lot, and although they kinda look the same, I am really glad they are carrying it on. My only real criticism of "da yoof" is that they are nowhere near as original as my generation, however this isn't really their fault. It's all about availability. I mean a kid can borrow their mum's debit card and head over to Flannels and bag themselves a nice Goggle jacket, a Stone Island sweater, an Aquascutum scarf and a pair of trainers and hey presto, you've got a ready-made Casual!'

Or, as Lenny Urban accurately describes them: 'The new generation of Flannel gift card wankstains.' Pisser!

Paul Johnston (Aberdeen):
'The older lads know no different from the styles and labels we wore when younger and still wear today, it's just toned down a lot more; the younger lads see the labels as a way of identifying themselves as Casuals/Ultras and are basically just carrying it on.'

Are we just being narrow-minded and biased (absolutely) when we don't allude to the possibility that the older lot are stuck in a style rut, in an eighties/nineties time warp? When they themselves were youths, they were, as Gutu says, 'in the period of defining and forming their own moral codes, which most of the time are influenced by environments,' which in turn became represented by their choice in clobber. The imprint of such exhilarating times, the white-knuckle riding of the wave of the zeitgeist juxtaposes strongly against the heart-sinking realization that things will never be the same again. It's why we, the Casuals, the Mods, the Skinheads, the Punks, cling onto our particular subculture as best we can and representing it with all our might, defending it until the bitter end, forever in our (Northern) Souls.

You should never disregard your style, your subculture or your soul, no matter if it is perceived nowadays as outdated, cheesy or Chav. Kudos to other neo-tribes for also keeping their legends alive. Recently I was up Hanley duck and saw some young EMOs and an older Northern Soul couple who were absolutely true to themselves, their subculture and what they stand for. They dress unmistakably in their clobber so the whole world knows exactly what they represent and who the fuck they are! Good for them and good for us for keeping our scene alive and continuing to push against the norm and the mainstream.

The mainstream is all the Nouveaux Casuals have. The lull in their own creativity over the past decade is evident in the formulaic brand choices. It is easy for them to mimic the 'alpha-Casuals' and theoretically the 'yoof' consumers would 'recycle a series of consumer goods, logos or niche brands, which they culturally assume, they prescribe them a strong symbolic connotation and they draw borders of their own culture.' Gutu writes about this 'bricolage' effect which appears to make it easier for the sheep in wolf's clothing to appropriate and then add their own twist, frustrating the older Casuals in their own continued quest for differentiation from the pack. However, I am of the opinion, that they are not even this independent of thinking or imaginative of brand choices. Collective consumption or just herd mentality?

Jared Latimer:

'There are still some people in that culture, obviously like the original guys, who were bringing stuff over in maybe the seventies and definitely the eighties. It was about standing out and how the fabric felt to them and things like that. Things have changed now, where the masses are sort of jumping on the bandwagon of things, but have not necessarily got any background, any history, or any relevance anymore.'

Believing the creative vacuum is due to social media amongst other evils, he adds:

'This is why people are starting to copy off each other and have stopped coming up with their own ideas because it's so in your face. This is cool, that's cool, that's dead cool, so you want to be getting the brands and getting the look that is out there and cool, instead of being the one that is a leader, not a follower.'

The followers are doing more than following, they are empty-headedly carbon-copying off everyone and everything, which begs the question; why would the original Casuals still deliberately choose to wear such standout/iconic/notorious Casual labels as the Nouveaux? Do they still want to be perceived as being linked with this subculture, even though the dichotomy is that by the very definition Casuals dressed in unique, different, limited-edition clobber. And if so, how can you make it apparent you are a Casual without resorting to the cliches?!

61|

Modern Day Dressers; How to Spot an Original Casual Today

Preserving the sacred heart of terrace culture is not for the faint hearted. The elders of the Casual tribe are the guardians, the purists, the obsessives. We are well aware of the unconditional love towards the big players (Stone Island/CP Company), but what do they also wear to show their affiliation with this subculture without looking like a clueless Nouveaux wannabee. The dilemma is real. But does age also come into play? Is it more style and sensibility? Functional substance over style?

The answer appears to be in the hunt for more subtle brands or the more high-end, rare, or limited-edition pieces and keeping it on the down low between those in the know.

David Elders (Hibs/Original Casuals):

'CCTV killed a big part of the culture more than twenty years ago. What we are left with are guys who used to do the business on a Saturday afternoon, who still love their clobber and keep it alive. Probably a small proportion who still adhere to the same ethos and values and a larger chuck for whom it is teary-eyed nostalgia. I think some of the young lot get it but clearly lots don't…

'There is definitely a healthy amount of brands that bubble under the surface which are limited numbers, good quality and original design. Almost like a little secret that only some people in the know are aware of.'

Elders, along with Glenn Nixon, set up Original Casuals, one such brand to watch, and falls effortlessly into this category:

'Our passion for our product comes from growing up in a time when travelling hundreds of miles to get a limited piece was the done thing. All to look good and individual on the terraces, streets, and clubs on any given Saturday. At Original Casuals we are bringing back this exclusivity and distinctive attire of the 80s Casual scene by only producing each design to a limited quantity. An exclusive brand which is sorely needed in a time of repetitive, bland mass-produced clothing.'

This explains why many of the older original lot are choosing to wear brands such as Plurimus, Patagonia, Saurcony, Loro Piana, Brioni, Adidas Spezial, Haglofs. Brands that are practical, rare, sometimes even more expensive (prices out the pesky Nouveaux); Casual-esque in demeanor but more subtle than screaming, 'I used to be a football Hooligan/Casual and want everyone to know!' The lads are smarter than this and need their clobber to be just as smart, to be both visually and mentally stimulating:

'The brands I am into these days are Plurimus and CP Company. Fabio releases 99 jackets every now and then, not season by season. He was the main man behind 12th Man and his Plurimus jackets have that urban/military look that attracts a lot of the older lot. It is also the exclusivity – not everyone can get their hands on them. I like to buy vintage Stone Island and CP Company. My favourite pieces I have at the moment are my 1989 CP 1000 Mille Miglia and a Stone Island Ice Camo Jacket,' states Riaz Kahn.

Kahn is not, I repeat, not fucking about.

Hiker-chic poster boy Neil Summers has a similar preferred combo of relatively newer classy brands and old-school faves, believing there is 'an outdoor crossover' trend:

'Everything has gone very tech. I worked with CP Company and spent a lot of time writing about technical fabrics, and they're pushing the boundaries with garment dyeing, and it's all similar to outdoor brands.

'There's a shop in Manchester, This Thing of Ours, and that's very Japanese, Korean kind of stuff. I find a lot of that interesting, because I'm massively into the outdoor wear scene. I started Hikerdelic. Because again, there's that GOAT culture, and kids in London wearing North Face and it's like a trend. But if you're from round where I am, you've got the Peak District, North Wales and the Yorkshire Dales. We've always worn it.'

Big coat weather for hardened Northerners only.

When I asked more of the Clobber Connoisseurs (the Clobberati) what brands they wear now, Jay Montessori tells me:

'I love a bit of Belstaff, vintage Stone Island and CP, partial to some M & S basics and Mephisto Rainbow or Superga all whites. M & S knitwear has always been an excellent quality understated go-to for me as are some of their shirts. Love Mephisto Rainbow, I rarely feel comfy in trainers these days (feel scruffy), so these are again an understated two fingers to the three-stripe bumming masses. And Superga Cotu classic are so clean and appeal to my Italian heritage.'

Simon Dowling:

'There are no new brands that make me go wow. There's a few like (Nigel) Cabourn, Hawkwood Mercantile and Club Stubborn who are carving a nice, niche area. It's about mixing it up and getting that balance. I don't know anyone now who has completely tailored outfits, people buy the whole look off the rack. I tip my cap to old school tailoring.'

62|

Get the S(m)ock In

Missing the Dandyist influence, both Simon and I lament the lack of sharp, custom-made tailoring which would no doubt bring the uniqueness back to this homogeneous market. It is also sad to see the Dandyist/Casual connection dim throughout the years, the subverting and appropriating of high-end garms and their nuances diminishing in favour of more loud and brash brand allegiances.

Legendary Professor Andrew Groves writes about the background of such subversions from his research and readings of Routledge et al:

'A Crombie overcoat (almost always a snide) was worn in winter months with a tie pin and silk hankie in the top pocket – red to match your red socks, and then various colours from bright yellow to orange to fluorescent green followed. This shift away from the hypermasculine uniform of the booted Skinhead towards a more refined, inconspicuous appearance was driven in part by some football grounds banning men wearing boots. This pivotal moment of transition is recalled by an impressionable young fan, who later became a Casual.'

The Dandyesque version of Get the Badge In was reimagined by the early Casuals. Groves continues:

'The Casuals' travesty in appropriating and distorting the leisure class's iconic brands (e.g. Burberry, Lacoste, Sergio Tacchini) exemplifies their carnivalesque mode of transgression.'

In *Fashion Crimes: Dressing for Deviance*, Turney focuses on Casuals and the fashioning of the handy dandy; she argues: 'Here, power is obtained through subversion; both social and cultural norms are upturned, the ordinary becomes extraordinary and vice versa, and innocuous clothing becomes invested with fear and violence; it becomes a sign of the hard man.'

Many of the originals still persevere creatively with the subtle subversions and thankfully certain brands do offer a tailor-made service. I was lucky enough to have my measurements taken by James Darby, a clothes designer and bespoke tailor who creates stunning parkas and smocks; quality Casual couture at its finest.

Manchester based Darby talks to me about his background, his influences, and who wears a smock jacket the best:

'I started designing when I was 14 and from there, I started to teach myself to pattern cut and sew. I was working in retail, shirt makers and bespoke tailors, then when I was 30, I opened a tiny bespoke shirt shop in the Northern Quarter in Manchester where I made and designed men's shirts. I started to make more of my designs to sell as stock so moved to a bigger shop where I started to create designs for coats, jackets, shirts and my piece de resistance, the Macintosh coat.'

Darby was influenced by Casual culture, quite apparent by his designs, and due to his age/location (50 from Manchester), it would have been hard to ignore the subculture sweeping the city as a teenager.

'I used to see mobs of lads at the football and train stations when I was 12, wearing loud checked scarfs, amazing coats and stood in works of art on their feet, that is, Adidas and Nike trainers.'

Unsurprisingly for a tailor, Darby cites cutting edge design icons as his other influences aside from the Casual clobber:

'Once I found the bug for sportwear, I then discovered designer boutiques and at the age of 14, I would travel to different cities finding amazing shops stocking Yamamoto, Issey Miyake, Stone Island and

Commes des Garcons. But since the age of 14, I have really been in awe and inspired by Sir Paull Smith, the guy is amazing.'

Darby is tapping into the market of the transitioning Daduals, understanding that older, original Casuals are looking for something more than just the usual Stoney:

'My customers are a mixture of young males with a disposable income and the more mature gents wanting quality and limited edition.'

Promoting his brand through social media platforms including football fan-based pages, such as Real 80s Casuals, Clobber and Brands from the Stands, by choosing public figures who fit the criteria (Fenners, Bez, and somehow me?!), he is getting his exquisite custom-made pieces to the intended target markets and beyond. Maybe the Nouveaux will see the craftmanship and customisation and want to add a smock to their collection. Darby insists smocks are so integral to Casual clobber as they, 'look cool and keep you warm.' When asked who wears one the best, he answers diplomatically, 'Just a person who has good taste in music and clothes.'

Smocks, Parkas and capes are unmistakably Mod in background and still influence the Casual aesthetic even today. Stone Island's Autumn Winter '22/'23 presentation showed the celebration and reimagination of the 40th Anniversary _82/22 edition, a glorious reinterpretation of the '982 Tela Stella cape. Surely no Nouveaux would wear the more 'Avant Garde' new pieces and pick the easier, non-scary, safe-bet overshirt? The cape is most definitely a nod to the brand's golden age and I for one, am all for it.

Smock fan Fenners, has like me, been sent a custom-made piece from James Darby clothing as has Bez from Happy Mondays. It's an iconic bit of clobber, synonymous with the Casual subculture which is evident from the chosen few selected to promote one.

Smock horror!

Fenners:

'What I like about them, I like the sort of oversized-ness of them. I like the fact that they're really old-fashioned, just really simple. It's very hard to put your finger on why they're so... I think for middle-aged men, it covers a multitude of sins. They are quite flattering. It's all about who's making them, and the cut and things.

'I think as well, it's like if Liam's wearing something then regardless of what it is, it's going to do big numbers isn't it?'

Ah yes, we couldn't discuss smocks or indeed terraces and the future of Casual culture without mentioning perennial once more the smock/parka/Stoney wearing Liam Gallagher:

'I don't drive cars and I don't buy Rolexes, but I've got enough parkas that I could whip out and still blow people's minds.'

Part 3: The Future

Terrace Renaissance? The fate of Casual Culture

63|

The Spezial One

The parallels between Bowie's undeniable impact on the birth of the Casuals and Gallagher's staunch loyalty to the subculture even today are undeniable; even more so when you consider the iconic garment for which their inspiration and style is epitomised. The duffle coat and the smock demonstrate, arguably, in the words of Mackenzie, the 'influence of that one outfit as a medium of Casual style.'

Every modern day Nouveaux Casual wannabe trips off Liam Gallagher, and the older lot will always respect him for sticking to his football Casual roots. When lads see him wearing something, as we have already seen, it will fly off the shelf. If he does a collab with any brand, it will fly off the shelf.

Jared recalls this influence on Terraces customers, which chimes in with we know from earlier in the book:

'Liam Gallagher, he gets a jacket, people literally ring us up for the exact jacket. Fair enough, he's your idol. But you don't want to be a like a lookalike. That's the way I think things have changed. People want to copy off people, instead of coming up with their own ideas.'

Fans love to feel involved, noticed even, by their heroes. And judging by the amount of Daduals and Nouveaux wearing bucket hats at Knebworth in June of this year, his star quality in terms of Casual hero and man of the people shows no sign of abating.

Neil Summers, close friend of CP Company and Pretty Green explains:

'He's a musician. Again, it's musicians, isn't it? That's me as well, when I've been at the football matches, I'm thinking, "Most of the people here are scruffy fuckers." Whereas musicians, before the internet, people like the Gallaghers, the Roses and the Happy Mondays etc., were the people you looked to as influences.

'They're like, "Oh, my jacket is from…" It's interesting how Liam has still got that, hasn't he? If you put a jacket on Liam, it's like amazing.'

Gallagher was involved in Pretty Green, a contemporary take on the Mod/Casual style. Arguably more taken up with non-footies and Daduals than the Nouveaux, perhaps because its retro tones are subtly classic and in keeping with mod, as opposed to football hooligan, culture.

Simon Dowling was also involved in the initial set up of Pretty Green. Allegedly Liam wanted to set up his own brand with the kind of clobber he himself wore and a mutual friend got in touch with Simon, aka tailor-extraordinaire, Stone Island aficionado and just THE guy to know in terms of clobber (even letting me rummage through his archives and let me play dress up in Marina), to help advise on the label.

Simon: 'It was amazing when it first came out, there was a real buzz about it. The ethos and aesthetic were like (Nottingham based brand) One True Saxon in its quirkiness and mod-ness (unsurprising as several of the team were ex-Paul Smith). With its paisley prints, strong parka and smock silhouettes, Fred Perry style sharp polos, the brand appeared to cherry pick the best bits of the Casual and mod look.'

Pretty Green continues to be a success, its musical credentials extended through events, Q & As and exhibitions they have in-store (my brother, Tom Oxley's photography exhibition of music artists, being one of them).

Liam Gallagher is connected to another 'newer' brand that has very much been adopted by the Casuals, Adidas Spezial.

High Snobiety reports:

'Since 2015, the premium sub-line of Adidas – which is curated by Gary Aspden – has become renowned for diving into the Three Stripes' extensive archives, and reimagining heritage styles through a modern lens for each of its collections.

'For Spezial, music is paramount. Since its inception the brand has continually drawn inspiration from British music scene and the various subcultures that surround it. Whether its linkups with Liam Gallagher and New Order, or a homage to British soul and the Second Summer of Love, music remains at the brand's core.'

Fenners is close to Gary Aspden, and we discuss Spezial's place within the latest version of Casual culture, collaborations, and Gallagher's Mancunian Midas touch.

'If Liam's wearing something, then regardless of what it is, it's going to do big numbers. He's such a popular figure, he's a big style icon for so many lads of all generations. Like my generation and the younger generation coming through.'

Consumers today are savvy as fuck, so anything that Liam does with Adidas, is a perfect fit. Liam embodies it with the clothes, the attitude, that nineties zeitgeist personified. Creating a collab with Adidas Spezial x Liam Gallagher was bound to hit the D (for Dadual) spot in terms of credibility and sales. Adidas anyway is the brand that surpasses all, transcends generations and countries, the footwear of choice. It's no wonder Adidas Spezial is doing so well; add a collaboration with everyone's favourite Casual-esque rogue, then it's bound for success.

High Snobiety continues:

'Nothing quite gets an Adidas dad going like Liam Gallagher. Whether in a pub eight pints deep howling *Don't Look Back in Anger* arms aloft or wearing a knee-length parka with their hands behind their back in the middle of the summer heat, the former Oasis front man has a certain unexplainable effect on a myriad of British men in particular.'

Game, set and match made in clobber heaven for Aspden.

Fenners:

'I know Gary really well. We've got a lot in common. Our careers have gone in different paths, but we've got common values. What he's done with Spezial is, he's not just created clothes or shoes, he's created his own subculture within a subculture. And he's created events. Like the Liam thing at Blackburn.

'When there's a Spezial drop, everyone's talking about it. Everyone's excited about it. Everyone wants to see it. Everyone sees the Instagram post, with the work that's gone into it. There's nothing like it really. And to have the collaborations with Liam, you know, doing stuff with Luke Shaw at Darwen…'

In October 2021, the heart of the industrial textile industry, Darwen, Lancashire, became home to an exhibition in conjunction with CP Company and Adidas Spezial. Most of the prominent Clobberati movers and shakers attended and/or were part of it including Lorenzo Osti, Aspden, Fenners, Neil Summers, Riaz Kahn, Professor Andrew Groves, photographer Neil Bedford, head designer Paul Harvey, Aitor Throup, the Happy Mondays et al et moi!

Soccer Bible proclaims:

'Looking to celebrate the upcoming collaboration between Adidas Spezial and premium Italian Casual wear brand C.P. Company, a huge mural of England and Manchester United left back Luke Shaw has been unveiled in the small Lancashire town of Darwen.

'So, for those unaware, Darwen is the town that gave birth to professional football globally back in 1870. It also happens to be the hometown of Gary Aspden, designer and curator of Adidas Spezial. Add to that the fact that it is also the chosen location for Cinquanta, a retrospective exhibition of C.P. Company's illustrious archive as part of the British Textile Biennial, and the town becomes something of a hub for the upcoming collaboration between Adidas Spezial and the Italian label. And that's why you'll find a 40-foot-tall painting of Luke Shaw on the side of an iconic period building in its town center. Got it?'

Got it.

64|

Darwen's Theory of Evolution

We have observed the life cycles of clobber, and the natural selection for the success (or not) of Casual brands. This is the new wave. This is the first instance for many years that there seems to be a synergy with clobber, Casuals, cultural icons and future brands.

Fenners:

'I hosted the panel (at the Cinquanta retrospective in Darwen) with Lorenzo and Gary and Paul and it was really interesting because Gary asked me to do it, which I was flattered by. And it's the only time I've taken any time off work on a Friday, ahead of *Soccer AM*, to do something.'

The whole event was different; real fans interacting with the Clobberati, all up in Darwen to discuss key pieces of clobber and the timeline of a brand that has had such a monumental impact on Casual culture. We are witnessing CP almost pass the mantle on to Adidas Spezial, a brand with the same core values of quality and innovation, visionaries at the helm and are both just cool as fuck to the Casual crowd. A clobber partnership for the post-pandemic generation? And it was held in the North! Not London! Thank fuck, for once!

The choice to present this exhibition was not only an inspired choice to show in Darwen, but it was also the only choice. Aspden is from Darwen, the centre of the UK's textile heartlands, and has a strong football heritage. The North West is a stronghold for football culture, it is where (arguably depending on if you are North or South) Casual culture first appeared and still thrives.

The same goes for former industrial Pottery manufacturing city, Stoke-on-Trent. We have been economically and politically abandoned since the whole process moved overseas. A few strong Pottery brands remain; Steelite, Churchill, Wedgewood, Burleigh... but there remain too many ghostly kiln shadows across the empty city landscape. There is nothing here, apart from a fading football Casual culture. As Jarvis Cocker sings in *Common People*:

'And you dance and drink and screw, because there's nothing else to do.'

The irony of showcasing one of the world's most stylish sport-luxe designer brands in the Grim up North is not lost on us. CP Company head designer Paul Harvey said in an interview for Sevenstore:

'The idea of this company that comes from Bologna, a very exotic and beautiful city in Italy and the way it clashes with this world in Darwen, is I think incredibly interesting. It's something incredibly risky, I mean, I don't think that many brands would do it, but I think it's been a brilliant idea.'

Brilliant, and extremely successful. To see so many CP Company fans loyally turn out at Darwen, all wearing their favourite pieces, old and new, is testament to the power of the brand. Photographer Neil Bedford was on hand, shooting the 'real folk' whose images were used in campaigns and as part of the exhibition itself. This bottom up, inclusive approach is what CP does best; not turning their back on anyone who is a fan, instead wanting anyone and everyone to adopt the label in their own individualistic way.

Lorenzo adds, building on something he said earlier in the book: 'The CP Company book...Neil made very nice portraits and as you see in the book, these people have an attitude, they have charisma, but they are not models. We want first of all to personalise. I mean, we have a connection to the people, we want to have this connection and then we want to have regular people. We don't want to have models. The same way we did the book and Neil was shooting the people passing by, we will do the campaign for the next seasons, so it'll be just regular people. Authentic people in love with the brand.'

These regular people are disciples practising at the Church of CP Company where Massimo Osti has an absolute God-like status, something that is not so much felt in Italy itself but Casual strongholds such as the UK and the Netherlands.

'Lorenzo confessed that it was only relatively recently he realised the almost fanatical adulteration that Northern men had for his father, Massimo Osti and C.P. Company. Indeed, this obsessiveness was on display at last Thursday's private view, with as many grails on display on the men attending the event as in the actual exhibition,' Sevenstore writes.

Lorenzo and I also had a confessional, him telling me the revelation he had in realising how devout the CP disciples are:

'We are very surprised, because believe me in Italy, nobody outside the industry knows our family, so, it's not popular at all. But then I realised there is a lot of love and affection to my father and his friends, and I start chatting with these guys, lovely people. I first came to the North three years ago to see Gary Aspden, and I mean it was weird, I was treated like a superstar!'

Who would have thought a label with such Italian panache would become such a constant and resolute part of British Casuals' clobber collections to wear on cold, grizzly match days. Or as Fenners puts it:

'I don't think Massimo Osti was sitting there going, "Right, I'm going to make a jacket for people to go and wear at the Britannia stadium of a Tuesday night." I don't think that was the intention, it's just the way that things have been adopted.'

It's how nature intended. The evolution of clobber continues.

65|

Mama Miglia: Going Back to My Roots

It is testimony to the big Casual labels that their brand equity has never crashed despite the consensus that they have sadly been diluted. The love-in for the big two just never diminishes; no matter how much the elders perhaps want it to, the brands just mean too much to them. It's part of them, and because of this, they will always have a longevity in the market and a place in the Casuals' heart:

'It's always Stonie, because I've got a big heart for Stonie. CP is losing its way a little bit, but I still love CP, Belstaff. I tend to like brands that have got a big history. So yes, they are probably my favourite three,' explains Jared Latimer from Terraces.

Heritage brand Belstaff is definitely a fave of other original Casuals with Paul Walters and the Shelton Casual both wearing it today, with the latter explaining it's 'a lovely make'.

Jay Montessori agrees:

'Belstaff is class and not over worn by the masses (plus originally from Stoke but now owned by Italians). Vintage Stone Island still takes some beating and worn with a bit of style separates you from the click Casuals that have took the shine off for men ... same applies for CP Company.'

Riaz Kahn:

'The only problem with the culture is the 'clone' every bleeder dress very similar! So, there are labels out there that the young 'uns haven't caught wind of like Hawkwood Mercantile, Uniform Bridge, Adidas Spezial etc. CP will definitely stand the test of time, and Stone Island. I try to wear Ghost or Shadow. Even I go for the vintage stuff. Both labels have been strong since the mid-eighties and seem not to waver. More collaborations and an injection of new designers have kept both labels strong. I believe it will continue for many years. As for future classics? Any Stone Island Tela Stella or CP Mille Miglia will be future classics along with some of the collabs that have appeared; CP x Adidas Spezial and CP x Barbour for example.'

David Elders:

'Without any doubt the two brands that have had their 'specialness' diluted the most would be Stone Island and CP Company. Ironically though, these are still the two brands which continue to come out with some of the best, most original pieces to this day. It's about seeing past the stuff which is squarely aimed at the Instagram massive out there and finding those pieces that are original.'

Elders also believes that the brands that do end up being future classics are:

'The ones who maintain originality and quality and steer clear of sacrificing those for bulk-shifting are the ones that will stick around...Some 'sell out' and start lowering quality to maximise profit, some go for the lowest common denominator in their designs-sacrificing exclusivity, some give crap customer service. All of these are nails in the coffin.'

Disagreeing, Matt Snell says:

'I wouldn't say brands have been diluted. More that they have advanced and gone where the money is. Which is understandable as they are running a business. The advances in technology in garments and the colours used are to cater to a different and a wider audience. I feel some have stayed closer to their roots more than others. CP have smashed it in the last two years, and I've started to prefer what they are coming up with than Stone Island. The price point is much more realistic too. The prices these days are alienating a lot of the people that were loyal to the brands ten/fifteen years ago.'

In these post-Covid, fuel-mongering days, there is a palpable, heavy concern in the air about how we will survive the absolute piss-take in the price hike of absolutely everything. If we can't even fill our cars with petrol, or must choose between heating or eating, how the fuck can we explain spunking money on frivolities such as high-end clothes?

66|

Casual-Lites; the Age of Jacomo & the New Alternatives

This is where the 'cheaper' Casual brand alternatives will really come into their own, brands such as Peaceful Hooligan, Weekend Offender, Terrace Cult, Marshall Artist; these Casual-lite brands for a fraction of the cost are becoming increasingly popular with the European Ultras and UK Nouveaux, playing their part in 'modern Casual trends', says Paul Smith.

Local store Terraces also stocks these brands with Jared Latimer saying:

'They're really good sellers, maybe it is the price point and a cheaper entrance into the Casual life.'

Matt Banks adds: 'Yeah, we do really well with Weekend Offender, Peaceful Hooligan, Napapijri, MA. Strum, Lacoste and Barbour online.'

There has even been schooligans posting pictures on #Get the Badge In, not with Stone Island, but Marshall Artist and Weekend Offender, proof that the younger generation perceive these as 'Casual' whereas the older ones do not.

Followers of Casual Client Clothing and Matt himself were asked their thoughts on these brands, along with Peaceful Hooligan:

'I have started to buy more Marshall Artist recently. Their overshirt quality is bang on at a third of the price of a top brand.' Matt Snell, Casual Client Clothing.

'I have all, but Marshall Artist's softshell jackets are just quality.' (@alfie_rattigan).

'Bovva says it's a cool brand.' (@nomoreheroes3).

'Close to working class.' (@dynamoCasuals_).

'Not too bad for price.' (@simonmckenzie).

'Got value for money and like the style of their stuff.' (@therealtommyegan).

'Smart jackets, affordable pricing.' (@andymc_1).

'They actually cater for people who prefer food to exercise.' (anonymous).

A mixed bag of public opinion then, but speaking of bigger gentleman, this is an interesting point as the average Joe is not necessarily always going to fit into the typically smaller Italian sizing.

But who cares when we've got Jacamo!!

More of my Casual heart sank on seeing that Napapijri was stocked by those Jacamo fucks. I mean, they can keep their Lyle and Scott, and Firetrap, but Clarks?! Berghaus?!! Noooooooo! There is a plethora of middle of the road, mediocre brands for middle aged guys who do it missionary. Along with Jacamo, who as an almost online catalogue cater for the normal guy (wears bootcut jeans and black pointy shoes whilst out/watching rugby but wants to go 'Casual' when he's been invited to hospitality at the Etihad), there are labels like Jack Jones and Superdry, the messieurs James Blunt and David Gray of the clothing world. How do these brands have such omnipresent, massive high street stores? Who buys this Newquay-teenager-getting-leathered chic? The mind boggles.

And then to add to the confusion of what is/is not Casual and furthermore what is allowed to be assumed of as Casual, are the newer kids on the block; Canada Goose, Moose Knuckles, Palm AJack1t and Trench. These newer brands may look the part, they may have glossy displays in Selfridges and slick TikTok ad campaigns, but would you feel comfortable wearing any of these brands? With no real story, no background, no heritage, just appearing from nowhere? Are these types of labels wannabee pretenders to the Casual throne? Perhaps their social media strategy will pay off and they will infiltrate the heart of the Casuals?

Director at Marshall Artist, Ed Quiligotti discusses his thoughts on the modern Casual crossbreeding of brands and our new intrepid visionaries of the gleaming Casual-lite urban look spearheaded by the North West:

'The attitude towards 'Casual' or 'Scally' in cities like Liverpool and Manchester for example has always been progressive and looking to add to the culture rather than just copy what's gone before. Both cities have long embraced the outdoor look which has diluted into the scene over the years, brands such as North Face, Berghaus, Mountain Equipment, Patagonia & Rab, alongside the more progressive sport brands such as ON Running, Under Armour & Nike.

'The scene within these cities is much more diluted due to the amount of lads attaching themselves to the scene for a variety of reasons. While Stone Island/CP remain the go to labels that have stood the test of time they are regularly paired nowadays with brands such as Valentino, Canada Goose, Moncler, Dsquared. Prada, Para Jumpers etc.... Think Flannels and shiny and that will give a closer representation of Liverpool and Manchester. There are a lot of lads who still embrace the original look but it wouldn't be the dominate look you see at Old Trafford or Anfield.'

Riaz Kahn adds:

'The younger generation try (to be Casual) but you'll see the odd Nike trainer or Yeezy trainer slipping in every now and then along with that bollocks label Balenciaga. I have seen young lads wear Alexander McQueen T-shirts under a CP jacket.'

All you need next is hair transplants and veneers from Turkey to accessorise this look which is pretty much typical and ubiquitous of many young lads today.

67|

Made In Italy; The Italian Job

Neil Primett and his team at 80s Casuals Classics have done an amazing in job in putting some iconic Casual brands back into the public domain.

The relaunch of Patrick was extremely successful and there appears to be this continued love in for a revamped Italo-classico brand, as Neil says:

'New doors to heritage revivals constantly come our way and customer support is overwhelming.'

As well as old skool brands such as Lois, Ellesse and Tacchini, there have been relaunches of Pouchain and Left Hand and ST-95.

Speaking with Pouchain's Mario, I have started to develop a crush on the label, and not because they sent me a mint trackie ☺. I like the fact that it's an older Italian sports label that has not been thrapped by the masses. It's cool, under the radar and definitely one for the daduals to adopt.

Me: 'What spurred on the relaunch of Pouchain?'

Mario: 'Since the 1980's a lot of sport brands disappeared. Only Adidas, Puma and Nike survived. Nowadays, people embrace old sport brands again. Mostly the brands with a great heritage. That is why Italian brands like Fila, Ellesse, Tacchini and Australian were relaunched.

Our fans are mostly men between the age of 35-44. We think online communities are the most important channel to inform consumers about the brand, heritage and collections; and as mentioned before, smaller sports brands with a great history are being successfully relaunched.'

Mario believes the resurgence of Casual brands is due to certain trends; the Against Modern Football movement, sportswear finding its way to streetwear and a growing interest for uniqueness and personal expression. Pouchain realise the older Casuals are part of their target audiences, explaining their ideal customers are:

'People interested in the combination of athletic lifestyles with more classic styling who seek to distinguish themselves with distinctive, functional products.'

This trend of the gents of the Casual scene turning towards the more distinguished of labels, the practical labels combined with a swish aesthetic, and not so much the obvious brands that have been clobbered to death, has seen the increase of relaunches of old favourites and other brands that never quite made it massively mainstream. Such examples would surely include Left Hand and ST-95 which were originally founded by Our Father, Massimo Osti and fit the brief for the future of Casual clobber?

'On a gathering storm comes a tall handsome man in a dusty black coat with a red LEFT HAND.'

Left Hand and ST95 are from the hallowed roster of Osti brands so naturally come with pre-ordained credibility. Started as side projects to experiment even further than the innovative garment-dyeing techniques he became so synonymous for, Osti's Left Hand label today states:

'Left Hand's first 1993 collection debuted two new materials, the first was Micro, a nylon that was produced by using an advanced pressing technique traditionally used in paper manufacturing. It resulted in a thin microfibre layer that maintained breathability and durability despite being paper-thin.

'The second material was Thermojoint, a lightweight cotton with a PVC base that resulted in a highly durable, 100% waterproof and nuclear radiation-resistant material. Osti's developments around this time transcended the sportswear ideas he set out with and brought the idea of clothing as protection to the forefront.'

So far, so Stoney, so CP, so Osti.

The most iconic piece in that of Left Hand is the Thermojoint, but what has happened to a brand with such promise and allure? Does anyone wear it and if not, why not? What's the story?

Oliver Beer gives me the low down:

'I had a few bits of Left Hand stuff over the years, cracking quality. I haven't seen any of the new stuff in the flesh apart from a few things online but nothing has really caught my eye! I have a BNV jacket from the last release and it is really good, but it seems like sales were low on the relaunch.

'I think if you are going to re-release an old brand you should do it justice by having it made in Italy and use quality fabrics and not just release second rate items. Most younger people will never have heard of BNV (Bonneville), Left Hand or ST95. In my opinion most of it should have been left in the past!'

It would have been great to hear from the brand itself about their reasons to relaunch. Appointing a forward-thinking, award-winning designer, Christopher Raeburn demonstrates the aim to progress the brand.

The official blurb:

'In 2020 Left Hand was acquired by Left Hand Studio Limited, along with another of Osti's original brands, ST95. Left Hand has been re-launched in 2022 with a collection under the creative helm of

Christopher Raeburn and his award-winning RAEBURN Lab in East London.

'Raeburn is renowned for his forward-thinking and sustainable approach to fashion, making him the perfect designer for the baton to be passed on to, continuing the late designer's interests in military technology, aesthetics, and experimental fabrics.

'Left Hand's new beginnings will see the brand continue to produce understated and design-focused pieces of outerwear and apparel that subvert outrageous branding and allow the strengths of good design, the use of sustainable fabrics and manufacturing processes to speak for themselves.'

'Made in Italy' himself Jay Montessori (😊) gives me his authoritative take on the Italian job:

'Early 90s, Osti sold his share in Stone Island and started his own brands which were Massimo Osti Production and ST95. It's a common misconception that Left Hand was a brand as such, it was an experiment, a collaboration between Osti and the renowned outdoor coat makers, Allegri. In my opinion, an absolute thing of beauty well ahead of its time. If you actually look into it the fabrics, they were all kinds of madness like radiation proof...just really typically deep military Osti, and absolutely beautiful. But more than anything, I used to love the advertising. If you look at old Arena mags and stuff like that, The Face, the adverts were always absolutely beautiful. I hold it right up there in high regard.

'ST95 in a nutshell, I thought it was shite, to be honest, I just thought it was much more downmarket, it aimed to be younger, bit more affordable, was in places like Scotts. Just didn't work for me.

'Production, I thought production was nice if not a little bland compared to Left Hand. Put a Left Hand jacket next to a Production, and I've got a few of both in my collection, the Left Hand wins hands down. But Production was nice and always loved the little M badge, Massimo Osti badge, again one of the best badges I've ever seen.'

So why aren't these labels really mentioned in the Casual connoisseurs' arsenal of clobber? Is it, as Oliver Beer describes, that you shouldn't just release something for the sake of it? Or as Jay says that it's just not up there in terms of beauty anymore? Perhaps it's because Left Hand and ST95 have been snaffled up into the Scotts/Tessuti stable of used-to-be-decent brands and now that Mike Ashley by affiliation with stakes in everything, has got his grubby, greedy mitts into the brand, they've gone tits up in terms of being Casually adored? And as a result, the quality isn't matched as when it was Made in Italy?

Brands such as Twelfth Man, Mandarina Duck, Namen along with early CP, Left Hand et al, all had that Italian simplistic yet stylish aesthetic; clean, minimal, innovative and top-notch quality no doubt from being manufactured in Italy itself. Geopolitical influences ought not be overlooked; it has an impact on the design, the designers, and the brand itself.

Alessandro Deserti writes:

'In many cases, Italian brands display a strong connection between their identity and the tangible nature of their offering, which is qualified by craftsmen's skills and/or by industrial capacities in an intricate system that is at the base of their brand equity. In some of these brands, the very stylistic codes are built over these capacities, and are so attached to them to become linguistic elements that make the brands recognisable and appreciable at a worldwide level.'

Barile agrees:

'Being Made in Italy is a potential booster of international success, and despite the risk of flattening complex identities over a stereotype the majority of Italian brands are somehow exploiting it, as a meta-brand attributing intangible values to specific local productions.'

Credibility is automatically, and correctly, assumed with the 'Made in Italy' insignia, and furthermore, as our Casual brands are often crafted in Bologna, a notoriously industrial and left-wing city with a strong student presence, does this have a lasting affect and the reason they are so damn good in design and technique?!

Speaking with Fabio at Plurimus HQ in Bologna, he tells me:

'Bologna has aways been very left-wing since World War 2. But this does not have any impact on my designs, to be honest. They are very military inspired so you could say they are not 'left-wing' – Massimo Osti was very left-wing and he still drew a lot of inspiration from the army world. I believe that, at the end of the day, no matter your political views, men like to look good and after all, the styles we use in everyday life are all very much influenced by the army world: Parkas, Anoraks, Bombers etc.'.

The dichotomy between Osti's left-wing background and militia designs becomes more striking throughout my research. Lorenzo talks to me about his father's hippy student background, prevalent in Bologna in the seventies:

'In the seventies, there was a big opposition between the young, the fathers and sons, or parents and sons and there had been the '68 hippy culture. All this generation was really heavily against the previous one or trying to flip the status quo. What my father did with CP Company actually was very similar within his field. So, what he did, he took the garment of that time, more like the garment of the parents in a way, and that garment was particularly stiff.

'Stiff in two different ways. One, from I mean a fabric perspective like a stiff new looking coat. And that was the value, when a family saved money to buy a new coat, you want the new coat to look new. You want people to see it was new. All the fabrics were like this, you know, an out of the box effect.

'What my father does, he says, "I hate that, I want garments that look old!" so, he started to garment dye everything and it was very unusual because people went into a nice shop, a coat was about 700/1000 euros, and it looks old! At that time nobody was doing that. Now it's pretty common, we have all the vintage, fascination of the vintage and old things, but at that time was weird.'

Throughout the interview, left-wing politics underpins the explanations of much of CP's background; when Lorenzo uses 'left-handed' it could be interpreted as left-wing, therefore the region's political environment and own familial allegiance perhaps has a bearing not just on design, but on the brand 'Left Hand's' own identity. These left-wing, rebellious beliefs had quite an impact on design, subverting the upper classes notion of the portrayal of wealth, and bringing exquisite craftmanship to the cool kids, which would then be adopted by the Casuals, and later the mainstream masses:

'When my father started CP before Stone Island, I mean, the kind of man (customer) he had in mind was very different; sophisticated, intellectual, left-handed. Very close to the kind of people he was hanging out with. So, the cultural scene, the political scene in Bologna, someone who could really appreciate the products, the people with knowledge. And that's what happened. They picked it up but then the big boom came from the Paninaro.'

A letter written by Osti (released by authors Tony Rivers and James Burnett behind the upcoming *Magnetic* book) discusses Osti's forthcoming launch of Left Hand. He describes the origin of the name simply: 'To those who ask me the reason for this name, my answer is that I am in fact left-handed'.

68|

Ol' Money, Mo Problems

Category is Old Money Realness! Much like the drag queens in ballroom competitions of yesteryear, Gen-Z are being inspired by an 'old money' aesthetic and plastering it all over my favourite place, TikTok. The channel, I hate; the concept, I approve. What's not to love about aspirational dressing and nicking high-end brands to make your own?! A clear parallel between the origins of Casual dressers and the WASP look, the young 'uns are clearly tripping over looking like posh old dears in pearls or Polos, evident with a gazillion views of #OldMoneyAesthetic on the social media site.

American kids are swooning over the clean-cut all-American preppy visual; think Ralph Lauren on a Kennedy. Then cue the Italians with typical flair, as described by *NSS Magazine*:

'In Italy, the trend comes to life thanks to old photos of mansions on Lake Como, castles once inhabited, and through a dress code made of white Ralph Lauren shirts, Loro Piana pullovers, Patek Philippe watches, loafers and logoed belts.'

Mwah!

Paninaro for the new millennium? With strong sporting references including yachting, skiing and tennis, and a desire to look as pristinely rich as the luxury brands acquired, the similarities between the louche, slouchy, Paninaro and this newer wave of Gen-Z, are uncanny.

It must be quite a moral dilemma for our delicate, woke, post-millennial flowers, however. Here they are wanting to look like part of the Agnelli family, or portray that they went to an Ivy League school, or that they study History of Art at Edinburgh in headbands and cardies. Yet this controversially draws inspiration from what is basically 'white privilege' and being part of the (typical old white and male) political elite, which totally conflicts with their inclusive ethics. As they would say, 'the struggle is real'. Like, literally.

Our beloved Casuals aren't bothered by such annoyances and distractions, are they? Nah. Couldn't give a fuck. And wha?

69|

Casual Core

Old Money Core is a thing. All things with the suffix 'core' are now a thing. Very millennial, very TikTok, very lazy. Adding 'core' simply translates to a minor fashion trend the TikTokers all jump over. Barbie Core. Ballet Core. Casual Core?

No such 'core' for the Casuals currently, thank fuck. But there is such a thing as 'Gorpcore'.

'Gorpcore takes its name from the phrase from the staple food source for hikers around the globe: Good Ol' Raisons and Peanuts. This hiking and mountainwear aesthetic have been gathering momentum in recent years; North Face, Patagonia, Hoka One One and On Running adopted by fashion insiders,' High Snobiety writes.

Thinking of Neil Summers as soon as I heard of this particular 'core', I immediately invited him for comment:

'Raisons LOL!!' he says.

In the same article, genuine hikers, you know, people who actually like being outside, were asked what they thought on city folk wearing the same labels and starting to encroach on their territory. No 'bitch stole my look!' from Tom, a 60-year-old walker. In his response, he was more wistful:

'I wish they wouldn't.'

His wife Barbara then adding pragmatically when asked about the new urban influx:

'We went up Snowdon when there was loads of snow and there were people going up in trainers. Somebody slipped off and died, because they just don't have any respect for…'

For what? For hiking? For outdoor brands? This is what happens if you wear snazzy, too cool for school outdoor fashion – all the gear, no idea. As Babs says, it's dangerous; you fall off Snowdon, you die.

City dwellers wearing Patagonia to hike to the tube or salivating over North Face x Gucci tents that will never get used already tolls the death knell for Gorpcore.

Patagonia owner Yvon Chouinard pretty much gave his company away earlier in 2022. A favourite of Daduals and a Gorpcore stalwart, this eco-hippy-esque decision will only favour the brand to the Gen-Zs and increase the equity of the brand, old and new. Vintage Patagonia is now becoming extremely sought after; on the day the company 'sale' was announced, vintage site supreme Too Hot limited, presented their full Patagonia archives to much acclaim.

'Billionaire founder of outdoor clothing company Patagonia has given the company away!' shrieked Unilad in September 2022. Clarifying, Patagonia themselves said:

'Instead of "going public", you could say we're "going purpose". Instead of extracting value from nature and transforming it into wealth for investors, we'll use the wealth Patagonia creates to protect the source of all wealth.'

This act of anti-corporate, anti-greed, anti-bank was met with huge praise from social commentators who observed this as an act of rebellion to highlight climate change, sustainability and the condemnation of war:

'Incredible. The founder of Patagonia, Yvon Chouinard, has given away his company and will donate all of Patagonia's profits to fight climate change. Patagonia also sanctioned Russia very early on in the war – and closed their Russian stores to help Ukraine. Thank you, Patagonia.'

The brand with a conscience now to be hijacked by sustainable-loving Millennials and City Slickers falling off mountains.

I feel your pain, Tom ☹.

70|

Independent Day

Catering for the modern-day Casual is no mean feat. Aside from the recent crippling factors of Brexit, Covid, the Ukraine war and the circus that is politics today, they all add up to create a ripple effect of tough economic circumstances. Hard enough as a global brand but even tougher for the smaller independent brands. And even if the brand becomes a success, how will they maintain longevity and brand loyalty in the consumer world today?

I spoke with Steve Lumb, owner of Terrace Cult; we discussed at length his background, his hopes and dreams for the brand's future, and the critical understanding of how to foster brand loyalty today:

'That's why you don't really see up and coming brands last a great deal of time because no one has loyalty to them, they think they've got to build it. With us, with Terrace Cult, we knew, that no one's just gonna walk in a shop and demand our stuff. A) it's got to be quality, b) it's got to be affordable and stand out from the rest, and c) we've got to do things online now and stuff that attracts people to us and make them have a sense of belonging.'

Brand loyalty can be earned as we know through the personal touches, the little details, the attention and care taken towards the customers. Steve gets this:

'We try to include all our customers, our influencers in anything and everything we do. We take feedback off them which is important.

If you sent an email to Stone Island that said, "I don't really like this zip, can you change it," you're not going to get anything. But with us, we take it on board and when we have a meeting, we'll say, "What do you reckon about this zip?" you know. There's things we've nearly brought to market, and then we've put on a poll on our website.'

This inclusion, this total transparency and welcoming manner absolutely helps build brand loyalty. Another savvy strategy is to not only use influencers, but also key Casual film icons to help promote the brand. In the same vein as Weekend Offender's choice to integrate *Green Street's* Leo Gregory into campaigns and collaborations (which was also a happy coincidence due to organic personal relationships), Terrace Cult have used Zeber-fuckin-dee from *Football Factory*, aka Roland Manookian, as their brand ambassador.

Steve: 'Zeberdee's never been used before, you know, no one has ever seen Roland Manookian as Zeberdee, they've seen him as Craig Rolfe in the *Footsoldier* films. So, we used him as Zeberdee and we got great feedback of it, he was good for us, the brand. We used him, and we did it in a nice way, we didn't overkill him and ruin Zeberdee, we just used him nice. There are brands out there milking it to death. We won't go into that, that's not my way, you know what I mean. I think people see through it. And I think people think, bleeding hell, I'm sick of seeing you.'

Similarly to CP Company, Terrace Cult aren't afraid to use 'unmodel' types in campaigns, often asking local fans to turn up as extras in any filmed campaigns. I mention this comparison of using real, genuine fans of the brand to Steve:

'We're in a totally different market. We've got to try and get there. And I'm not saying we're gonna be on the level of CP, but if I didn't sit here now and think that's what I aspire to, I'd be doing my brand and the people who work for me an injustice, because I'm driving this brand to the very top, and we're trying to get there by being real, and being affordable, being loyal to the Casual scene.

'We're a British brand. We're owned by Casuals, we're lads that have been there and done it, we can associate ourselves with the customer, our target customer. And you know, back British, back a local brand, you know what I mean? Back us, you know, cos we're trying our best. We're trying to do something. We've come out of our comfort zone. We've all had normal jobs doing something we've never done. We're taking our time and we've turned down big offers for stakes in the brand, we've turned down stores, big stores that wanted it, we just didn't feel we were right for it yet and we're happy building how we're building now.'

Clocking onto the economic concerns and trends of consumers, Steve can position his brand as a high-quality alternative to the bigger labels:

'With our brand, we're trying to keep it real. We try our best, sourcing the best materials all the time. We're now bringing some real quality stuff out at the right money. We try to make it affordable. I could put a Terrace Cult coat out there for £500 but I'd just be ripping people off. So, we're trying to be loyal to the movement, we're trying to bring something affordable to the market, we're trying to bring bigger sizes to the market. We're trying to cater for the modern day Casual.'

Describe this modern-day Casual?

Steve:

'Somebody who likes to wear clobber, might be on the larger size – we are all growing, and drinking! We've got fiercely loyal fans of Terrace Cult who will put us up against anyone, and we've also got people who look down on the brand going, "oh yeah you think you're Stone Island…" We don't think we're nothing. But all I think is the quality of our clothes is quality, the price point is on point, and we're having a go. That is all it is. We're having a go. We're the underdog in the Casual clothing market, and always beware of the underdog.'

Terrace Cult, Plurimus, Original Casuals and Transalpino. These fiercely independent brands are continuing to put two fingers up to the corporate world of retail and consumerism, which has been a pleasing feature throughout this book. They are all doing things their way for their much-valued customer with whom they have personal and direct contact with.

Beware indeed.

71|
This Thing of Ours

So, here we are. We are coming to the end of the book after galivanting all over the show in the name of all things Casual and clobber. But we still need to find the answer, the crux of the book, the whole point of the research, the $64,000 question: why do we still dress in terrace clobber if there's apparently no terrace culture anymore?

Why??

If the Casuals are the proverbial peacocks, historically prancing and preening at the match, and they no longer go to the match, or because match days are less naughty, is the whole thing redundant? What's the point if there's no audience? Matchday would be a fashion show, but if there aren't any attendees, why bother?

Fashion and trends ebb and flow, easy come, easy go. We have heard first hand from Casuals, commentators and collectors, that terrace culture does not exist as it did in the golden era of the eighties and nineties, but there is still something intrinsically there that pulls them into retaining their style and the fashion affiliated with the football Casual culture. A fire that will never die, this thing of ours is just that. It's ours. And we want to show its ours by the clobber we wear. No days off, you're either Casual or you're not. You've either got it or you don't.

The coolness of Casuals is contagious, and if you haven't got it by now, you'll never get it. Everyone wants to be Casual. The originals love it, the Nouveaux love, it, every fucker loves it. But you can't just be Casual. Stay fucking Casual and if you don't know how, you're not!

Terrace fashion has become globally adored, universally copied and mainstream as fuck. But the legend of Casual culture lives on in memory and sartorial practice.

As of Friday 5th November 2022, whilst concluding this book, Dave Hewitson from 80s Casuals has co-created the first exhibition on this: 'The Art of the Terraces', which was held at the Walker Gallery in Liverpool, and it celebrated all aspects of this subculture and featuring many of the Clobberati's own collections and contributions. The exhibition is a long time coming but is testament to the absolute cultural power the Casuals have had on our society with influences still being felt today.

Terrace culture may have died, the world perhaps has lost its soul, but we just want to hold on as tightly as possible to the good 'ol days, less red tape, no political correctness, just freedom, fun, friendships, fashion, football.

Why do we still consume Casual brands?

Fenners: 'I know a lot about clothes, it's always been a passion, it's becoming more of an obsession now. But what you find is, there's a lot of old-school people who love brands. They love the brands, and they sort of support them, passionate about them, like a football team. It's like you don't go away. And they see themselves as the gatekeepers of the brands.'

Oliver Beer: 'The reason why I dress, when I go out, I want to look nice, and someone gives you a compliment, it's ace. It makes you feel good, you want the feel-good factor. It takes away from your humdrum life.'

Simon Dowling: 'Everything has become so diluted, I used to go to get inspired at the football, but it doesn't happen anymore. It's nothingness. On the pitch it's so shit, we need some excitement instead of forcing the issue, let's be a Casual. It's a bit manufactured...bashed up sniff, Stone Island, generic football culture. But! When you grow up, it's something you can never drop, it will always be in your blood. The music, the fashion, it will always be there.'

Paul Smith: 'Casual culture will never die, NEVER!! It's just too good to ignore. The Casual lifestyle just has an edge to it that makes you wanna be involved. It's cool as fuck, sometimes naughty and always a laugh, and the clobber is to die for!'

David Elders: 'It's not so much now whether the stuff I wear is seen as terrace brands or not, more just if it looks the part or not and if it's a little different to what everyone else is wearing.'

Giovanni Calandras: 'It's in my DNA and forever will be. I got inspiration from tailoring as my father worked in a gent's tailors from the late fifties to early nineties. In my opinion, a football Casual should be celebrated more than just for the obvious wearing brands that have been catapulted into premium brands status.'

Matt Snell: 'I will always buy these brands. And the affiliated brands with the culture. Looks better than a pair of Nikes and an oversized hoodie. I'm 33 now and the clothing looks good for any age. Plus, none of it goes out of fashion, I still have stuff I first bought and cannot part with it. Buy cheap, buy twice.'

Jared Latimer: 'I think there are a lot of people who are into brands who have actually got no clue about the football side of things. But there are lads who are into the football side of things, where it is a uniform. It's important for their culture, their whole weekend lifestyle.'

Steve Lumb: 'I think we're at the forefront (of the spread of Casual culture), and anything we bring out here will spread eventually. I just think we've got to keep it fresh. I'd love one of these brands to come out and do a big campaign and put all the hooligans and the Casuals in.'

Davy Pennings (Terrace Cult Nederland): 'My love has grown for it over the years, it's an expensive hobby but you love it, and I love to go out well dressed and to this day I still buy (the brands). Who doesn't want to be Casual these days?!'

Casual Ultra: 'I think people want to feel part of something and that's why the terrace culture will always be supported. Why do I still wear the brands? Well, that's because I like the style. Wearing some Adidas trainers, Stone Island jeans, MA. Strum sweatshirt and a CP Company goggle jacket. Still my favourite style!'

Derek Diablo: 'There isn't a better subculture to be part of as I see it. Casuals' style is unique in that it simultaneously stands out if you know what you're looking at but isn't as definable. There is the old Casuals adage which states that "it isn't what you wear, it's how you wear it". Our footy scene is growing. Soccer is becoming more and more popular every season, it's not where it needs to be but is growing and eating into the market share of the other American major sports. With international Football/Soccer, you have the traditions of Terrace Culture that are unique to it. The Casuals are a special, elite even part of that equation and no other sport has anything comparable within its culture.'

Kyle Dixon, Archivio Clothing: 'Terrace culture will always be here as places like Asia try and replicate it, its seen as something to aspire to. The fashion, the music, the drugs, the lifestyle, the character and the family you make along the way, there's so much to be said about it.'

Ed Quiligotti: 'A lot of brands that found themselves inadvertently involved in the Casual movement over the years have learnt how to market it to the masses of ordinary match going fans, this has allowed the look to take on a more commercial approach widening their reach. There are also retail stores such as Terraces, 80s & Scotts that have not only kept the culture alive but introduced it to a wider more commercial audience.'

Neil Primett: 'I think the more premium brands have moved into a sector not necessarily seen as football fashion. The heritage revival resonates from much more than just football culture, music resonates as much if not more. Obviously, the passion started in the eighties but ever since music has brought back retro style with the Manchester scene. Brit Pop nineties nostalgia is often more linked to music evoking memories. Heritage (brands) evoke the feel-good feelings for the older generation and is embraced by a new younger generation who it seems are educated enough to identify what it all meant versus today's somewhat fake world.'

Matt Banks: 'The scene won't die out in my opinion. I see kids at the football with more expensive jackets than their dads nowadays, much different than in the eighties-noughties. We took inspiration from fashion from Europe and created our own unique Casual uniform. There's a massive link with British football and terrace wear style. The culture is still strong, people want to look their best wearing designer labels whether you're off to the football, going to a gig, or a night out on the town, I'm confident this culture isn't going anywhere. We take influences from musicians we see on TV, on the terraces, or see on social media, and then add that to our own Casual identity.'

This subculture has impeccable taste, but in whose eyes. Beauty is in the eye of the beholder so it's all about personal perspective; however, I'm the author and the Casual style is second to none.

And wha?!

And it's not just me who thinks this. I asked the (h)oi polloi on my insta – generally made up of 'lads' – and asked them the key question: why do we still wear terrace fashion and Casual brands if there's no terrace or, arguably, football culture anymore. The response was rousing and backs up what I believe strongly myself. It is and always will be this thing of ours.

'Because it's to keep the history of the terraces alive. It's a way of life wearing Stone Island, Lacoste, Aquascutum. People go mad for Gucci, Versace, Prada and all that bollocks. We have the Casuals look...' @sheffufc1520.

'You are what you wear. All my clothes have and serve a reputation.' @martynhyde1967.

'Because for some of us of a certain age it's indoctrinated into us for over 30 years. And we'll never be seen dead in mainstream gear. They'll bury us in Italian terrace wear. It's our personality. Our choice. Our life.' @martin_kimberley1966.

'It's all to do with identity and still feeling part of something you grow up with. Casual brands are the only constant in life as you get older.' @leonard15shaun.

'Old habits die hard.' @burty2603.

'I think we/ myself, a 48-year-old male who started wearing Stone Island, Armani etc when I was about fourteen/fifteen, then it became an addiction, a lifestyle as I still wear it now.' @glennsmith1974.

'Why do people still wear Casual clothes? I think its that it reminds them of a culture and a time where they felt they belonged to. I'd say it's similar to the reason why the Mods still dress in that style, as that's where they felt they belonged, and to identify themselves as part of something.' @jplinc82.

'If you grow up with very little, it was aspirational, a culture of standing out, yet belonging. My memories are of laughs and friendships; the football, the clothes, the fights, the drugs, the music. I guess now I have money, I buy a little of those memories, each time I buy.' @nickcameron74.

Just like video killed the radio star, CCTV killed the Casuals, and then with Covid being the sartorial cock block, the weakened subculture was almost finished off by the pandemic. And Drake. But, as we know, everything goes full circle and it was inevitable that terrace culture, with a smattering of football violence and the strength and longevity of Casual brands, along with a heritage revival of terrace fashion, would remain strong. Get that fucking badge in.

As Fabio Cavina says, you can't recreate the same magic, but we're sure as fuck going to have a good time trying. We wear Casual brands because we are Casual! We still want to be affiliated with a subculture that is ingrained in our sense of self, to conspicuously display the correct brands, to consume is to still be part of it, even though the methods of consumption have drastically changed.

If the gladiatorial arenas of football are decaying through corporate gluttony and snowflake rules, where is left for us to strut and show off? Every pavement is a catwalk, just strut, what the fuck! We've still got it; in clobber we trust.

We have but one moment to sum someone up, to size up their character. And we do. We all make judgements whether we want to or not. And clobber is the conduit, a mutual sizing up. In a split second your clothes will represent you and what you're about without uttering a single word. Boom.

Without sounding like an X Factor cliché, writing this book has been a personal journey, and I feel so privileged to have been able to speak with so many of the key protagonists of the Clobberati. We have only just scratched the surface of looking into the developing Casual scene in the new worlds, and more research needs to be undertaken regarding the small but committed number of female Casuals. This book has shown me there are many others with the same passion for terrace culture within them, a force that will never die, and we will never be able to shake this thing of ours, and why the fuck would we want to?

'These Northern dickheads might have been onto something.'
– Neil Summers.

Reclaim the Game

Cold rain. Hard rain. With the unyielding, relentless wind smashing into his face, he shrugs to rid his new piece of droplets. Undeterred, he nonchalantly ignores the wet seeping into him, zips up the newly acquired coat and begins to bowl and bounce into town.

Past the decaying white bricks of Spode, he quickens his pace, bolstered by the pride he has of displaying his new attire to his mates; a magnificent, majestic peacock, strutting in all his glory, with all his might.

Today was a big game. He knew it, the lads knew it, the away fans knew it. Clearly by the amount of Old Bill lining the streets and guarding the shops and pubs in Stoke, the authorities also knew it. Sucking hard on a ciggie, he starts thinking about the old times, when he was younger going to the match.

Beer, Bovril and bothered!! When Stoke scored in the Victoria Ground's Boothen End, he was chucked around with delight by the old boys, whooping with solidarity. This is our club! Our ground! City!! City!! Tell the lads in red and white everything will be alright!! A working-class game for working class men. They claimed the terraces as theirs. Their manor, their fortress against anyone who dared to venture into their territory.

He looks back with a heavy heart; terraces desolate, the spirit of the community ripped open when the decision was made to relocate to the Bet365 Stadium, the coldest place in the world. Too many rules and restrictions now, the heart and soul gone forever.

In a society where there is so little stability to cling onto, in a community where there have been few economic prospects, to save enough money to buy expensive knitwear, coats and clobber in a game of one-upmanship at the match, and to support and sing your heart out in inebriated solidarity, was what the boys lived for. Thinking nothing of spending hundreds of pounds on the latest, finest brands of Casual culture, they were spending this huge amount of money and time on looking the best, when paradoxically they were living and existing in an area with no money, future or opportunities.

We are Casuals, we are Stoke, and what?! Like a finely dressed, suited and booted army, the lads would wear their clothes with passion and integrity, like a soldier's uniform, easily identifiable to both sides. No one hit shirters. They knew who to look out for.

Striding along quicker now, having a few scoops all along London Road, the alcohol warming his insides. For the first time in a long time, he felt excited. His disdain for the ground, for Stoke, for the management and for modern football was beginning to wane. The smell of anticipation was intoxicating, the air dense with trepidation, with excitement.

Grabbed in a chocking tight headlock, he laughs as the rest of the clan hooked him by the scruff of his neck into the boozer. All of the lads look sharp, proud, Casual; accessorised by Stella, the atmosphere was electric despite the streets outside bleak with a never-ending grey drizzle. They didn't care though, inside they belonged. He belonged.

Times have changed, with the only commodity the working-class man having as their own, football, being snatched away from corporate yawns. He hates the suits in the business boxes who choose the match as a backdrop to schmoozing potential clients. He despises the families who choose to take little girls to the game, wriggling in their chairs, clearly not caring a jot for the game in front of them, but then why would they? This is the audience the team plays out to now on a weekly basis, people who turn around in their red chair looking with disgust if they hear swearing or inappropriate behaviour.

It's a football game!! He wants to shout. What do you expect happens here! It's ours! The only bit of the world we want and you've still taken it, thrown money at it, installed seats instead of terraces, TV rights, sponsorships, advertising, branding, extortionate player wages. You've killed it!

Being in the pub, with his mates, wearing the gear, there is still some spirit about them that will not rest in peace. The cheek, the charm and the charisma will always be there, it's a part of him, his life and his culture, that cannot and will not be modernised, made politically correct or told to be quiet. Rising against authority, nothing will quell the fires being stoked within that pub today.

Maybe it was because they were playing old rivals, maybe because they were all out together for the first time in ages, or maybe just because he wants to reclaim his club and get that passion back, but today's match was going to be different. The old sparks were there, his new piece glistening from the rain, bristling to attention, on constant alert for the away fans.

Take out the core of the city, move it to the top of the hill, ban loads of people from going to it, but you still cannot banish the identity of Stoke's fine Casual element. A sub-culture that may have been destroyed, but never forgotten, it lives on in memory, in soul and in pride. A reputation that was fought hard for, it takes more than a couple of seats to fully dismantle a movement that was so integral and synonymous to the city itself.

Hearts beating, beer flowing, banter swapping, it was almost time to down pints, zip coats, pull hats/hoods firmly down. The people, the humour, the culture; that is what makes Stoke-on-Trent. He doesn't know whether it's the alcohol or the adrenaline, but he starts to feel an intense affection for this noble city.

The status of the club and the city feeds inadvertently into his own ego. He is Stoke. Stoke is him. It is time to fix up, look sharp and give his head a wobble. Swallowing hard, feeling the emotion run through his veins, glancing at his loyal, unconditional mates, for a fraction of a second, his love and ardour for SCFC returns.

Quick they're here!! Someone shouts as a brick crashes through the pub window, fragmented glass flying all over his new coat. He feels alive again.

THE END END.
END OF THE ROAD.
END OF.
AT THE END OF THE DAY, END OF.
LATERS.

Bibliography

Books

Bourdieu, P. (1984) *A Social Critique of the Judgment of Taste*. London: Routledge & Kegan Paul.

Brown, L. and Harvey, N. 2006 *A Casual Look: A Photodiary of Football Fans 1980s to 2001*, Brighton: Football Culture UK.

Baudrillard, J. (1994) *The Illusion of the End*. New York: Stanford University Press.

Chester, M. (2003) *Naught*, Wrea Green: Milo Books

Dunning, E., Murphy, P. and Williams, J. (1988) *The Roots of Football Hooliganism*, London: Routledge.

Durkheim, Émile, 1858-1917. (1995). The elementary forms of religious life. New York: Free Press

Firth, Simon (1986) *Performing Rites: On the Value of Popular Music*, Cambridge MA: Harvard University Press

Guilianotti, R., Bonney, N. and Hepworth, M. (eds) (1994) *Football, Violence and Social Identity*, London: Routledge.

Hall, S. and Jefferson, T. (eds) (2006) *Resistance Through Rituals: Youth Subcultures in Post-War Britain*. 2nd edition, London: Hutchinson.

Haynes, R. (1995) *The Football Imagination: The Rise of Football Fanzine Culture*, Aldershot: Arena.

Hebdige, D. (1979) *Subculture: The Meaning of Style*, London: Routledge.

King, A. (1998) *The End of the Terraces: The Transformation of English Football in the 1990s*, London, Leicester University Press.

Lowles, N. and Nicholls, A. (2005) *Hooligans 2: The M-Z of Britain's Football Hooligan Gangs*, Lytham: Milo.

Maffesoli, M. (1996) *The Time of the Tribes: The Decline of Individualism in Mass Society*. London: Sage Publications.

Muggleton, D., 2000. *Inside Subculture*. Oxford: Berg.

Redhead, S. (eds) (1993) *The Passion and the Fashion: Football Fandom in the New Europe*, Aldershot: Avebury.

Redhead, S. (1997) *Post-Fandom and the Millennial Blues: The Transformation of Soccer Culture*, London: Routledge.

Redhead, S., 2017. *Football and Accelerated Culture: This Modern Sporting Life*. London: Routledge.

Routledge, W., 2012. *Northern Monkeys*. Cheshire: Thinkmore.

Sampson, K., 1998. *Awaydays*. London: Vintage Books

Thornton, P. (2003) *Casuals: Football, Fighting and Fashion, The Story of a Terrace Cult*, Lytham: Milo.

Turney, J. (2020) *Fashion Crimes: Dressing for Deviance*, London: Bloomsbury.

Willis, P.E. (1978) *Profane Culture*, London: Routledge.

Willis, P.E., Canaan, J. and Hurd, G. (1990) *Common Culture: Symbolic Work at Play in the Everyday Cultures of the Young*, Milton Keynes: Open University Press.

Journal Articles

Armstrong, G. and Harris, R. (1991) "Football Hooligans: Theory and Evidence," *The Sociological Review*, Vol.39. No,3, pp. 427-458

Ball, D. and Tasaki, L. "The Role and Measurement of Attachment in Consumer Behaviour," *Journal of Consumer Psychology*, 1992, Vol. 1, No. 2 (1992), pp. 155-172

Bennett, A. (2011) The post-subcultural turn: some reflections 10 years on, *Journal of Youth Studies*, 14:5, 493-506

Blackshaw, T. (2008) "Contemporary Community Theory and Football," *Soccer and Society*, Vol.9. No.3, pp.325-345.

Bodin, D. and Robène, L. (2014) Hooligans, Casuals, Independents: Decivilisation or Rationalisation of the Activity? *The International Journal of the History of Sport*, 31:16, 2013-2033

Chandon, J., Laurent, G., and Valette-Florence, P. 2016. "Pursuing the concept of luxury: Introduction to the JBR Special Issue on "Luxury Marketing from Tradition to Innovation"," *Journal of Business Research*, Elsevier, vol. 69(1), pages 299-303.

Cova, B. (1997) "Community and Consumption-Towards a definition of the 'Linking Value' of Products or Services," *European Journal of Marketing*, Vol.31. No.3/4, pp.297-316.

Crabbe, T. (2008) "Fishing for Community: England Fans at the 2006 FIFA World Cup," *Soccer and Society*, Vol.9. No.3. pp.428-438.

Davari, A., Iyer, P., Guzmán, F., Veloutsou, C. (2022) "Determinants of Luxury Purchase Intentions in a Recessionary Environment." *Journal of Marketing Management*

Davari, A., Devinder Pal Singh & Justin, P. (2020): The consumer behavior of luxury goods: a review and research agenda, *Journal of Strategic Marketing*.

Derbaix, C., Oecrop, A. and Cabossart, 0. (2002) "Colors and Scarves: The Symbolic Consumption of Material Possessions by Soccer Fans," *Advances in Consumer Research*, Vol.29. pp.511-517.

Dean Cooke, M. (2021) "The Development of Sport in the Potteries during the Nineteenth Century: An Initial Survey, Midland History, 46:2, 178-191 during the Nineteenth Century: An Initial Survey," *Midland History*, 46:2, 178-191.

Doidge, M. and Lieser, M. (2018) The importance of research on the ultras: introduction, *Sport in Society*, 21:6, 833-840

Ebrahim. R. (2020) The Role of Trust in Understanding the Impact of Social Media Marketing on Brand Equity and Brand Loyalty, *Journal of Relationship Marketing*, 19:4, 287-308,

Goworek, H., Oxborrow, L., Claxton, S., Cooper, T.H., Hill, H. and Mclaren, A, 2020. Managing sustainability in the fashion business: challenges in product development for clothing longevity in the UK. *Journal of Business Research*, 117, pp. 629-641.

Grix, J., Brannagan, P., Grimes, H. and Neville, R. (2021) The impact of Covid-19 on sport, *International Journal of Sport Policy and Politics*, 13:1, 1-12.

Groves, Andrew (2022), 'A Casual obsession: Inside the British Sock Fetish Council', *Critical Studies in Men's Fashion*, 9:2, pp. 187–206.

Gutu, D. (2017) "'Casuals' culture. Bricolage and consumerism in football supporters' culture. Case study – Dinamo Bucharest Ultras', *Soccer & Society*, 18:7, 914-936.

Hobbs, D. and Robins, D. (1991) "The Boy Done Good: Football Violence, Changes and Continuities," *The Sociological Review*, Vol.39. No.3, pp. 551- 579.

Holt, D.B. (1995) "How Consumers Consume: A Typology of Consumption Practises" *Journal of Consumer Research*, Vol.22. pp.1-16.

Kim, A. and Ko, E. (2010) "Impacts of Luxury Fashion Brand's Social Media Marketing on Customer Relationship and Purchase Intention," *Journal of Global Fashion Marketing* 1(3):164-171.

Ko, E., Kim, K., Lee, M., Mattila, P., & Kim, K. H. (2014) "Fashion collaboration effects on consumer response and customer equity in global luxury and SPA brand marketing," *Journal of Global Scholars of Marketing Science*, 24(3), 350-364.

King, A. (1997) "The Lads: Masculinity and the New Consumption of Football," *Sociology*, Vol.31, No.2, pp.329-346.

Lee, S. and Workman, J. (2015) "Determinants of brand loyalty: self-construal, self-expressive brands, and brand attachment," International Journal of Fashion Design, *Technology and Education*, Vol.8, No.1, pp. 12-20.

MacKenzie, M. (2019) Football, fashion and unpopular culture: David Bowie's influence on Liverpool Football Club Casuals 1976-79, *Celebrity Studies*, 10:1, 25-43.

Michallat, W. 1989. "The Macho Factor." *The City Gent* (23): 32–33.

McAlexander, H., Schouten, J. & Koenig, H. (2002) "Building Brand Community," *Journal of Marketing*, Vol.66, No.1, pp. 38-54.

Muniz, A.M. and O'Guinn, T.C. (2001) "Brand community," Journal of Consumer Research, Vol.27, March 2001, pp.412-432.

O'Cass, A. and Frost, H. (2002) "Status Brands: Examining the Effects of Non-Product Related Brand Associations on Status and Conspicuous Consumption," *Journal of Product and Brand Management*, Vol.11. No.2. pp.67-88.

Oeppen, J and Jamal, A. (2014) "Collaborating for success: managerial perspectives on co-branding strategies in the fashion industry," *Journal of Marketing Management*, Vol.30, No.9, pp.925-948.

Oliveira, M. and Fernandes, T. (2020): "Luxury brands and social media: drivers and outcomes of consumer engagement on Instagram," *Journal of Strategic Marketing*, Vol.30, No.4, pp.389-407.

Perasović, M. & Mustapić, M, (2018) Carnival supporters, hooligans, and the 'Against Modern Football' movement: life within the ultras subculture in the Croatian context, *Sport in Society*, 21:6, 960-976.

Power, D. and Hauge, A. (2008) "No Man's Brand- Brands, Institutions, and Fashion," *Growth and Change*, Vol.39. No.1. pp.123-143.

Rao, A. and Ruekert, R. (1994). "Brand alliances as signals of product quality," *Sloan Management Review*. Vol. 36, No.1, pp. 87-98.

Redhead, S. and McLaughlin, E. (1985) "Soccer's style wars," *New Society*, 73 (1181), 225-228.

Redhead, S., 2009. Hooligan Writing and the Study of Football Fan Culture: Problems and Possibilities. *Nebula*, 6 (3), 16–41.

Redhead, S. (2010). "Little Hooliganz: The Inside Story of Glamorous Lads, Football Hooligans and Post-Subculturalism," *ESU*, Vol.8, No.2.

Redhead, S., 2012. 'Soccer Casuals: A Slight Return of Youth Culture. International Journal of Child, *Youth and Family Studies*, 3 (1), 65–82.

Redhead, S., 2015a. "The Firm: Towards a Study of Four Hundred Football Gangs," *Sport in Society*, 18 (3), 329–346.

Redhead, S., 2015b. "Terrace Banter: Researching Football Hooligan Memoirs," *Sport in Society*, 18 (3), 313–328.

Rehling, H. (2011). ""It's About Belonging": Masculinity, Collectivity, and Community in British Hooligan Films," *Journal of Popular Film and Television,* Vol.39, No.4, pp162-173.

Richardson, B. (2004) "New Consumers and Football Fandom: The Role of the Social Habitus in Consumer Behaviour," *Irish Journal of Management.*

Richardson, B. and O'Dwyer, E. (2003) "Football Supporters and Football Team Brands: A Study in Consumer Brand Loyalty," *Irish Marketing Review,* Vol.16. No.1, pp.43-55.

Seo, L. and Buchanan-Oliver, M. (2015) "Luxury branding: the industry, trends, and future conceptualisations," *Asia Pacific Journal of Marketing and Logistics*, Vol.27, No.1, pp. 82-98.

Schouten, J.W. and McAlexander, J.H. (1995) "Subcultures of Consumption: An Ethnography of the New Bikers," *Journal of Consumer Research*, Vol.22, June 1995, pp.43-61.

Schiele, K. & Venkatesh, A. (2016) "Regaining control through reclamation: how consumption subcultures preserve meaning and group identity after commodification," *Consumption Markets & Culture*, 19:5, pp.427-450.

Spaaij, R., 2007. Football Hooliganism in the Netherlands: Patterns of Continuity and Change. *Soccer & society*, 8 (2–3), 316–334.

Voss, k. and Gammoh, B. (2004) "Building Brands through Brand Alliances: Does a Second Ally Help?" *Marketing Letters*, Vol.15, No.2, pp.147-159.

Wu, G. and Chalip, L. (2014) "Effects of co-branding on consumers' purchase intention and evaluation of apparel attributes," *Journal of Global Scholars of Marketing Science,* Vol.24, No.1, pp 1-20.

News

Al Jazeera, 2022. Deadly Indonesia football stampede caused by tear gas. [online]. Available at: Deadly Indonesia football stampede caused by tear gas: Minister | News | Al Jazeera [Accessed October 2022].

BBC News, 2006. Football Hooligans Attack Police. [online] Available at: BBC NEWS | England | Staffordshire | Football hooligans attack police [Accessed October 2021].

BBC News, 2010. West Midlands Police unit tackling football hooligans. [online]. Available at: West Midlands Police unit tackling football hooligans - BBC News [Accessed October 2021].

BBC News, 2010. Football Fans in England and Wales still 'Over-policed.' Available at: Football fans in England and Wales still 'over-policed' - BBC News [Accessed October 2021].

BBC News, 2010. Increase in young football hooligans, say Police. [online]. Available at: Increase in young football hooligans, say police – BBC News [Accessed October 2021].

Brotherly Game, 2018. No one likes us, but we care. [online]. Available at: No one likes us, but we care: Millwall fans object to Philadelphia adopting signature song – Brotherly Game [Accessed August 2022].

Contrast.Org, date unknown. The Immediate Aftermath. [online]. Available at: The Immediate Aftermath – The Media Reaction – Hillsborough Football Disaster (contrast.org)

Daily Mail, 2018. Steward hurt and 11 fans arrested. [online]. Available at: Steward hurt and 11 fans arrested after bottles, flares and seats are thrown at Port Vale | Daily Mail Online [Accessed November 2021].

Greater Manchester Police Online, 2021. Three million pounds worth of goods seized in counterfeit crackdown. [online]. Available at: Three million pounds worth of goods seized in counterfeit crackdown | Greater Manchester Police (gmp.police.uk) [Accessed December 2021].

The Guardian, 2000. Football Hooligans Raise Their Game. [online] Available at:
www.guardian.co.uk/uk/2000/aug/14/footballviolence.football>
[Accessed 15 June 2011).

The Guardian, 2003. Hooligans Ready for big kick off [online] Available at: Hooligans ready for big kick-off | UK news | The Guardian [Accesses 15 June 2011].

iNews, 2022. Missguided in administration as Love Island teams with eBay. [online]. Available at: Missguided in administration as Love Island teams with eBay - Gen Z is falling out of love with fast fashion (inews.co.uk) [Accessed June 2022].

iNews, 2022. Ukraine's football hooligans put combat training to use in fight against the Russian enemy [online]. Available at: Ukraine's football hooligans put combat training to use in fight against the Russian enemy [Accessed June 2022].

Manchester News, 2022. Pretty Little Thing rapped over seriously offensive advert for jeans [online]. Available at: PrettyLittleThing rapped over 'seriously offensive' advert for jeans – *Manchester Evening News* [Accessed June 2022].

The Scottish Sun, 2019. Rangers react as Peaky Blinders leader Tommy Shelby says, 'We are the People,' [online]. Available at: Rangers fans react as Peaky Blinders leader Tommy Shelby says 'We are the people' | *The Scottish Sun* [Accessed August 2022].

The Sun, 1989. The Truth. Not Available.

The Times, 2022. How Gen Z fell for Kate Bush. [online]. Available at: *How Gen Z fell for Kate Bush | Times2 | The Times* [Accessed June 2022].

Blogs/Interviews/Articles

Achille, A. and Zipser, D. 2020, April 1. A perspective for the luxury goods industry during-and after-coronavirus [online article]. Retrieved from: The luxury industry during--and after--coronavirus | McKinsey

Brain, E. 2022, July 11. Liam Gallagher Goes Back to Basics for his Adidas Spezial LG2 SPZL [blog post]. Retrieved from: Liam Gallagher x adidas Spezial LG2 SPZL Release | Hypebeast

Bilderbeck, P. 2022, September 15. Patagonia founder gives away $3 billion company [online article]. Retrieved from: US news: Patagonia founder gives away $3 billion company (unilad.com)

Chouinard, Y. 2022, September 15. Earth is now our only shareholder [blog post]. Retrieved from: Yvon Chouinard Donates Patagonia to Fight Climate Crisis

Cochrane, L. 2012, April 18. Tale of two macs: Aquascutum goes bust while Burberry booms [online fashion article]. Retrieved from:

Tale of two macs: Aquascutum goes bust while Burberry booms | Fashion | *The Guardian*

Eror, A. 2017. Why Drake & Streetwear are ruining Stone Island for Soccer Fans [blog post]. Retrieved from: www.highsnobiety.com/p/drake-stone-island/

Ginsberg, B. 2022, March 2. How fashion brands have optimised their ecommerce efforts to survive the pandemic [blog post]. Retrieved from: How Fashion Brands Have Optimized Their E-Commerce Efforts to Survive the Pandemic – *Rolling Stone*

Halil, T. 2021, October 12. The rise of Stone Island: From hooligan to high fashion [blog post]. Retrieved from: THE RISE OF STONE ISLAND: FROM HOOLIGAN TO HIGH FASHION (culted.com)

MacNeil, K. 2022, June 23. How getting the Stone Island badge in became a way of life [blog post]. Retrieved from: How getting the Stone Island badge in became a way of life - The Face

Monteton, T. 2022, March 7. How the pandemic changed the luxury industry [online article]. Retrieved from: How the pandemic changed the luxury industry - article - Kearney

NSS Magazine, author unknown, 2021, November 4. What's the Old Money aesthetic and why it's going viral on TikTok [online article]. Retrieved from: What's the Old Money aesthetic and why it's going viral on TikTok (nssmag.com)

Pavarini, M. 2016, May 05. Stone Island, the brand adopted by the streetwear crew [online interview]. Retrieved from: Interview: Stone Island, the brand adopted by the streetwear crew (the-spinoff.com)

Persaud, R. 2012, November 13. Hillsborough - The Real Truth: How the Media Twists into a Baying Mob [blog post]. Retrieved from: Hillsborough – The Real Truth: How the Media Twists Into a Baying Mob | *HuffPost* UK News (huffingtonpost.co.uk)

Raymond, M. 2012, April 18. Tale of two macs: Aquascutum goes bust while Burberry booms [online fashion article]. Retrieved from: Tale of two macs: Aquascutum goes bust while Burberry booms | Fashion | *The Guardian*

Rogers, M. Date Unknown. Six Essential Brand Qualities for Building Millennial Loyalty [blog post]. Retrieved from: Six Essential Brand Qualities for Building Millennial Loyalty (digsite.com)

Sandercock, H. 2022, July 6. Missguided UK administration: why did firm collapse? [online article]. Retrieved from: Missguided administration: how fast fashion firm collapsed | NationalWorld

Scotts Menswear, Ultrafication of British Football [blog post]. No longer available.

Smith, M. 2022. July 11. Travis Scott's Dior x Cactus Jack Collab releasing July 2022 [blog post]. Retrieved from: Travis Scott's Dior x Cactus Jack Collab Releasing July 2022 (highsnobiety.com)

Soccer Bible, author unknown, 2021, September 29. Luke Shaw Mural Unveiled For adidas Spezial x C.P. Company Collaboration [online article]. Retrieved from: Luke Shaw Mural Unveiled For adidas Spezial x C.P. Company Collaboration – *SoccerBible*

The Graduate Store. Author and date unknown. The keys to the success of the Stone Island brand [blog post]. Retrieved from: The keys to the success of the Stone Island brand (graduatestore.fr)

Transalpino, 2016. Paninaro. [blog post]. No longer Available. Willson, T. 2022, August 5. Adidas Spezial is a curated marriage of now and then. [online interview]. Retrieved from: adidas SPEZIAL Summer 2022 Gary Aspden Interview (highsnobiety.com)

Magazine Articles

Gallagher, B. 2021. Fenners: Me, Myself and Mental Health. *Paninaro*. Issue 002.

McLean, A. 2020. Paninaro: Football...Fashion...Culture and how we thought it was a great name for a magazine. *Paninaro*. Issue 001.

Oxley, R, 2020. Where have all the subcultures gone? *Proper Magazine*. Issue 35.

Smith, M. 2012. Paul Heaton Interview. *Proper Magazine*. Issue unknown.

Songs

Cave, N., Harvey, M. and Wylder, T. 1994. Red Right Hand. Nick Cave and the Bad Seeds. *Let Love In*. UK: Mute Records.

Cocker, J., Senior, R., Mackey, S., Banks, N. and Doyle, C. 1995. Common People. Pulp. *A Different Class*. London: Island Records.

Lennon, J. and McCartney, P. 1966. I'm Only Sleeping. The Beatles. *Revolver*. London: Parlophone Records.

Seal and Sigsworth, G. 1990. Crazy. Seal. *Seal*. London: ZTT Records.

Tennant, N. and Lowe, C. 1986. Paninaro. Pet Shop Boys. *Please*. London: Parlophone Records.

TV

Frontline Hooligan (2022). Popular Front. Available at: You Tube.

Pose (2018). Color Force. Available at Netflix.

The Real Peaky Blinders (2022). BBC. Available at: BBC iPlayer.

The Terror (2021). AMC Studios. Available at: BBC iPlayer.

Film

It's a Casual Life. 2004. [film]. Jon S. Baird. Dir. UK. Logie Productions.

Quotes

Fashion fades, only style remains the same" Coco Chanel, 1965

"It's not about football, nothing to do with it. It's about tribes." Alan Clark (2011).

"My style comes from football and all this Casual thing…" Liam Gallagher (2012).

"I don't drive cars and I don't buy Rolexes, but I've got enough parkas that I could whip out and still blow people's minds." Liam Gallagher (date unknown).

"When you got PMQs at 1 and Millwall at 3." Glenn Kitson (2022). Instagram.

"Youth culture now really looks back and embraces the past but keeps it contemporary but not sticking to one particular style." Alexander McQueen (2009).

"When I was growing up, the cultural reference points that defined your character were music, clothes and football." Paul Weller (2014).

Meme

'Wearing Stone Island to the Christmas family meal in case anyone wants sparking out.' (unknown).

Acknowledgments

Without question, thank you to my family for allowing me to not feel like the black sheep for once, and also thanks Mum for letting me have your Cambridge University log ins for the online academic papers. At last I have made you proud, thank you for everything Mum and Dad. To my siblings, Sarah, Tom and Lizzie, thank you for absolutely everything and your unwavering support.

My mates for not busting my balls, or in fact busing my balls, about when the book will be done so I can come out to play.

Jasper (Mark Chester, N40) Thank you for all your help and advice in navigating my fledgling first attempt into the literary world. Thanks for believing in me. Casual!

Jason Marriner for being on constant standby.

The Prof (Richard Kelly).

My sister Liz Oxley.

All the interviewees and Clobberati including:

Adam Keyte, Aidan Tregay, Bill Routledge, Casual Ultra, Casual Client Clothing followers, Casual Connoisseur, Col Tiv, Dan Butler, Darren Broomfield, Dave Hewitson, David Elders, Davy Pennings, Derek Diablo, Ed Quiligotti, Fabio Cavina, Fenners, Fine Casual Element, Giovanni Calandras, Harry Butler, James Darby, Jared Latimer, Jay Montessori, Jude Moore, Kevin Feliz, Kyle Dixon, Lenny Howlett, Lorenzo Osti, Matt Banks, Matt Williams, Matt Snell, Mirko Budimir, N40 (anonymous), Neil Primett, Neil Summers,

Oliver Beer, Olmes Caretti, Original Casuals, Our friends in Norway/Montenegro, Patrick, Paul Johnston, Paul Smith, Paul Walters, Mario from Pouchain, Riaz Kahn, Richard Kelly, Robert Van der Weijden, Shawn Paul Gordon, Simon Dowling, Steve Lumb, Terrace Cult, The Chaps Club, Tom Oxley, 80s Casual Classics, Special thanks to Jay Montessori, Simon Dowling, Riaz Kahn, Oliver Beer, Lorenzo Osti, Steve Lumb, Jasper, Fabio Cavina, Neil Summers, Neil Primett and Matt Snell for patiently responding to my random, any time of the day or week, questions that were coursing through my head at that time. Always great, probably not printable and definitely not repeatable, answers given too.

Simon again, thank you for allowing me to play dress up in your epic, inimitable Stoke Island and CP Company collections. Kid in a sweet shop etc etc but thank you for the warmth hospitality especially when doing the front cover.

Neil Primett and the 80s Casual Classics team, the unwavering support you guys have given me is much appreciated...as is the amount of clobber you send me.

Steve Lumb and the whole Terrace Cult family for believing in me from the start and welcoming me into the fold.

Mike McDonald aka Head of Parking Services aka my mate letting me park on the car park next to the train station. All the codes you have given me to get out after travelling for interviews (sometimes just for shopping). But nice one anyway 😊

Roo Oxley is a freelance writer born and bred in Stoke-on-Trent. A football girl, Roo has long attended Stoke City football games both home and away. With a master's degree in marketing and a successful career in marketing following this, Roo has written about subcultures, music, fashion and football but with a particular interest in terrace casuals. Dressed impeccably always, Roo ultimately knows her clobber, inside and out. One of the leading and most well-known female casuals today, Roo intends to continue to write about her one true passion: Casuals.

Find her online:
@missroooxley
roo.oxley@oxleycontinproductions.com

Printed in Great Britain
by Amazon